Land and Landscape in Nineteenth-Century Ireland

In this series

Land and Landscape in Nineteenth-Century Ireland

Úna Ní Bhroiméil & Glenn Hooper

EDITORS

FOUR COURTS PRESS

Set in 10 on 12.5 point Bembo for
FOUR COURTS PRESS LTD
7 Malpas Street, Dublin 8, Ireland
e-mail: info@fourcourtspress.ie
and in North America
FOUR COURTS PRESS
c/o ISBS, 920 N.E. 58th Avenue, Suite 300, Portland, OR 97213.

A catalogue record for this title
is available from the British Library.

ISBN 978–1–84682–065–6

Printed in Great Britain
by Athenaeum Press, Gateshead, Tyne and Wear.

Contents

Foreword

FINTAN CULLEN

This collection of essays is the eleventh in an impressive series of publications that began life as conference papers at the annual meetings of the Society for the Study of Nineteenth-Century Ireland. The fact that the Society has consistently published many of the papers delivered at its conferences testifies to the quality of the scholarship being carried out across the Anglophone world on issues relating to nineteenth-century Ireland. I delivered a paper at my first conference of the SSNCI over a decade ago in Galway in June 1996 and I have attempted to attend subsequent meetings ever since. My memories of those few days on the campus of NUI, Galway, are of stimulating papers followed by fruitful networking with academic colleagues and convivial evenings of further conversation. The 2005 conference at Mary Immaculate College, now part of the University of Limerick, out of which the following papers have emerged, was no different. The list of talks was impressive, the range of academic interests was even more interdisciplinary than ten years earlier and the exchange of ideas was as intense as ever.

Having been asked to deliver the plenary lecture of the 2005 Limerick conference, I was in the enviable position of not having to worry if I would get an audience. As the final speaker of the conference, all the parallel strands merged in the one lecture hall and with a conference dinner to follow, there was nowhere else to go. I can only hope that my talk on 'Appropriating new landscapes: the Irish in London' was an apt conclusion to two days of intellectual exchange as well as giving the audience sufficient appetite for the conference banquet. So what of the theme, land and landscape? As an art historian, my talk at the Limerick conference, which came out of work I had recently been doing on the representation of Irish women in London, focussed on the way that that city helped certain individuals to succeed in a variety of professions most particularly that of the artist's model. The London landscape was given an Irish complexion most particularly in the 1860s and 1870s, as women such as Jo Hiffernan, Kathleen Newton and Mary Ryan frequently featured in works by such artists as James McNeill Whistler, James Tissot and Julia Margaret Cameron, respectively.[1] Due to a variety of circumstances, these women chose an alternative landscape from their native land in which to succeed.

The theme of the Limerick conference allowed a range of scholars from a good mix of disciplines to further complicate definitions of the relationship between land and landscape. For too often, the study of land in nineteenth-century Ireland

---

1 Fintan Cullen and R.F. Foster, '*Conquering England': Ireland in Victorian London* (London, 2005).

has been dominated by either who owned it or who wanted it. Equally, it has been about those who stayed on it or those being removed from it. By focussing on the land and landscape in its inimitable interdisciplinary way, the SSNCI has broadened the topic to include Ireland transplanted, in my own study on London, or Ireland imagined, as in so many of the essays in this volume which focus on literary examples. We must thus thank the SSNCI for allowing scholars the opportunity to address a wider range of approaches to the nineteenth century – gender, ideology, regional identity, religion, amongst many others. In an imaginative contribution to Irish nineteenth-century studies, the Society recently commissioned the publication of an immensely useful series of essays on research in the field, again covering a wide range of disciplines.[2] Maybe one day a whole conference and subsequent publication will address the role of the visual in nineteenth-century Ireland.

2 Laurence M. Geary and Margaret Kelleher (eds), *Nineteenth-Century Ireland: a guide to recent research* (Dublin, 2005).

Introduction

ÚNA NÍ BHROIMÉIL & GLENN HOOPER

Land in nineteenth-century Ireland is a contested terrain. This collection recognizes the centrality of land to the discourse on nineteenth-century Ireland and explores what Howes and O'Neill call the 'complex, almost bottomless historical layering that characterizes landscape in Ireland'.[1] The essays do not focus on the land question and land legislation or on the grievances of the challenging collectivity. Neither do they dwell on nineteenth-century aesthetic models of landscape painting or on mere descriptions of a wild or romantic landscape. Rather they stress the human interaction with land and focus on perception and memory and on the symbolism of land and landscape as key determinants for the formation of character, of self identity and of 'situated knowledges'.[2]

Land and landscape are thus linked in a cultural code as critical signifiers of a specific Irish identity. In attending primarily to the rural landscape these essays conjure up the places that Heaney suggests 'stir us to responses other than the merely visual'.[3] In the unsettled political and social context of nineteenth-century Ireland the land provides a space for negotiation – of identity, of nationality, of ownership. The changing landscape over time provides a link between past and present, between real and imagined communities. Throughout, the essays testify to Simon Schama's concept of landscape as the 'work of the mind . . . built up as much from strata of memory as from layers of rock'.[4]

This is an interdisciplinary or even transdisciplinary collection. There are however key points of intersection between the essays and common themes. More than just territory, the transforming power of the land is conveyed in Dabundo's and Murphy's essays. The characters' experiences in and of the land change and remake them and to live in Ireland as Dabundo suggests is to be 'reborn by the force of the land'. Nature is thus exalted and recognized as a power for good and made visible in the morality of the characters portrayed by Edgeworth and Owenson. This connection between land and a person's sense of self and identity is again emphasized in Murphy's discussion of *The O'Donoghue* by Lever. Key relationships are based in the land which reflects the impact of human imprint and which is at the same time a well-spring for the creativity of the human imagination. The practical use of the

1 Marjorie Howes and Kevin O'Neill, 'Introduction: Toward a history of the Irish landscape' in Vera Kreilkamp (ed.), *Éire/Land* (New Bedford, MA, 2003), p. 13. 2 Joan Vincent and Marilyn Cohen, 'Anthropological and sociological studies' in Laurence M. Geary and Margaret Kelleher (eds), *Nineteenth-century Ireland: a guide to recent research* (Dublin, 2005), p. 112. 3 Seamus Heaney, *Preoccupations: selected prose, 1968–1978* (London, 1980), p. 132. 4 Simon Schama, *Landscape and memory* (London, 1995), pp 6–7.

land as a force for good is explored in Walsh's essay on the nineteenth-century district asylum. In pursuing a regime of moral treatment the land and landscape
surrounding the asylum came to play a key role in the recuperation and ultimate
cure of mental patients although as she points out 'the healing properties of land,
so often cited for the men, was rarely mentioned in the women's records, beyond
the necessity for the patients generally to take the air in the exercise yards'.

People are core to Pierse's discussion of George Moore's use of landscape as a
medium for presenting ideas. Pierse suggests that the visual and sensory images
used to convey landscape invariably encompass political agendas and social problems and that Moore presents landscape scenes to provoke discussion and evoke
thought. Indeed landscape used in this way may be considered subversive in that
messages and agenda are obscured and secreted behind a veil of popular landscape
imagery both verbal and visual and delivered to a reading and seeing public when
they least expect it. In drawing attention to Moore's belief that landscape should
be 'more about the reality of living than the picturesque' land is presented as a
'humanized space' where life is lived and social and political matters are enacted.
As much as the land marks people and is an 'unseverable aspect of self', people too,
as Garavel claims in his essay on Somerville and Ross, impress themselves upon the
land and leave impressions of their histories, culture and even something of their
characters behind as markers of their physical presence.

Traces of past human activities are addressed by Ní Cheallaigh in her discussion of archaeological sites and the conundrum they pose for contemporary
viewers. On the one hand, people use these sites as observation points from which
to view the past. This past, covered at times superficially and at others overgrown
to the point of near extinction can lead to perceptions of things that literally are
not there. On the other hand, the past is so obviously present in some sites and

monuments that they need to be destroyed in order to obliterate painful historical
memories. This material past and present is also evoked by Wein's view of the Irish
sublime in which she identifies the 'subliming of history' as a key feature. The land,
she maintains, like its people is 'unknowable' and its aesthetic conditions 'haunted,
if not deformed' by the moulding of history onto the land. The Irish sublime she
contends, is dark and full of despair because of the nexus between past and present.

Certain places and the landscapes associated with them embody this connection between past and present and, according to Cronin in her essay on balladry,
they acted as 'veritable codes linking past and present' in the popular consciousness
of the people. The appropriation of the landscape if not the land itself is a common premise uniting the essays. While Cronin does cite particular instances of
mound building, bonfire lighting and the take-over of hills in particular as evidence
of actual land appropriation and indeed of popular mobilization in pre-famine
Ireland, it was the capture of the landscape in the songs and ballads of the common
people that was significant in claiming it and the events associated with particular
landscapes as their own. Similarly, Egenolf stresses the metaphorical appropriation

of picturesque scenes by Owenson's Horatio to convey his sense of 'colonial entitlement' to the land. By making the landscape of Ireland familiar to the reading
public she suggests that even the wildest parts of Ireland, particularly the west
where 'the potential for insurgent activity lies unnoticed but radically present',
rights to the landscape are asserted and rights to the actual land justified.

These rights to landscape are developed further by Benatti in her essay on the
Dublin Penny Journal. This was the first time average Irish readers were presented
with 'good quality depictions of their own homeland' and Petrie's aim, she submits,
was to develop a sense of shared identity amongst Irishmen and women, that was
located in their appreciation of and ultimately their appropriation of their own
landscape. The loyalist press on the other hand emphasized land as the basis of their
shared oppression by both nationalist sectarianism and British liberalism. The rights
of loyal and propertied individuals to the actual land, Jones maintains, was summed
up by the fact that 'in southern unionist discourse "the land" was often framed as
a prefixed right of the "ascendancy classes"'. In a close reading of the nineteenth-
century loyalist press she concludes that the issue of land provided official unionism
with the opportunity to present loyal individuals as victims as well as an 'effective
propaganda weapon to counter self-government for Ireland'. Within the context
of opposing assertions of ownership and community in nineteenth-century Ireland
the symbolic claiming of land and landscape by different factions attest to the
power of what Nash terms 'an authentic identity and relationship to place'.[5]

Rights to the profits provided by land and landscape are claimed in a more concrete way in the essays by Furlong and Mulligan who deal with opposite ends of
the country and with very different aspects of Ireland's economic life. As Ireland
'slowly awakened to the economic potential of tourism' the gentry began to realize the potential of their estates and this lead in 1896 to the cordoning-off of the
Giant's causeway and charging for entry to what had been a public space. Furlong
points to 'indignation meetings' which were held to protest the 'seizure of the
causeway' as testament to the notion that certain locations were imbued with
meaning for a people and belonged to them as of right. The filching of this right
to walk and view their own space was protested vehemently. In his discussion of
mining ventures in Cork and Waterford, Mulligan suggests that the potential for
economic success was always overestimated by mining promoters who attributed
repeated failures to poor management rather than changing world markets or
overly optimistic projections. While the possibility of gaining wealth from the land
existed, Mulligan claims that this was located more in the imaginations of mining
promoters rather then in reality. In both Furlong's and Mulligan's essays the surrounding poverty of the countryside is emphasized in contrast to economic
prosperity.

5 Catherine Nash, 'Remapping and renaming: new cartographies of identity, gender and
landscape in Ireland', *Feminist Review*, 44, Nationalisms and national identities (Summer
1993), 39–57.

The rich and textured descriptions of land and landscape in this collection make visible places and events and locations as they were and as they appeared to contemporary observers. In reading text and image simultaneously we too become participants in this observation and can look beyond the symbolism and the economics of land in the nineteenth century to the reality and the actuality of that which surrounded and encompassed its inhabitants. What is conveyed above all through making visible these locations is the importance of place, of a sense of place, of rootedness and of the assertion of nationality, of identity. As Edward S. Casey suggests, 'texts and traces are *found in place*: the place of landscape itself. A given landscape retains and presents the evidences of history that come to enter its generous embrace; more exactly, it both withholds these evidences and renders them visible.'[6] As the essays in this volume demonstrate, the intersection of history and memory, and of place and identity, are represented on the land, and in the very landscape itself – as tracings and lines, as territorial markers, but fundamentally as a series of texts from which we must speak of, and towards, ourselves.

---

6 Edward S. Casey, *Representing place: landscape painting and maps* (Minneapolis, 2002), p. 275.

Land and landscape in the
Dublin Penny Journal, 1832–3

FRANCESCA BENATTI

This essay focuses on how the themes of land and landscape were represented in the *Dublin Penny Journal* through the articles of its two editors, George Petrie and Caesar Otway. It examines how the authors provided their readers with a framework for interpreting Ireland and Irish identity, and how they attempted to reconcile their cultural goals with the commercial goals of a periodical publication.

It is essential to identify Petrie and Otway's writings with the medium they chose for publication – a weekly journal aimed at a popular audience. Periodicals were the mass media of the nineteenth century, and their production and consumption shaped the lives of millions of readers in the United Kingdom. The 1830s saw the growth of a new market that developed in addition to the established one for expensive quarterly reviews and monthly magazines. It centred on weekly periodicals, and was aimed at the emerging working and lower-middle classes of the great cities.[1] The *Dublin Penny Journal (DPJ)* shared in this milieu when it began its career on 30 June 1832. It was the property of Dublin printer John Sewell Folds and, as the title implies, it was sold weekly for the price of one penny. Caesar Otway was its first editor, but, seven weeks into his enterprise, George Petrie joined him as co-editor.[2] Otway, besides being a renowned preacher and antiquarian, also possessed significant journalistic experience, as he had been the editor of the monthly *Christian Examiner* from 1825 to 1831.[3] Petrie, on the other hand, had never worked in an editorial capacity before, though, as a member of the Royal Irish Academy, he was already renowned as a scholar in the field of antiquities. He was also an accomplished landscape painter, and the driving force behind the historical department of the Ordnance Survey.

In its general publishing format, the *DPJ* was following in the footsteps of the *Penny Magazine of the Society for the Diffusion of Useful Knowledge*, whose extraordinary success in Britain had launched a new periodical genre in March 1832.[4] The circulation of the *DPJ*, which peaked at close to 40,000 copies per week, was meagre compared to the 200,000 of its British model, but far surpassed anything published in Ireland at the time. Indeed, post-Union Ireland had proven particularly

---

1 See Richard Altick, *The English common reader: a social history of the mass reading public, 1800–1900* (Columbus, 1957; 1998), p. 82. 2 Caesar Otway, in *DPJ*, 1:7, 11 August 1832, p. 56. No title given. 3 Barbara Hayley, 'Irish periodicals from the Union to the *Nation*', in *Anglo-Irish Studies*, 2 (1976), 86–7. 4 Scott Bennett, 'Revolutions in thought: serial publication and the mass market for reading', in Joanne Shattock and Michael Wolff (eds), *The Victorian periodical press: samplings and soundings* (Leicester, 1982), p. 244.

unfavourable to periodicals in general. Of the over 150 periodicals begun in Ireland between 1800 and 1848, less than a quarter survived for one year or more.[5] With its four-year run, the *DPJ* definitely ranks among the success stories, especially in terms of its influence on subsequent journalistic ventures.[6]

The *DPJ* consisted of eight pages, printed on two columns and on cheap paper. Each issue may have been published with a cover or wrapper, but this cannot be ascertained since the magazine has only survived through bound copies (fig. 1). It was an unstamped publication, meaning that its customers did not have to pay the onerous duty of 4*d.* per copy that was imposed upon the readers of daily or weekly newspapers. While this choice kept the price of the *DPJ* low, it also placed some clear restrictions on the subject matter the journal was allowed to cover. The newspaper stamp duty had been introduced to monitor and limit the circulation of printed news. As such, unstamped publications could not include 'any Public News, Intelligence or Occurrences, or any Remarks or Observations thereon, or upon any Matter in Church and State'.[7] The British *Penny Magazine* chose therefore to fill its pages with articles on geography, manufactures, statistics, natural science and topography, as well as descriptions of British monuments and locations.

Otway and Petrie chose to emulate this model, but with at least one significant difference, enshrined in the title of the periodical itself. The new venture was firmly rooted in its Irish basis, as exemplified by the reference to the Irish metropolis, Dublin. This choice of a local denominator in the title perhaps followed on the other success story of the popular press, the Scottish *Chambers' Edinburgh Journal*. To state that a periodical was from Dublin or Edinburgh was a signal for a nineteenth-century reader that the magazine partook of the national character of, in this case, either Ireland or Scotland. It indicated that unlike other examples of the same genre, the text in question focused on more than universal (or English) themes. The *DPJ*, by declaring itself a 'penny journal', implicitly shared the belief in 'useful knowledge' of the new penny periodicals, but arranged its programme from an exclusively Irish perspective. The two editors stated that their periodical would move 'on new and entirely national ground',[8] meaning that, not only would the bulk of their material be Irish, but that they would also include as many original articles as possible. This in itself was unusual in cheap periodicals, as reprints were a common way to keep costs low. Out of over 500 articles published under Otway and Petrie, only 81 were not original. A further 136 were anonymous, but all of the remaining 300 bear a signature of some kind, even if in most cases it was just an initial.

Otway and Petrie began their work 'with national as well as useful objects in view'.[9] They would not merely educate the masses, but use their periodical to create 'a national and concordant feeling in a country in which there is, as yet, so much of

5 Hayley, 'Irish periodicals', p. 83.   6 For example, see Charles Gavan Duffy, *Young Ireland: a fragment of Irish history, 1840–1850* (1880; New York, 1973), p. 75.   7 Quoted in Joel H. Wiener, *The war of the unstamped: the movement to repeal British newspaper tax, 1830–1836* (Ithaca, NY, 1969), pp 4–5.   8 Caesar Otway and George Petrie, Preface, *DPJ*, 1, 1832–3.   9 Ibid.

THE

DUBLIN PENNY JOURNAL.

1832—3.

CLAYTON. S⁰

DUBLIN:

JOHN S. FOLDS, 5, BACHELORS' WALK;

SOLD ALSO WHOLESALE BY

W. F. WAKEMAN, AND W. CURRY, JUN. & CO; IN LONDON BY SIMPKIN & MARSHALL, AND J. ROBINS;
WILLMER & SMITH, LIVERPOOL; BANCKS & CO. MANCHESTER; DRAKE, BIRMINGHAM; WRIGHT,
NOTTINGHAM; R. GRANT & SON, EDINBURGH; J. NIVEN, JUN. GLASGOW; JACKSON, NEW YORK;
WARDLE, AND DOBSON, PHILADELPHIA; GRAY & BOWEN, BOSTON; AND G. G. BENNIS, PARIS.

Price 5s. in Twelve Monthly Parts, and 6s. 6d. bound in Cloth.

1 Frontispiece of the first collected volume of the *Dublin Penny Journal*, 1833.

discord and party' and to stimulate 'a taste for literature among a people to whom it
has been but little known, except as connected with political and polemical discussions'.[10] By deliberately avoiding news items, Petrie and Otway had committed the
DPJ to providing a representation of Ireland that was not predicated upon allegiance
to 'sect or party'.[11] The two editors embarked upon the complex task of creating this
alternative and inclusive definition of Ireland, independent of religion and politics,

10 Ibid. **11** Ibid.

and centred instead on instruction and knowledge. They needed the *DPJ* to construct and disseminate a version of Irish identity that could be both authoritative and engaging for their intended audience. What Petrie and Otway required was a sufficiently neutral ground that would allow them to construct their representation of Ireland, and yet remain within the legal remits of a penny journal. The editors opted for a range of subjects, which they believed were 'most likely to attract the attention of the Irish people, next to those of politics and polemics ... namely the history, biography, poetry, antiquities, natural history, legends and traditions of the country – subjects which can never fail to interest the feelings of a people'.[12] The Irish landscape and its human, natural, and monumental contents proved to be the ideal embodiment of these disparate topics, and its exploration formed the backbone of the *DPJ*.

The first and most obvious way in which the *DPJ* addressed the Irish landscape was through its illustrations. The *DPJ* usually included about three per issue, in line with its British models, but far in excess of anything previously within the financial reach of its Irish audience.[13] Illustrated books on Ireland had been in existence long before the *DPJ*, and indeed Petrie had contributed engravings to several of them, most recently to *Ireland Illustrated* in 1831. However, the vast majority of the Irish reading public, limited as it was, had been prevented from owning these images by their extremely high price. For the first time, the *DPJ* made available to average Irish readers some good-quality depictions of their own homeland. The success of this strategy can be judged by the lawsuit filed by the owners of *Ireland Illustrated*, Fisher of London, against the *DPJ* for infringement of its copyright. It appears that the *DPJ* had actually copied some of the illustrations from the book, and was 'selling for pennies what they [*Ireland Illustrated*] sold for pounds'.[14] The Fisher firm evidently saw the *DPJ* as a threat to its market position, despite the fact that the considerable price differential should have placed the two publications within clearly distinct reading spheres.

Petrie, with his training as a landscape painter, was perfectly qualified to supervise the visual side of the journal, but the other sections of the *DPJ* show clear signs of his involvement as well. He wrote sixty-five articles in total, although he signed none of the illustrations (many of which had indeed been reproduced from *Ireland Illustrated*). He also engaged the services of other artists, like Andrew Nicholl from Belfast, the self-taught Drogheda housepainter, Robert Armstrong, and Dublin engraver Benjamin Clayton.[15] A cursory glance at these illustrations could lead one to believe that Petrie was merely using the visual side of the *DPJ* to construct an image of Ireland as a picturesque and romantic land. Indeed, such had been the effect

12 Ibid.   13 For the role of illustrations in the penny journals, see Patricia Anderson, *The printed image and the transformation of popular culture, 1790–1860* (Oxford, 1991), pp 54–7. 14 'Fisher and Others a. Folds' [*sic*], in *DPJ*, 1:36, 2 March 1833, p. 288.   15 The entry for Nicholl in the ODNB erroneously states that his connection with the *DPJ* began in 1834. See Martyn Anglesea, 'Nicholl, Andrew (1804–1886)', *Oxford Dictionary of National Biography* (Oxford, 2004) [http://www.oxforddnb.com/view/article/68446, accessed 25 Oct 2005].

of his work for the expensive guidebooks over the previous decade.[16] There is, instead, strong evidence to assert that, in the *DPJ* at least, Petrie adopted a more complex stance, one that combined his talents as both scholar and painter. In the guidebooks, Petrie had been relegated to the role of illustrator, a mere commentator on content that others had composed. In the *DPJ*, his role as an editor allowed him instead to emerge from the limbo of the paratext into the text itself, shaping the entire structure of the journal.[17] He produced or supervised both text and paratext in the articles that were joined to the illustrations, and, with Otway, he determined what material to include in every issue and where to place it within the journal, guiding the readers through its pages. Petrie and Otway as editors were surely behind the decision to open all numbers of the *DPJ* with an article that can be defined as topographical. Petrie authored more such articles than any other correspondent, and thus shaped the policy of the entire *DPJ* on the subject of the Irish landscape.

The vast majority of Petrie's articles centred on the built heritage of Ireland, as opposed to its natural beauties, and always included historical as well as visual information. On one level, most articles acknowledged the romantic attraction of a castle or ruined abbey, especially in the illustrations. At the same time, the text of the article usually conceded very little to sublime rapture and lyrical description, focusing instead on historical and factual data. This apparent discrepancy stems from the fact that, with his landscape articles, Petrie tried to answer two distinct imperatives. The first was commercial, the need to attract the audience's attention, so that they would purchase his journal and continue to receive his message. As the lawsuit confirms, he achieved this mainly through the well-crafted image on the front page. However, the target audience of the *DPJ* was not rich foreign tourists contemplating an exotic country. It was instead composed of Irishmen and women (though the *DPJ* never addresses its audience as including females),[18] who needed to learn more about their homeland in order to develop a sense of shared identity. Petrie claimed, for example, that the inhabitants of Dublin did not appreciate the variety of its suburban landscapes: 'The more solitary and sublime scenery of the country is wholly deserted', while Dubliners crowd on the way to Kingstown out of 'mere fashion'.[19] Petrie found numerous causes for this 'apathy'. Some, like 'political excitements', were outside the bounds of the *DPJ*, while others, like 'the want of cultivation of intellectual tastes, we shall apply ourselves to remove'.[20] Therefore, when Petrie and the other artists of the *DPJ* put Ireland on display, and presented it as a spectacle worthy

16 For an analysis of Petrie's work in commercial illustration, see Eve Patten, *Samuel Ferguson and the culture of nineteenth-century Ireland* (Dublin, 2004), pp 91–5. **17** I am following Gerard Genette's definition of paratextuality, which includes illustrations; see Gerard Genette, *Paratexts: thresholds of interpretation* (Cambridge, 1997), pp 7; 405. **18** Women are never explicitly mentioned as part of the audience of the *DPJ*, except in the opening editorial. They are portrayed as mere adjuncts to the intended reader, a male Irish artisan, who is envisaged as reading aloud to his family. See 'The Age of Brass', *DPJ*, 1:1, 30 June 1832, p. 3. **19** George Petrie, 'The Needles, Howth', in *DPJ*, 1:21, 17 November 1832, p. 165. **20** Ibid., p. 166.

of the attention of Irishmen of all sects and parties, they were only fulfilling the first part of this plan. The picturesque scene on the front page would draw readers into the text and into the history and cultural achievements of Ireland.

Petrie used the verbal side of the articles to accomplish the second part of his strategy. The illustrations would save beautiful Irish locations from oblivion and apathy; the body of the article would rescue Irish history from 'the prejudices of partisanship' and 'lay open the pages of history with an impartial hand'. [21] Petrie's articles included, apart from the illustration itself, a description of the location being represented, and the most significant events connected with it, supported by references to chronicles and documents. The piece on Newgrange, written by Petrie and illustrated by Andrew Nicholl, is a good example of how the *DPJ* approached topography.[22] The article opens with a statement on the beauty of Newgrange and its merits in comparison with the Pyramids and Stonehenge. It proceeds then to describe the tumulus through a series of precise measurements, which comprise everything from the number of stones in the roof to the minimum and maximum height of the passage. Only when he has laid out concrete facts does Petrie proceed to speculate on the age of Newgrange, making references to previous antiquarians and dismantling their claims with the use of further evidence. Newgrange had not yet become the tourist attraction it is today, being described by one of Petrie's antiquarian correspondents as 'curious'.[23] Likewise, most of the other locations chosen by Petrie for his articles would not have featured very prominently in the guidebooks, with only one appearance of a tourist favourite like Killarney[24] and none at all of Wicklow. Nicholl's illustration depicted the central chamber of Newgrange in partial darkness, and called the reader to enter the tomb and discover its true origin (fig. 2). It was an invitation to learning more about the subject of the picture, rather than an excuse to admire it.

While typical in its methodology, the article on Newgrange was unusual in subject, since most of the topographical features, whether Petrie's or not, focused instead on medieval monuments, perhaps since they were both more visible and easier to document than prehistoric locations. The review of documentary sources from chronicles and annals usually occupied a large portion of the topographical articles of the *DPJ*, longer than the description of the present state of the monument. In this choice to focus on history, Petrie was certainly influenced by the fact of writing for an unstamped journal (too easy to stray into forbidden territory when mentioning the present), but he was also consciously making a decision to link place with past, to borrow an expression from Joep Leerssen.[25] Petrie's choice of subjects

21 George Petrie, 'Bridge and Castle of Shruel [*sic*], Co. of Mayo', in *DPJ*, 1:33, 9 February 1833, p. 257.   **22** George Petrie, 'New Grange', in *DPJ*, 1:39, 23 March 1833, pp 305–6. **23** Edward Benn to George Petrie, 27 November 1832, in NLI, MS 789.   **24** In one of the last articles Petrie wrote for the *DPJ*. See 'Mucruss Abbey, Killarney', in *DPJ*, 1:52, 22 June 1833, pp 409–11.   **25** See Joep Leerssen, *Remembrance and imagination: patterns in the historical and literary representation of Ireland in the nineteenth century* (Cork, 1996), p. 103.

THE

DUBLIN PENNY JOURNAL,

PUBLISHED EVERY SATURDAY.

| No. 39. Vol. I. | J. S. FOLDS, 5, BACHELOR'S WALK. | March 23, 1833. |

East Recess of the Sepulchral Tumulus at New Grange. County of Meath.

2 Andrew Nicholl, 'First Recess of the Sepulchral Tumulus of New Grange, County of Meath', *Dublin Penny Journal* 1:39 (23 March 1833).

to describe and illustrate tried therefore to construct in the pages of the *DPJ* a symbolic map of Ireland by emphasising the past achievements of its inhabitants. The physical remains of Irish history were invested with a significance that went beyond directing the gaze of the tourist. They became the embodiment, the *locus* of what constituted Irish identity. For Petrie, Ireland lay neither in the uncultivated wastes so dear to the British imperial traveller (because they implied Irish backwardness), nor in the 'cyclopean works' of ancient Phoenician-Irish civilisation, held by nationalist scholars as the symbol of the pure, undisturbed greatness of their native ancestors, unmarred by any conquerors. Irish identity for Petrie meant recognising that several groups had participated in the shaping of the visible landscape, and that, where they worked together, they had produced, or preserved, works of art as great as those of any other nation (fig. 3). To change their condition of strife and division, the people of Ireland should be required to learn more about their past, and Petrie proceeded to instruct them by pointing out the places where that past became part of the physical landscape of their present. By investing specific places with national significance, Petrie showed the readers of the *DPJ* how to join the dots in order to draw a new symbolic map of their country, one location at a time as the issues of the *DPJ* unfolded.

To lend further strength to his arguments, Petrie chose not to stop at the surface of Ireland, at the picturesque illustration, or even at the history that was visible above ground. The Irish land itself contained further proof of the past achievements of its inhabitants. It bears remembering that when Petrie joined Otway at the helm of the *DPJ*, he had just submitted his essay on 'The Uses and Origins of the Round Towers of Ireland' to the Royal Irish Academy. He was therefore defining the scientific approach to the study of the Irish past that would make him the founding father of Irish archaeology. His passion for research emerges in the *DPJ* through the twenty-seven articles he wrote on the finds he and other antiquarians had collected. These articles were also illustrated, probably by Petrie himself, and usually positioned in the middle pages of the *DPJ*. Petrie believed that, if scholars could look beyond the surface of the Irish land and probe its depth, they would find in it the proof of the accomplishments of their ancestors.[26] Similarly, if readers could read beyond the first page of the *DPJ* and its glittering illustration, they would be enlightened with critical information on their own country, of a kind rarely available to a mass audience. After the spectacle, the pictorial teaser to get the reader into the journal came the evidence of Petrie's finds.

Another considerable element in the strategy of representation of the *DPJ* was the space dedicated to O'Donovan's Irish translations. Most of them came from the Annals of Dublin, therefore supplementing the historical content of the *DPJ*, and furthering its reliance on documentary sources. A few addressed indirectly the theme of land in Ireland. O'Donovan, for example, presented the reader with proof of the antiquity of wheat farming in Ireland, thus implicitly demonstrating the evolved nature of pre-conquest Irish civilization.[27] These articles supported Petrie's investigations into the Irish landscape and further presented the land of Ireland as, quite literally, the common ground that united Irishmen of all origins and faiths. Petrie and O'Donovan's efforts were supplemented by those of a host of voluntary correspon-

---

26 See George Petrie, 'Fine Arts. Historical sketch of the past and present state of the fine arts in Ireland. First article', in *DPJ*, 1:11, 8 September 1832, p. 84.   **27** John O'Donovan, 'Antiquity of corn in Ireland', in *DPJ*, 1:14, 29 September 1832, p. 108.

3 Andrew Nicholl, *Ruins of the King's Castle, Ardglass, County of Down.*
Dublin Penny Journal, vol. I, no. 40 (30 March 1833).

dents, who through the *DPJ* could disseminate their knowledge of specific locations or events to a nationwide audience.

By contrast, Otway's more limited efforts on the subject of the Irish landscape followed a more precise if narrower plan. They were organised in a coherent series entitled 'A Tour to Connaught', and described the journey of Otway's alter-ego, Terence O'Toole, from Dublin to the Shannon. Unlike Petrie, who broke new ground with his topographical articles for a mass audience, Otway was following in a consolidated scheme of travel literature. Otway described the various towns and villages his characters were crossing, recollecting major historical events, but these were not the main focus of his pieces. Proportionally, he devoted more space to the material aspects of the Irish land and its economic prospects, transforming the locations he visited into parables of Ireland's woes. The first article, for instance, contained an account of a woollen factory in Celbridge, and its vicissitudes were transformed by Otway into an *exemplum* of the obstacles faced by manufactures in Ireland (lack of a poor law, lack of skilled labour, no 'spirit of industry' among the Irish).[28] Similarly,

---

28 Caesar Otway, 'A tour to Connaught part 1', in *DPJ*, 1:14, 29 September 1832, p. 107.

crossing the estates of the duke of Leinster provided Otway with the chance to discuss the need for an Irish yeomanry,[29] while the bogs of Meath had him launch a tirade against lazy landlords who did not improve their lands.[30] There was a humorous exchange between O'Toole and the character of an enterprising Irish tobacco grower, who was however dodging the law forbidding such cultivation,[31] and the regular confutation of another character, the 'Manchester bagman' and his ignorance of everything Irish.[32] The physical landscape was certainly present, but it seemed to take second place to the moral considerations Otway extracted from what he observed. Interestingly for a preacher like Otway, religious matters were presented only in an indirect way. For example, the neat appearance of Moate and its surrounds provided Otway with a platform to praise the Quakers who lived in the town,[33] but there was in the eight issues no converse deprecation of Catholic superstition. Indeed, the history of the Catholic cathedral of Clonard was given as an example of the combination of learning and scholarship in ancient Ireland.[34] This oblique approach to a theme dear to Otway was due certainly to the strict limitations imposed on unstamped periodicals, but arguably it also sprang from the editorial goals of the *DPJ*. When Otway republished the articles as a part of his book *A Tour in Connaught*, they were immediately followed by a condemnation of Catholic super-stition at Clonmacnoise.[35] His description of the college in Maynooth also changed from a large building 'more like a large barrack than a college' in the *DPJ* article,[36] to 'a great factory, where strong machinery is applied to the purpose of bending mind' in the book version.[37] The woes that Otway observed on his journey with the readers of the *DPJ*, however, were equally spread between native and conqueror. Otway seemed to suggest that Ireland's problems could only be solved if all the components of Irish society dedicated themselves to improving their country. It was therefore necessary to induce the Irish of all classes to know and admire their country, which was the ultimate objective of the *DPJ*.

What was slightly unusual about Otway's articles is the fact that they were not illustrated, as might have been expected from a travelogue. They were not given pride of place either, as might have been the case for the production of the editor of *DPJ*, but were instead tucked away in the middle pages of the journal. The intervals between the first six articles were moderately regular, between two and four weeks, but they mysteriously lengthened to seven between parts six and seven, and an unusual eighteen between seven and eight. Thus, if they surpassed Petrie's articles in

29 Caesar Otway, 'A tour to Connaught part 2', in *DPJ*, 1:16, 13 October 1832, p. 127. **30** Caesar Otway, 'A tour to Connaught part 4', in *DPJ*, 1:23, 1 December 1832, p. 179. **31** Caesar Otway, 'A tour to Connaught part 5', in *DPJ*, 1:24, 8 December 1832, pp 186–7. **32** Caesar Otway, 'A tour to Connaught part 4', p. 178.   **33** Caesar Otway, 'A tour to Connaught part 8', in *DPJ*, 1:52, 22 June 1833, p. 414.   **34** Caesar Otway, 'A tour to Connaught part 3' in *DPJ*, 1:19, 3 November 1832, p. 151.   **35** Caesar Otway, *A tour in Connaught* (Dublin: Curry, 1839). The reprints from the *DPJ* form chapters 1 and 2. **36** Caesar Otway, 'A tour to Connaught part 2', p. 126.   **37** Caesar Otway, *A tour in Connaught*, p. 15.

coherence by having a common thread, they certainly lost out on visibility. Overall, Otway's voice is harder to trace within the journal he had personally founded.

But Petrie's editorial approach also had serious limitations, which manifested itself in the absence of a guiding plan behind the locations described. In the one surviving letter from Nicholl to Petrie, the Belfast man offered some of his drawings, all on northern Irish locations, but regretted not being able to provide anything on Omagh.[38] The exchange suggests that Petrie had commissioned some illustrations, but that he had not imposed absolute requirements on Nicholl, perhaps simply asking for Ulster subjects. The strategy of publishing articles from external correspondents was also a dangerous one. On the one hand, it strengthened the bonds between the audience and the magazine, by allowing readers to cross the divide from consumers of meaning into producers. On the other, it introduced an outside voice that could partly elude the control of the editorial team, if not firmly managed. Both Petrie and Otway appear to have dedicated only some of their time to the conduction of the *DPJ*, the first being involved with the Ordnance Survey, the second with the birth of the *Dublin University Magazine*. As a result, they were probably always in need of original articles to fill their pages. In the topography department, areas where correspondents were more numerous, like Dublin or Ulster, were the subjects of numerous articles, while others remained completely untouched. One example of this situation is the extraordinary figure of Robert Armstrong, a Drogheda-born housepainter who had turned to artistic and antiquarian pursuits. He wrote and illustrated several articles quite capably, but concentrated exclusively on the areas he was familiar with, Drogheda and its environs, and Dublin, where he was working as a teacher. There was however no such correspondent writing from Connacht, for example, and therefore the land and history of the province were the subject of no article at all. Petrie's efforts in presenting the Irish landscape to his readers were therefore episodic and inconclusive.

Petrie and Otway's articles did not appear in isolation. Each was read and understood as part of a multiple text comprising the other articles within a single issue, and also articles by the same authors or on similar topics in preceding and subsequent numbers of the *DPJ*. If properly managed, such complexity would greatly reinforce the efforts of the *DPJ* in creating a neutral Irish identity. The two editors, however, seemed only capable of profound but disorganised insights into Irish history, or of entertaining but sporadic descriptions. Both these approaches were unsuitable for their chosen publishing genre. Periodicals depend on the repetition of structures and motifs at fixed intervals of time. These recurring formats are what persuade readers, week after week, to return to a familiar, routine object, and identify with the point of view of the journal.[39] Petrie and Otway instead provided their readers with no such continuity, thus complicating the chances of survival of their magazine.

38 Andrew Nicholl to George Petrie, 14 March 1833, in NLI, MS 792. **39** See Margaret Beetham, 'Towards a theory of periodicals as a publishing genre', in Laurel Brake (ed.), *Investigating Victorian journalism* (Basingstoke, 1990), p. 26.

Moreover, it appears that the strategy of combining spectacle with instruction did not fully work. After the first few months, sales started to drop and in June 1833 they had fallen to less than 10,000.[40] Proprietor J.S. Folds had to sell the *DPJ* to a new owner, and Petrie and Otway lost their jobs. The *DPJ* continued for another three years under editor/proprietor Philip Dixon Hardy, but with different aims and different contributors. Petrie and Otway's failure stems from chiefly another misjudgement of their chosen medium. The penny journal was perceived as too popular to attract the patronage of upper-class readers, who were more likely to cultivate an interest in history and archaeology. At the same time, the illustrations alone did not make it sufficiently spectacular or entertaining to captivate a lower-middle-class readership. Its lack of an openly political stance probably impaired its sales, as neither unionists nor nationalists could easily subsume its meaning into their discourse. Pride in a shared landscape was not enough to create an Irish identity independent of politics and religion. It would take an openly political journal like the *Nation* to exploit more fully the cultural potential of the Irish landscape, and call for a nationality that could transcend religious lines, devising clear politics for the Irish land.

40 Philip Dixon Hardy, letter to the editor, *Saunders's Newsletter*, 6 December 1839.

Claiming the landscape: popular balladry in pre-famine Ireland

MAURA CRONIN

Broadside ballads, narrative songs printed cheaply for public sale, were a significant form of entertainment for pre-famine Ireland's *cosmhuintir* or common people, that is, those below the ranks of the middle classes. Mostly in English, the ballads frequently echoed the themes and refrains of Irish compositions, their themes including political invective, tragedy, romance and love of place. Printed in jobbing shops throughout the island, particularly in Dublin and Cork, ballads were sung and sold through streets, fairs and markets – or wherever else crowds gathered – and were considered by contemporaries to both reflect and shape popular opinion.[1]

To what extent did the printed ballads and the orally transmitted songs, Irish and English, reflect a popular consciousness of landscape? Did they follow the current literary trend of equating the character of the landscape with the character of the people – a trend that was also visible in print culture outside the literature of the elite? Tourists' accounts, for instance, were peppered with parallels between scenery and *mentalité,* while works whose focus was primarily factual were equally susceptible to a preoccupation with the romantic.[2] Lewis' *Topographical Dictionary* of 1837, besides detailing local population figures, economic pursuits, topography and prominent landmarks, also pursued the scenic and sublime, making specific references to 'lofty mountains', 'sublime and beautiful scenery', 'view which is the most magnificent imaginable', 'most picturesque and romantic scenery'.[3] Contemporary trade directories and tourist guides, too, mixed practical information with descriptions of awe-inspiring landscape, and although guides to Irish beauty-spots, especially Killarney, continued to be produced mainly by Dublin and London publishers, provincial entrepreneurs took up the initiative from 1840 onwards. Windele's 1840 *Guide to the Cove and the Harbour of Cork,* for example, included scenic, antiquarian and historical material,[4] while in 1843, the canny proprietor of the recently opened Kilkee Baths published what was really an extended advertisement for his own business, but which doubled as a general tourist's guide to the beauties of Kilkee and its environs.[5] Newspapers, too, used descriptions of landscape to further two distinct ends. Firstly, such descriptions were a verbal substitute for visual representation – a

---

1 The research for this chapter has been facilitated by the award of an Irish Research Council Senior Fellowship 2004. 2 Glenn Hooper, *The tourist's gaze: travellers to Ireland, 1800–2000* (Cork, 2001), especially pp 55–59; 67–73; 85–94. 3 Samuel Lewis, *Topographic dictionary of Ireland* (London, 1837), pp 283–4 et passim. 4 John Windele, *Guide to the Cove and Harbour of Cork* (Cork, 1840).

veritable painting in words, accurate enough, though frequently sharing the painting's tendency to 'touch up' nature. Secondly, landscape descriptions, like those in litera-ture, were used as a metaphor for the perceived qualities of the people who populated the landscape. Accounts of meetings, outings and communal pastimes, all becoming increasingly newsworthy in the 1830s, provided an opportunity for the newspaper writers to exploit to the full this descriptive-cum-metaphorical function of landscape. Such was the *Waterford Mail*'s account of a purely local event, the Dunmore East regatta of August 1833:

> We do not think that the majestic scenery of our River ever appeared to more advantage. At one side the bold and precipitous cliffs of the County Waterford reared themselves, bearing upon their broad shoulders the varied and animated population [watching the event]. Opposite to this, and well contrasting with it was the flat coast of the County Wexford, studded with neat villages and villas, and terminated by the Hook Tower light house, the useful and cheering beacon of the wearisome mariner. Between the two shores the River of Waterford expands its broad bosom and joins the broader sea. Innumerable yachts and boats of all descriptions and of every size and tonnage were upon the water, and by the fluttering of their white sails and the heaving motion with which they were wafted along, completed the picturesque character of the scene. Steamers and other large vessels arriving and departing added, if possible, still more to the effect.[6]

To what extent did such a consciousness of landscape, either in its pictorial or symbolic sense, enter the consciousness of the *cosmhuintir*? Some Irish language poetry of the eighteenth and early nineteenth century certainly implies an intense awareness of scenery and natural beauty in a local setting. Merriman's 'Cúirt an Mheon Oíche', for example, gives a sense of the combined serenity and menace in the landscape of east Clare, as well as the impact of that landscape on the individual:

> Do ghealladh mo chroí an uair chínn Loch Gréine,
> An talamh, 's an tír is íor na spéire,
> Taithneamhacht aoibhinn suíomh na sléibhte
> Ag bagairt a gcinn thar dhroim a chéile.[7]

5 *New guide to the Scenery of Killarney by a Visitor* (Dublin: O'Flanagan, 1830); *A directory of Kilkee in the County Clare on the West Coast of Ireland with a map showing the situation and number of the lodges, to which is added some useful information relating to warm and vapour baths, and the mineral waters of the locality, which have been analysed by Dr. Gore of Limerick. Published by and for Hugh Hogan, proprietor of the Kilkee Baths* (Limerick, 1843). **6** *Waterford Mail*, 31 August 1833. **7** Brian Merriman, *Cúirt an Mheon-Oíche*, ed. Liam Ó Murchú (Baile Atha Cliath, 1982), p. 19; Ciaran Carson (translator), *The Midnight Court* (Oldcastle, Co. Westmeath, 2005), p. 19. Carson's translation runs as follows: 'The sight of Lough Graney would dazzle my eyes, / As the countryside sparkled through the blue skies. / Uplifting to

At least some individuals from within the *cosmhuintir*, though admittedly from its higher ranks, were not only well acquainted with Merriman's lines, but could also apply them to the landscape that they observed in their daily lives. Half a century after Merriman penned his poem, Humphrey O'Sullivan, a Kerry-born schoolmaster who plied his trade in the south Kilkenny town of Callan until his death in 1838, quoted the lines in his diary when he looked at the snow-covered Wicklow mountains on his way from Callan to Dublin in April 1831.[8]

Such consciousness of landscape, its sights and – equally importantly – its sounds, was peppered throughout O'Sullivan's diary, as is obvious in one of his entries for early January 1832:

> The little thrush is singing sweetly on the branch in every sheltered bush; the wild lark happily singing high up in the sky, and many other birds enhance the beauty of the morning with their sweet song. The bright daisy, the yellow dandelion, the star-like celandine and the yellow flower of the furze adorn every glen. A fine soft quiet cloudy day.[9]

Such timeless consciousness of landscape is equally apparent in his somewhat clipped description of the dawn scenery as he travelled from Callan to Clonmel in December 1831:

> First signs of dawn came at Tigh na Naoi Míle / daybreak at Muileann na gCloch Chapel; the first blush of aurora at the opening of Glen Bodhar; rosy blushes before sunrise at the end of Glen Bodhar; sunrise shortly after that. The view of Gleann an Óir and the Commeraghs was beautiful.[10]

Whether such an awareness of landscape was the preserve of a culturally attuned and literary minority is not clear, though that it penetrated down into local communities is suggested by the longevity of some songs at regional level, where local scenes (admittedly less minutely and more formulaically described than by Merriman or O'Sullivan) set the scene for the ensuing story. Máire Bhuí Ní Laoire's 'Cath Chéim an Fhia', perpetuating the memory of the armed clash between locals and the authorities at Keimaneigh in January 1822, evokes the sights and sounds of the countryside around the pass in which the event occurred:

> Cois abha Ghleanna an Chéime in Uibh Laoire 'sea bhímse
> Mar a dtéann an fhia san oíche chun síor chodhladh sóil
> Ag macnamh seal liom féinig, ag déanamh mo smaointe,
> Ag éisteacht i gcoilltibh le binn-ghuth na neoin.[11]

see how the mountains were stacked, / Each head peeping over a neighbouring back.'
8 Tomás de Bhaldraithe (ed.), *The diary of Humphrey O'Sullivan, 1827–1835* (Dublin and Cork, 1979), p. 105. **9** Ibid., p. 116, 8 January 1832. **10** Ibid., p. 113, 28 December 1831.
11 'Cath Chéim an Fhia', written by Máire Bhuí Ní Laoire of Inchigeelagh in West Cork.

In the broadside ballads, however, though many were in praise of place, landscape descriptions were stylised and formulaic, just like the classical allusions with which they were inter-layered. The language used was pedestrian, with many 'floaters' or stock lines and phrases used more to fit the requirements of metre and internal rhyming (borrowed to some extent from contemporary Irish language poetry) than to capture the essence of the scene described.[12] As a result, sentiments in harmony with Irish language idiom and poetic convention frequently descended into combined hyperbole and banality. The 'Praises of Cove', printed in the 1830s by Haly of Cork, was a typical combination of the allegorical and the humdrum:

> What pleasant prospects are near to Cove,
> From Passage Ferry to Belgrove,
> Where nymphs and swains do range and rove
> To take sweet recreations.[13]

'Sweet Castle Hyde' was in the same vein. Written in the late eighteenth century in praise of an estate on the banks of the Blackwater near the north Cork town of Fermoy, its composer was reputedly chased away from the gates of the said demesne when its owner thought the song was one of ridicule, so exaggerated were its sentiments:

> The richest groves throughout this nation,
> In fine plantation you will see there,
> The rose, the tulip and sweet carnation
> All vying with the lily fair.[14]

Some researchers of broadside balladry consider that the woodcut heading the broadside was as great a selling point as were the words of the ballad.[15] This woodcut was the obvious place for visual representation of landscape, but relatively few landscape-based woodcuts exist. Granted, a number of castles, bridges, rivers, woods and urban skylines figure in the woodcuts, but these are based less on representation of a real scene than on a stylized pattern applicable to any one of many familiar land-scapes. Thus, 'Sweet Castle Hyde' printed in the 1830s by Haly of Cork whose

For an outline of this event, see Brian Brennan, *Máire Bhuí Ní Laoire: a poet of her people* (Cork, 2000). 'I [wander] beside the Keim Glen river in Uibh Laoire, Where the deer goes at night to sleep, Where I think and meditate, While listening in the woods to the sweet song of the birds.'   12 Michael N. Joy, 'The everyday uses of nineteenth century broadside ballads and the writings of John Clare' p. 12, http://www.jrc.sophia.ac.jp/kiyou/ki22/ mjoy.pdf: accessed 10 November 2006.   13 'The Praises of Cove', Madden Ballads, Reel 12, frame 607.   14 'Sweet Castle Hyde, a much-admired song', Madden Ballads, Reel 12, frame 8497; Andrew Carpenter (ed.), *Verse in English from eighteenth century Ireland* (Cork, 1998), p. 520.   15 Michael N. Joy, 'The everyday uses of nineteenth century broadside ballads', p. 5.

woodcuts were superior to those of many contemporary printers, bore at its head the woodcut of a stately turreted castle built in the fold of two hills, skirted by woodland, and overlooking a graceful bridge over a broad river. But this was, in fact, a less accurate representation of the palladian-style Castle Hyde than of Lismore Castle some twenty miles distant on the shores of the same Blackwater river in the neighbouring county of Waterford, and described by Lewis as 'an imposing object, rising majestically from the elevated bank of the river, and occupying the verge of a precipitous cliff, partly clothed with wood and towering above the foliage which conceals its base'.[16] Similarly, 'Cork's Own Town' was headed by an urban skyline, complete with steeples, towers and river, equally applicable to Limerick and Waterford as to Cork – as obvious in the use of the same or similar woodcuts in other contemporary broadsides, while 'A New Song in Praise of the River Lee' had as its woodcut a generic illustration of a bridge over a tree-lined river – which could represent any river in any age and was, indeed, used also to head another Haly number, 'The Lovely Sweet Banks of the Suir'.[17] In most ballads, however, the use of woodcuts even vaguely representative of local landscape was dispensed with, and the text was headed by pictorial representations only tangentially linked with the place and scene celebrated. Thus, 'An Admired Song on Youghal Harbour', its third line describing how 'sol appeared with pomp most charming', was surmounted by a stylised sun, while 'The Praises of Cove' was headed by a woodcut of a three-masted ship, appropriate as an indicator of Cobh's maritime role, but only barely linked with the theme of the ballad.[18]

In most broadside ballads, it is clear that reference to landscape was simply a backdrop to the adulation of individuals, groups or idealized types. The ballad praising Cobh focussed primarily on the 'Irish heroes' who manned the naval vessels in the harbour and the barracks on the hill; 'The Lovely Sweet Banks of the Suir' simply provided a backdrop to the adulation of the poet's 'own grá mo cree'; and 'Sweet Castle Hyde' – despite the unfavourable reaction of the castle's owner – was dedicated more to praising the family's wealth and hospitality than to describing the local scenery:

> If noble princes, from foreign places
> Should chance to sail to this Irish shore,
> 'Tis in this valley they would be feasted
> As often heroes had been before[19]

– surely an echo of the celebration and lament for the south Tipperary Butler family in the Irish language song 'Cill Cais' dating from the earlier eighteenth century:

16 'Sweet Castle Hyde', Madden Ballads, Reel 12, frame 8497; Lewis, *Topographical dictionary*, ii, 283–4. **17** 'A New Song in Praise of the River Lee', National Library of Ireland Broadside Collection, no. 243; 'The Lovely Sweet Banks of the Suir', Madden Ballads, Reel 12, frame 8387. **18** 'The Praises of Cove', Madden Ballads, Reel 12, frame 607; 'An Admired Song on Youghal Harbour', National Library of Ireland Broadside Collection, no. 25. **19** 'The Praises of Cove'; 'Sweet Castle Hyde'; 'The Lovely Sweet Banks of the Suir'.

An áit úd a gcónaíodh an deighbhean,
Fuair gradam is meidhir thar mnáibh,
Bhíodh iarlaí ag tarraingt thar toinn ann
Is an t-aifreann binn á rá.[20]

The local landscape, in both its visual and aural aspects, was also used in the popular songs composed in the early nineteenth century. Raftery, in his lament for Anthony Daly, hanged for alleged Whiteboy offences in Co. Galway in April 1820, interlinked landscape and personal tragedy:

Ni lasann na réalta
Is na héisc ní phreabann ar toinn,
Ní thagann drúcht ar an bhféar
Is na héanlaith ní labhrann go binn.[21]

Similarly, a bastardized broadside version of the Irish "Séan Ó Dhuibhir a' Ghleanna' a song lamenting a seventeenth-century Tipperary raparee, took up the original's evocation of landscape sounds:

One morning as I started
From the house of Morpheus,
The hounds and trumpets rattled
Which caused the earth to shake.[22]

Thus, landscape, while frequently implied rather than elaborated upon, was a pervasive presence in popular song, whether in the Irish or English language. Usually supplying the harmless picturesque, it could also be used as a code to facilitate the expression of popular resentments, real or imagined. In an era when politicisation was proceeding at an accelerated pace, not only among the upwardly mobile middle classes but also within the ranks of the *cosmhuintir*, there was an increasing tendency to link landscape with national identity.[23] If by the mid-1840s, the Young Ireland

20 'The place where the noble lady lived, Who was honoured above all women, Earls travelled there from over the sea ,And the melodious mass was celebrated'. Donal O'Sullivan and Micheál Ó Súilleabháin (eds), *Bunting's Ancient music of Ireland* (Cork, 1983), pp 3–4. 21 'Anthony Daly', Ciarán Ó Coigligh, *Raiftearaí, Amhráin agus Dánta* (Baile Atha Cliath, 1987), p. 133. 'The stars do not shine, Nor do the fish leap on the waves, No dew rests on the grass, And the birds do not sing sweetly'. 22 The melody to which the song was matched was widely sung, certainly from the late eighteenth century onwards, a version being printed in Bunting's *Ancient Irish Airs* (London: Preston and Son, 1796) most of the airs in which were collected from performers at the Belfast Harp Festival of 1792. The original text reads:'Ar m'éirí dhom ar maidin, / Grian an tSamhraidh ag taithneamh, / Cúl an úll á casadh / Agus ceol binn na n-éan'. A more elegant translation was produced in the later nineteenth century, beginning 'After Aughrim's Great Disaster ...' 23 Elizabeth Crooke, *Politics, archaeology and the establishment of the National Museum* (Dublin, 2001), pp

movement saw the Irish landscape as 'inescapably scored with historical signs', this tendency had already begun with O'Connell who constantly referred to local land-scape to make his audience conscious of current grievance and its imminent redress.[24] At Limerick he pointed to the 'majestic Shannon' as a symbol of Ireland's future destiny; at Cashel he outlined Ireland's past, present and future against the backdrop of the Rock; at Bagnelstown he gestured towards the surrounding 'verdant vales' from which the native had been displaced by the foreigner.[25] O'Connell's lieu-tenants at regional level, particularly during the anti-tithe agitation, took up this historicization of the landscape, coupling their scenic allusions with maledictions on 'heartless tyrants' and reminding their listeners, whether on the plains of Meath or on the banks of the Suir, of Cromwell's appreciation of the Munster landscape – 'This is a country worth fighting for'.[26]

The same interweaving of place, past oppression and future retribution was apparent in the broadsides and chapbook songs. A maudlin song on 'My Own Sweet Wicklow County' was transformed into a potentially inflammatory number by including a reference to 'my sires, the great O'Byrnes'.[27] Even more pointedly, the 'Church of Slane' openly equated the ruined state of the abbey in a Kildare village with the current humiliation of Ireland:

> This abbey once respected, alas, now stands neglected,
> I really did inspect it, which does increase my pain,
> That man's degeneration and Erin's degradation
> Which leaves depopulated the ancient church of Slane.[28]

Similarly, in 'The Abolition of Tithes' sung in Tralee in 1832, physical ruin, former reli-gious persecution and current grievance were all interlinked:

> Our clergy they were banished
> And our abbeys levelled down,
> All for the pampered Ministers
> By King Harry, the bloodhound.[29]

32–4.   **24** Sean Ryder, 'The politics of landscape and region in nineteenth century poetry' in Glenn Hooper and Leon Litvack (eds), *Ireland in the nineteenth century: regional identity* (Dublin, 2000), p. 170.   **25** *Freeman's Journal*, 21 April 1841; *Tipperary Free Press*, 24 May 1843.   **26** *Tralee Mercury*, 4;18 August 1832.   **27** 'My Own Sweet Wicklow County', Cambridge University Library Irish Ballads 446, folio 39: 'Home of my sires, the great O'Byrnes, / My birthplace dear to me, / Oh when that day of hope returns / I'll risk this life for thee. / But patiently I will await / The will of Heaven's bounty, / And night and day I'll always pray / For my own sweet Wicklow county.' Fiach MacHugh O'Byrne (1544–1597) defeated Lord Gray's forces at Glenmalure in 1580.   **28** 'The church of Slane', Cambridge University Library Irish Ballads 446, f. 179.   **29** 'The Abolition of Tithes', Chief Secretary's Office, Private Papers 1832, 1458, 31 July 1832.

Where references to landscape served to recall specific local events, the capacity of the ballad to fuel popular grievance was particularly powerful. Schama, in his work on landscape and memory, gives the historian a salutary reminder of the necessity to know a place and its landscape in order to understand its impact on events over time:

> Historians are supposed to reach the past always through texts, occasionally through images; things that are safely caught in the bell jar of academic convention; look but don't touch. But one of my best-loved teachers ... had always insisted on directly experiencing 'a sense of place', of using 'the archive of the feet'.[30]

This warning is certainly worth bearing in mind when exploring the link between landscape, balladry and popular political consciousness in pre-famine Ireland. It is clear that certain places – and the landscapes linked with them – acted as veritable codes linking past and present, codes best understood when historical exploration is accompanied by familiarity with the landscape. Thus, references to the Curragh of Kildare were frequent in popular songs and ballads, partly because the placename fitted into an endless variety of rhymes, partly because its association with the army made it a perfect location for songs about love betrayed, partly because the open and windswept landscape of the Curragh was one that remained in the imagination, and partly because it was the scene of a major defeat of the rebels during the 1798 rebellion – one of the most emotive events within living memory in the period under review. 'Young Bony's Freedom', for instance, sung not only in the Kildare town of Newbridge but also in centres as far distant as Kilmallock (Co. Limerick) and Broadford (Co. Clare) between March and November 1831 took up this coded message, promising that

> At the next Curragh meeting
> We will leave those bigots sleeping,
> Where they slaughtered Roman Catholics
> And made their blood to spill.[31]

In reality, then, the stress on landscape in ballads was to make an event 'visible' in the memory of the audience, to link that landscape and event with a memorable melody – capable of repeated recall over a long period – and ultimately to avenge that event.

This link between landscape, event, memory, melody and revenge was even more obvious in two interlinked songs, composed some thirty years apart, one in Irish and the other in English. Both songs were entitled 'Slievenamon', and were called after the south Tipperary mountain of that name from whose summit four counties can

30 Simon Schama, *Landscape and memory* (London, 1995), p. 24. **31** 'Young Bony's Freedom', Chief Secretary's Office, Private Papers 1831, 101, 3 March, 16 August, 22 November 1831.

be seen and which is inextricably linked with the heroes of the mythic Fenian cycle.[32] The first version was 'Sliabh na mBan', dating from soon after 1798, recalling the failed rising at Carrigmockler on the mountain's southern slopes near Nine-Mile-House. A haunting lament blaming failure on betrayal, the song's several stanzas were closed by couplets simultaneously stressing the link between heroic failure and the local landscape of Slievenamon, and promising revenge for the betrayal causing that failure. Thus, memory and aspiration were tied to a familiar landscape, and familiar local scenery and popular recall were, in turn, linked to a nebulous sense of wider identity:

> Dá mba dhóigh liom féinig go mb'fhíor an scéal sin,
> Bheadh mo chroí chomh h-éadrom le lon ar sceach,
> Go mbeadh cloí ar mhéirligh is an adharc dá shéideadh
> Ar thaobh na gréine de Shliabh na mBan.[33]

The second Slievenamon composition appeared in 1832, following a major incident in the escalating anti-tithe agitation.[34] This event was an attack by local people on a process server and fifteen policemen at the townland of Carrigshock in the hills above Knocktopher in South Kilkenny, some thirteen miles north-east of Slievenamon. In the attack, three locals were killed, while the process server and police were brutally stoned or beaten to death. This was not first such incident in the tithe war, but it was one of the most widely publicized and longest remembered, partly because it was so gruesome, and partly because of the outcome of the subsequent trials.

A number of arrests had been made after the incident, but it had proved impossible to bring a successful case against the attackers. The cholera epidemic disrupted the trials in early 1832, and when the trial was eventually held at the Kilkenny assizes of July 1832, it proved impossible to secure a conviction because of the local conspiracy of silence surrounding the affair. Thus, as the trials collapsed seven months after the original incident, a wave of popular elation spread and a number of ballads celebrating the event were composed – the most significant being 'The Downfall of Tithes', alternatively called 'Sleeve na Mon', which was sung throughout Munster and beyond up to late 1832.[35] Printed in inelegant but fluid English, its metre and refrain suggest it was probably sung to the air of the original 'Sliabh na mBan'.[36] The

---

32 From the summit of Slievenamon can be seen the Rock of Cashel and the flat expanse of mid-Tipperary and Kilkenny to the north, the Suir Valley and Comeragh Mountains to the South, and the Nore valley, Blackstairs Mountains and Mount Leinster to the East. **33** George Sigerson, *Poets and poetry of Munster* (Dublin, 1860), p. 108. 'If I could believe that this tale were true, My heart would be as light as the blackbird on the bough That traitors would be vanquished and the horn blowing On the sunny side of Slievenamon.' **34** The spellings vary from Slieve na Man to Sleevenamon to Slieve na Maun. **35** Georges Denis Zimmermann, *Songs of Irish rebellion: political street ballads and rebel songs, 1780–1900* (Dublin, 1967), pp 31; 206–7. **36** 'The Downfall of Tithes', Chief Secretary's Office, Private Papers

closing lines of each stanza not only echoed the equivalent lines of the original Irish song, but acted as an answer to the 1798 number's calls for revenge, for although the Carrickshock incident had not happened at Slievenamon, it had unfolded only a dozen miles to the north-east, within that mountain's natural hinterland, and certainly within the region in which memories of the 1798 defeat were still alive. A brief glance at two closing couplets from both the 1798 and the 1831 compositions illustrates the way in which, firstly, the earlier number's calls for revenge were answered and fulfilled by the triumphalist lines of the later broadside ballad and, secondly, a familiar feature of the landscape became a symbol of avenged defeat:

> Beidh cloí ar mhéarlaigh is an adharc dá shéideadh
> Ar thaobh na gréine de Shliabh na mBan ...
> Is go gcuirfeam *yeomen* ag crith 'na mbróga
> Is go mbuailfi coach iad ar Shliabh na mBan.[37](1798)

as against

> But all that's past is but a token
> Of what we'll show them on Slievenamon ...
> We'll free old Ireland from every traitor,
> Or die like heroes on Slievenamon.(1831)

The broadside ballad spread throughout the country like wildfire between January and October 1832, and with it spread the association of place and landscape with popular triumph, but now, interlinked with the 1798-related memories of Slievenamon, the scene in question was 'the narrow boreen of Carrickshock'.[38] Place and event thus passed into the codified vocabulary of the *cosmhuintir*, so that well into the 1830s when policemen were being taunted or threatened by hostile crowds, the phrases 'Give them Carrickshock!' and 'Knocktopher to them!' were used as rallying cries.[39]

But if place, landscape and popular triumph were closely interlinked in the subtext of the songs and broadside ballads, there was also a sense in which popular triumph was stamped both aurally and visually on the landscape itself. It was no coincidence that the song-narrated incidents of both 1798 and 1831 took place on hills – the earlier incident on the lower reaches of Slievenamon and the later at Carrickshock on the slopes of the Walsh Mountains. Similarly, when the ultra-loyalist candidate, Colonel Verner, won the Armagh election in 1835, both his supporters and opponents (fairly evenly divided in the south of the county) gathered on neigh-

1832, 1063, 1431, 9, 28 July 1832.   **37** 'The traitor would be vanquished and the horn blowing On the sunny side of Slievanamon; Yeomen would be made to shake in their shoes On the sunny side of Slievenamon'.   **38** 'The Downfall of Tithes', Chief Secretary's Office, Private Papers 1832, 1572, 14 August 1832.   **39** *Kilkenny Moderator*, 1 March 1832; *Waterford Mail*, 6 July 1833. Knocktopher is the village nearest to Carrickshock.

bouring hills to taunt and abuse one another, while three years earlier similar hill-sited confrontations had taken place in Sligo.[40] Many such attempts to monopolise landscape and locality were, particularly in Ulster and its borderlands, a manifestation of inter-denominational rivalry. But there were some rare occasions when opposing creeds joined together on the same hillside to present a common opposition to the authorities, as in 1830 when over a thousand people of all denominations assembled on the Co. Tyrone hill of Larnagar between Augher and Fintona to demonstrate against tithe.[41] In Munster, crowds seemed to gravitate automatically to a local hill when some issue of major local importance was brewing. For instance, in early 1846 a large crowd of country people assembled at Ardvarna near Ahane, between Limerick city and Newport, when rumours of impending evictions spread. Remaining there for three days, they were supplied by food from the village below, and kept themselves warm in the bitter weather by playing hurling.[42] Later in the same year, when the potato scarcity had begun to pinch, another crowd converged on Tory Hill near Croom on the other side of Limerick, to discuss how the crisis might be met.[43] This gravitation towards hills was largely a practical matter. Locals planning a foray or organising a meeting without official approval could more effectively watch out for approaching danger from a vantage point high on a hill, while control of the higher ground also gave them a psychological advantage over those whom they confronted. So much was the take-over of hills associated with popular mobilisation from the early 1830s onwards that in official reports to Dublin Castle the absence of shouting and horn-blowing crowds on hills was taken as an indication that no trouble was expected at local level.[44]

The acoustic quality of the landscape of hill and valley also facilitated the transmission of messages of warning and celebration across the miles. The human shout could carry long distances, particularly when magnified by a natural echo or when relayed from one valley to the next by successive groups of people. In 1822, when the confrontation between locals and authorities took place at Céim an Fhia, the great shout – 'an liú gur lean i bhfad i gcéin' – rousing the local community across several miles of hills lived on in song and folklore for over 150 years.[45] Similarly, during the tithe agitation of the 1830s, the ringing of chapel bells and the more resonant sounding of horns vibrating across a landscape rallied local communities as at Gowran in Co. Kilkenny where horns were blown in February 1832 to warn the locals that the police were approaching to arrest a man who had been involved in a murder, or at Desertserges in Co. Cork a year later, when similar sounding of horns

---

40 *Ballina Impartial and Tyrawley Advertiser,* 25 January 1835; Chief Secretary's Office, Private Papers, 1832, 1585, 15 August 1832.   **41** Chief Secretary's Office, Private Papers, 1830, 191, 15 December 1830.   **42** Chief Secretary's Office, Registered Papers, Outrage Reports 1846, 17/1045, 4125, 6, 8 January 1846.   **43** *Limerick and Clare Reporter,* 11 April 1846.   **44** Chief Secretary's Office, Private Papers, 1832, 223, 8 February 1832.   **45** 'The shout that carried afar off'. Brennan, *Máire Bhuí Ní Laoire,* p. 38; Cathal Ó Riada, 'Cath Céim an Fhia in its historical context', unpublished undergraduate research dissertation, Mary Immaculate College Limerick, 1984.

gathered people from far and near to fall, Carrickshock-style, on a posse approaching to collect tithe.[46] It was hardly surprising that songs in both Irish and English used the sounding of horns on the hills as one of the most popular motifs signifying popular vigilance and triumph:

> Is chuala fuaim na hadhairce
> Ar Sliabh Guille le sult is greann
> Ag Ó Conaill is a mhór-shluaite
> Go luath cugainn thar sáile anall.[47]

It was not simply a matter of using communication and vantage points to the greatest possible advantage: it was also a way of demonstrating to the hated 'other' (whether a rival community or an unwelcome representative of the central authorities) one's control of the local landscape.

But it was the visual rallying signs that most effectively staked popular claims to the landscape. Perhaps the most dramatic attempt to impress on the landscape the ubiquity and tenaciousness of anti-tithe sentiment at popular level was the wave of mound building – usually on hills or high ground – which occurred in the summer of 1832. The mounds, consisting of earth and rocks, were erected mostly in Leinster, though some ordnance survey-related mounds made in Munster by government engineers were mistaken for the anti-tithe variety.[48] Considered by nervous observers to serve as 'signal stations on corresponding heights' the anti-tithe mounds had little meaning in themselves – but stood as a physical sign of resistance to tithe, sometimes being erected within sight of the local police barracks. So symbolic did the mounds become that a veritable tug-of-war developed between locals on the one side, and law on the other, mounds demolished one day being re-erected the following night.[49] A major confrontation regarding the erection of an anti-tithe mound in the local landscape near the Wicklow village of Dunlavin in early July 1832 took place between locals on the one hand, and police, dragoons and yeomanry. Though the immediate issue was the demolition or retention of the mound, what lay at the heart of the confrontation was the settling of old scores (dating perhaps as far back as the 1798 rebellion) and the muscle-baring of an increasingly aggressive *cosmhuintir* intent on humbling a traditional elite.[50]

The second method of putting the common people's mark on the landscape,

46 Chief Secretary's Office, Private papers, 1832, 2175, 22 February 1832; *Waterford Mail*, 16 March 1833.   **47** 'Orange Grief, or Colleen beg na luchra', sung at Dunmanway, Co. Cork, 27 April 1841. Chief Secretary's Office, Registered Papers, Outrage Reports, 1841, 6/7015. 'I heard the sound of the horn on Slieve Guille with joy and delight, As O'Connell and his great band [came] swiftly to us over the sea'.   **48** Chief Secretary's Office, Private Papers 1832, 1609, 18 August 1832.   **49** Mounds were reported in July 1832 from as far apart as Eagle Hill near Hackettstown (Carlow) and Talbotstown, near Kippure mountain in Co. Wicklow. Chief Secretary's Office, Private Papers 1832, 1042, 1384, 8, 22 July 1832.   **50** Chief Secretary's Office, Private Papers, 1832, 1042, 8 July 1832

more transient but also more immediately powerful in impact, was the lighting in swift succession of bonfires or signal fires on neighbouring hills as soon as news of an event had broken:

> Céad moladh go brách le Rí na nGrást'
> Mar chonac-sa aréir na tinte cnámh,
> Do thóg mo chroí le h-áthas grinn.[51]

Thus, in August 1832, tithe-related excitement produced multiple signal fires on the hills around Sligo, while a parallel string of fires spread from the slopes of Nephin, above the Mayo parish of Addergoole, as far as Kilcummin – a distance of twenty miles. [52] A year later, a party of police and tithe collectors were ambushed at Drumtarriffe, in North Cork by a crowd of locals who had been 'assembled by the sounding of horns and the lighting of fires upon the hills'.[53]

But it was the Carrickshock affair and the subsequent acquittal of the prisoners that led to one of the most dramatic symbolic takeovers of the landscape by the *cosmhuintir* as bonfires blazed from hill to hill over a radius of some twenty miles. Within a few hours of the prisoners' liberation and their setting out on the twelve-mile journey home from Kilkenny city, fires flared from South Kilkenny to Slievenamon, on towards Fethard, Rosegreen and Cashel, and thence towards the Devil's Bit.[54] The broad landscape, centred on the Kilkenny and Tipperary lowlands and circled by ranges of hills and mountains from the Comeraghs in the south to the Castlecomer plateau in the north-east, became a natural amphitheatre in which the rising assertiveness of the common people literally blazed in the face of elite and authorities.[55] The letters flooding into Dublin Castle from frightened observers, particularly in the south of this amphitheatre, illustrated the rapidity with which the landscape was taken over by the bonfires. One observer in Cashel, for instance, described the scene thus:

> He first perceived a fire on the side of the hill – it was almost instantly answered by another at a short distance – that was rapidly replied to by a third, and, in less than five minutes, from fifty to sixty fires could be counted extending along a line of fifteen miles.[56]

---

51 'An Irish Elegy', Madden Ballads, Reel 12, frame 8356. This ballad refers to the 1835 Cork City election when the popular candidates triumphed. 'Praise for ever to the King of Grace, Since I saw the bonfires last night My heart rose with joy ...' **52** Chief Secretary's Office, Private Papers, 1832, 1585, 15 August 1832. **53** *Limerick Chronicle,* 9 January 1833. **54** *Freeman's Journal,* 10 August 1832. **55** The range of mountains, running clockwise from the south-east included the Walsh Mountains, Comeraghs, Galtees, Silvermines, Slieve Felim, the Devil's Bit, Slieve Bloom, to the west and north-west, the Castlecomer plateau, Mount Leinster and the Blackstairs. **56** Chief Secretary's Office, Private Papers, 1832, 1413, 24 July 1832.

Nor was the breathtaking effect of the scene lost on those who participated in or approved the celebrations: Humphrey O'Sullivan, the Callan schoolmaster, gave much the same account as he watched the domino-like spread of the fires from twenty miles east of the Cashel gentleman's vantage point:

> There are thousands of bonfires on the hills of Ireland all around as far as I can see on Sliabh na mBan, hundreds of fires on Sliabh Díle, on the Walsh Mountains, on Sliabh Ardach, on the Crannach Hills, on every hill and mountain in the four counties, Kilkenny, Tipperary, Waterford, Wexford, and of course on Carrig Seac itself.[57]

Local song and ballad singers took up the theme. One Irish composition, reputedly from the pen of one of the Cahill brothers of Killamery, celebrated not only the acquittal of the prisoners but also the killings for which they had been charged, by building up a veritable word-landscape in which the hated police barracks, one by one, were marked for destruction:

> Léifead díbh feasta *barracks* na méirleach
> Cill Lamhrach a haon díobh, is Leacht Breac a dó,
> Bearna na Gaoithe is Ceanannas aerach,
> Agus Callainn an aonaigh mar a mbíodh acu sport.[58]

Another triumphal song, probably from the same pen, and aptly entitled 'Oíche na dTinte Chnámh' (Bonfire Night), described both the swiftness and the *éclat* with which the landscape was claimed for the triumphant locals:

> Ní mire cú a rithfeadh ar thaobh cnoic,
> Ná sneachta gléigeal á shéideadh ar bhán,
> Ná oíche an adhmaid 'bhí á roinnt le féileacht,
> Níor rith chomh héascaidh leis na tinte cnámh.
> Ní raibh cnoc ná coill i radharc sa réim úd
> Ná raibh sop á shéideadh agus réabadh ar fál
> Ag tabhairt fios feasa don óg is aosta
> Gur bhuaigh oíche Fhéil Shéamais ar Oíche Fhéil' Sheáin.[59]

57 de Bhaldraithe, *Diary of Humphrey O'Sullivan*, 24 July 1832, p. 121. 58 'Carraig Seac'. Daithí Ó hÓgáin, *Dusnaire Osraíoch: Cnusach d'fhilíocht na ndaoine ó Cho. Chill Chainnigh* (Baile Atha Cliath, 1980), p. 43. 'The barracks of the traitors will be destroyed, first Killamery and then Laghtbrack, then Windgap and airy Kells, and Callan of the fair where they once enjoyed themselves.' 59 Ó hÓgáin, *Duanaire Osraíoch*, pp 18; 44. 'The hound that races on the hillside, The sparkling snow blowing on the bawn, The night when timber was shared out [for burning] – none ran as swiftly as the bonfires. There was not a hill nor a wood in sight in that region where hedges were not raided and sops were not burning, To let young and old know That St James' Eve was more splendid than that of St. John'. The traditional

Everything came together in this stanza: pastime, news-spreading and popular triumph, all woven together against the backdrop of the fire-illuminated landscape.

If landscape signifies 'a portion of land which the eye can comprehend in a single view' or 'a picture representing a piece of country', then nineteenth century broadside balladry paid little enough attention to it, except insofar as it provided a tapestry against which an event or individual could be celebrated.[60] Nor was the historicisation of the landscape in the ballads as sophisticated as that in contemporary literature, travel writing and newspapers, though it was eminently more vibrant since it very easily translated from word to deed. If, on the other hand, references to landscape provided a metaphor for emerging popular self-confidence, then the ballads – and the communities for and among whom they were composed – manipulated landscape (both literally and physically) to reflect the political and social aspirations of the *cosmhuintir* in an era of change.

bonfire night in Kilkenny was on 24 June, i.e. St John's Eve; the release of the Carrickshock prisoners was celebrated on 24 July, the eve of the feast of St James. **60** *The Cambridge English dictionary* (London, 1990).

Imagining the Irish landscape in novels by Maria Edgeworth and Sydney Owenson

LAURA DABUNDO

In Kenneth Clarke's great work, *Landscape into Art,* it is asserted that 'landscape painting, like all forms of art, was an act of faith; and in the early nineteenth century, when more orthodox and systematic beliefs were declining, faith in nature became a form of religion. This is the Wordsworthian doctrine which underlay much of the poetry and nearly all of the painting of the century.'[1] I would like to propose that what Clarke identifies as the faith behind landscape painting, the creed he demonstrated, can also be found in the word paintings, the landscape described in novels where setting suggests and reinforces meaning. And, just as he found this creedal understanding manifest in nineteenth-century art, it can also be located in selected works by Maria Edgeworth and Sydney Owenson, Lady Morgan, two leading women novelists of early nineteenth-century Ireland. These writers were Irish by lineage and birth, but cosmopolitan outsiders by upbringing and family ties, for Edgeworth's family was Anglo-Irish, and although Owenson's father was Irish, her mother was English. Nonetheless, both of them very clearly and closely identified with the land of their birth and sought through their fiction to inspire patriotic pride at home, to solicit sympathy and understanding from the 'alien' English reader and, at the last, to assert an Irish national identity in literature to the world. Moreover, many of these concerns were grounded in the Irish landscape. In particular, their Irish novels, including Owenson's *The Wild Irish Girl* (1806) and *The O'Briens and the O'Flahertys* (1827), and Edgeworth's *Ennui* (1809), *The Absentee* (1812) and *Ormond* (1817), feature travel through parts of Ireland that might well have been unfamiliar to an English readership, and all of these appeal, first, on political terms to the Protestant Ascendancy for the value of residence in situ, not in absentia; to the English nation for the rights of the Irish to their own homeland; and beyond that to the innate attraction for all to appreciate this unique and potent land.

Owenson's hero in *The Wild Irish Girl*, for instance, observes:

> I left the shore and crossed the summit of a mountain that 'battled o'er the deep,' and which after an hour's ascension, I found sloped almost perpendicularly down to a bold and rocky coast, its base terminating in a peninsula, that advanced for near half a mile into the ocean. Towards the extreme western point of this peninsula, which was wildly romantic beyond all description,

---

1 Kenneth Clark, *Landscape into art* (New York, 1976), p. 230.

> arose a vast and grotesque pile of rocks, which at once formed the scite [sic] and fortifications of the noblest mass of ruins on which my eye ever rested. Grand even in desolation, and magnificent in decay – it was the Castle of Inismore.[2]

Owenson herself, in a footnote, reveals that her inspiration is Antrim's Castle Dunluce, showing thereby her efforts to be faithful to an Irish original even as she invents her 'wildly romantic' scenery, which is grand in both its natural and archaeological formations, with authority deriving from ancient settlement and local landscape. Edgeworth, for her part, offers up this picture on the first morning of the sojourns in his native Ireland, of her hero of *Ennui*:

> When I awoke, I thought that I was on shipboard; for the first sound I heard was that of the sea booming against the castle walls. I arose, looked out of the window of my bedchamber, and saw that the whole prospect bore an air of savage wilderness. As I contemplated the scene, my imagination was seized with the idea of remoteness from civilized society: the melancholy feeling of solitary grandeur took possession of my soul.[3]

Like Owenson's Horatio, Lord Glenthorn is moved to Burkean categories of sublimity by the Irish landscape and will later find his life altered and his perspective infinitely enriched and transformed as he learns to claim his Irish identity. That is what it means to live in Ireland for these characters. It is to be reborn by the force of the land, of majestic Ireland, founded on that aforementioned Wordsworthian ideal: 'In nature and the language of the sense/ The anchor of my purest thoughts, the nurse, /The guide, the guardian of my heart, and soul/ Of all my moral being'.[4] This is the encompassing, defining response to the landscape that several Irish novelists promote.

Owenson's two Irish novels that I wish to consider in this context bracket Edgeworth's three, chronologically, but I want to begin with Edgeworth whose novels are replete with references to the Irish countryside. In *Ormond,* for instance, she describes 'a remote old abbey-ground, marked only by some scattered trees, and a few sloping gravestones',[5] and in *The Absentee* several characters pay sightseeing visits 'to round-towers, to various architectural antiquities, and to the real and fabulous history of Ireland'.[6] But, although these references suggest that these relics of the Celtic Church dotting the terrain have merely picturesque and historical interest, in truth she finds great moral and spiritual value in the landscape itself, and her characters are transformed by their developing relationships with it.

2 Sydney Owenson, Lady Morgan, *The Wild Irish Girl,* ed. Kathryn Kirkpatrick (New York, 1999), pp 44–5.   **3** Maria Edgeworth, *Ennui* in *Castle Rackrent and Ennui,* ed. Marilyn Butler (New York, 1992), p. 179.   **4** William Wordsworth, 'Tintern Abbey', in Stephen Gill (ed.), *William Wordsworth: the Oxford authors* (New York, 1984), lines 110–12.   **5** Maria Edgeworth, in Claire Connolly (ed.), *Ormond* (New York, 2000), p. 147.   **6** Maria Edgeworth, in Heidi Thomson and Kim Walker (eds), *The Absentee* (New York, 2000), p. 116.

In Edgeworth's *Ennui* the protagonist learns to live a meaningful and constructive life from his engagement with the Ireland of his patrimony. For instance, we can track how Lord Glenthorn becomes changed from his first travels around Ireland, of which he reports, 'The Giants' Causeway and the Lake of Killarney, were the only things I had ever heard mentioned as worth seeing in Ireland . . . Yet I was seized with a fit of yawning, as I sat in my pleasure boat, to admire this sublime spectacle.'[7] The yawning, of course, denotes the ennui of the title of the book, the rich young man's tedium borne out of idleness and dissipation, though the Burkean language of the sentence's close, 'this sublime spectacle', reveals that he is heading toward a newfound appreciation for what he had previously scorned in the landscape. And toward that end, his time in Ireland is marked by his loss, for a time, of his birthright, his property, and his beloved, stripped down to essential man, at which juncture he begins his Irish reformation. Thus, when the wrongful heir, who has supplanted him, burns the ancestral house down, the rightful Lord Glenthorn is restored to his lands, with himself remade to suit its demands. Now he can find redemption, and he returns to his estate, in 'one of the wildest parts of Ireland'[8] no longer alienated, and he can live and prosper anew. Thus, we see this character's progress against the backdrop of Irish landscape and under its tutelage. In a word, the land and his experiences in and of it have remade the man as a responsible steward for the land and its people.

As with the more well-known *Castle Rackrent*, Edgeworth excoriates what truant landholders have done to the Irish lands in *The Absentee*. *The Absentee* begins with the despicable attempts of Anglo-Irish landlords to secure their position in shallow, empty English high society by bankrupting themselves and their Irish domains in the process. For as the landlord and father of the protagonist declares, blaming his wife for their absence, aspirations, and indebtedness: 'If people would but, as they ought, stay in their own country, live on their own estates, and kill their own mutton, money need never be wanting'.[9] And his wife is indeed culpable, for she has bragged and looked to impress the English by declaring, 'there being no living in Ireland, and expecting to see no trees nor accommodation, nor any thing but bogs all along . . .'[10] She is rendered as depraved and as worthless as her opinions and her social climbing by the moral calculus of the novel's philosophy. In contrast, her son, as a young man, is drawn to Ireland: 'The sun shone bright on the Wicklow mountains. He admired, he exulted in the beauty of the prospect; and all the early associations of his childhood, and the patriotic hopes of his riper years, swelled his heart as he approached the shores of his native land'.[11] It is clear that his Irish properties will be in good hands when he comes into his inheritance, and the novel ends with the same kind of propitious marriage of English and Irish, Protestant and Roman Catholic, that Owenson in *The Wild Irish Girl* also promotes as the resolution of centuries of conflict and chaos.

Ormond, Edgeworth's last Irish novel, also features what she termed the wild parts

---

7 Edgeworth, *Ennui,* p. 250.   8 Ibid., p. 177.   9 Ibid., p. 19.   10 Ibid., p. 91.   11 Ibid., p. 77.

of the Irish landscape, the west. The hero travels to Paris, but he can only be satisfied in his kingdom of the Irish Black Islands, which evoke his best nature. For instance, before the end, 'his visit to the Black Islands revived his generous feelings, and refreshed those traces of early virtue which had been engraven on his heart'[12] and, at the last, 'they were associated with all the tender recollections of his generous benefactor',[13] when he purchases them and dwells there. Thus the geography is itself seen as positive and sustaining of goodness; characters may wander and stray from Ireland and what it nurtures, but the good ones are drawn back and ameliorated by the experience and the connection.

Sidney Owenson, too, equates the connection to the land with the morality of her characters. In *The Wild Irish Girl,* her hero Mortimer must be educated and acclimatised by Ireland, and the novel begins with his sense of himself in exile to Ireland from England, from civilization to savagery. He must learn the value of Ireland and its superior merits before he can be accepted and reside permanently. Once he learns this lesson, he practically crafts a travel brochure for Ireland:

> To him who derives gratification from the embellished labours of art, rather than the simple sublime operations of nature, *Irish* scenery will afford little interest; but the bold features of its varying landscape, the stupendous attitude of its 'cloud-capt' mountains, the impervious gloom of its deep embosomed glens, the savage desolation of its uncultivated heaths, and boundless bogs, with those rich veins of a picturesque champagne, thrown at intervals into gay expansion by the hand of nature, awaken in the mind of the poetic or pictoral traveler, all the pleasures of tasteful enjoyment, all the sublime emotions of a rapt imagination.[14]

In other words, Ireland appeals to a superior and cultivated mind that belongs to one who can appreciate what is profound, irrational, original, natural and sublime, all the positive values for the aesthetically attuned spirit of this time. Owenson, as I have intimated with Edgeworth's *Ennui*, would certainly have known the work of her fellow Irishman Edmund Burke and especially his *Enquiry into the Origins of our Ideas of the Sublime and Beautiful* (1757), which exalted the power and might in nature, leading to the infinite and the magnificent.[15] Clearly, what was picturesque is only for the narrow, limited, domestic and small-minded, not what Ireland might convey or teach. This response to sublime landscape is not only suggestive of Wordsworth, as Kenneth Clark would argue, but reminds us of Shelley's reaction to the Alps where he locates 'the secret strength of things/ Which governs thought',[16] the psychological reality and recognition of human consciousness and creativity revealed in sublime

12 Edgeworth, *Ormond,* p. 181.   **13** Ibid., p. 297.   **14** Owenson, *The Wild Irish Girl* (italics in original), p. 18.   **15** Marilyn Gaull, *English romanticism: the human context* (New York, 1988), p. 232.   **16** Percy Bysshe Shelley, 'Mont Blanc', in Donald H. Reiman (ed.), *Shelley's poetry and prose* (New York, 1977), lines 139–40.

natural settings: 'And what were thou, and earth, and stars, and sea, /If to the human mind's imaginings/ Silence and solitude were vacancy?'[17] Thus, there can be no creativity without nature, but there can be no acknowledgment of nature without the human imagination, and both Edgeworth and Owenson, as proper Romantics, argue for the Irish landscape in keeping with this understanding and developing tradition. *The Wild Irish Girl*, as already suggested, ends with a stirring affirmation of unity and hope, as a comedy of reconciliation, with a marriage of the young, attractive, educated Anglo-Irish and Irish lovers, so that the hero's father can declaim, 'let the names of [the two] . . . be inseparably blended, and the distinctions of English and Irish, of protestant and catholic, for ever buried. And, [I] . . . look forward with hope to this family alliance being prophetically typical of a national unity of interests and affections . . .'[18] Hence, where there is beauty and youth, education and culture, aristocracy and wealth, there can be assimilation of some sort, trumping differences in the name of love.

In marked contrast, *The O'Briens and The O'Flahertys*, Owenson's last Irish novel, is dark and despairing, over an increasingly ruined and destitute land, foreshadowing by a mere two decades the devastation of the famine. The people, too, are alienated and estranged from the land that previously inspired them. Here is one vision of the landscape for the protagonist:

> O'Brien . . . on the southside of the Liffey found himself in one of the most dreary and ruinous suburbs of the Irish capital. Swamps and wilds to the left, were edged with dilapidated buildings, the more melancholy in their aspect, when a glimmer of light, issuing from a broken pane, gave indication that there some victim of wretchedness had retired to die. To the right appeared the then neglected banks of the river, with the high walls of the various hospitals (the refuge for every infirmity, from the mental aberration, for which Swift had here provided, in a dreadfully prophetic spirit, to the most loathsome of bodily inflictions. [sic]) One dark mass, frowning and terrible above all, for a moment fixed his eye, and arrested his steps – the state prison of Kilmainham.[19]

Death, disease, both mental and physical, and imprisonment, are all enacted visually in the landscape. And that is just the city. In the countryside, however, some Ascendancy figures and their hangers-on venture toward a hunting lodge and, predictably perhaps, since there is to be no leadership from that quarter: 'Every trace of a road, or even of a path, was now gradually disappearing; and the horses floundered on, through rough masses of rock, rising out of the quaking swamps of a peaty vegetable soil, till the ravine terminated abruptly over one of those deep and deso-

---

17 Ibid., lines 142–4.   **18** Owenson, *The Wild Irish Girl*, p. 250.   **19** Sydney Owenson, Lady Morgan, *The O'Briens and the O'Flahertys: a national tale in four volumes* (London, 1827), iii, 173–4.

late hollows, which resemble the gaping crater of an extinct volcano.'[20] Thus, here too is to be found decay and void, despair writ in a valetudinarian Ireland, prostrate, infirm, and mortally afflicted.

The novel posits the late eighteenth century as a time of stressors of contemporary politics in the collision of Irish nationalism and Romantic idealism, figured in its hero, who begins life as the heir of one side of a Montague/Capulet, Lancastrian/Yorkist, American Scotch-Irish Hatfield/McCoy feud, here set in the west of Ireland. Says one O'Flaherty to an O'Brien, speaking perhaps for her author: 'Every thing in Connaught [. . .] is the sign of feuds and alliances, of hatreds and of loves, of ancient inheritances and recent usurpations. What an abridgment of the history of the land, for instance, is the story of the O'Brien and the O'Flaherty, names that to Irish ears speak volumes?'[21] the 'history of the land', as it were, as captured in this book. And at one point, Owenson succinctly represents this collision of family and legacy when she says her expatriate hero Murrogh O'Brien returns home, 'knowing nothing of modern Ireland, but her sufferings and her wrongs; knowing little of ancient Ireland but her fables and her dreams',[22] which detachment renders the sensitive, idealistic O'Brien ripe for Wolfe Tone's United Irishmen. O'Brien, like Tone, a Protestant, has been greatly influenced by revolutionary France of the 1780s,[23] and both fail in their efforts and end their days in French exile.[24] In the novel, O'Brien suffers personally for his brief dalliance with the United Irishmen, for he is 'rusticated for his rebellious views' from Trinity College.[25] Nonetheless, exile for misbehavior is his natural state in this novel. His patrimony is the Aran Island's fortress Dun Aengus,[26] which supports his role as the avatar of, as critic Julia Wright notes, 'a nationalist prophecy. [However,] he also has a tendency to get distracted by beautiful women' and constantly needs to be rescued for his troubles.[27] Thus, there is ever-steady conflict and diametrical opposition, in the land, in its politics, in its people, in its religion, in the self. Previously, Ireland was a source of strength. Now it is destitute, and its heroes are victims.

Indeed, O'Brien is a fugitive from one authority after another throughout the novel, and in flight, finally, from himself, from his destiny as a 'saviour of his country'.[28] His ignorance of Ireland, we have seen, is destructive, not just of himself, but of all he comes into contact with, for as he seeks his father, his dilapidated, disintegrating ancestral home in Dublin literally collapses around him during a thunderstorm: 'rafter after rafter gave way, and beam after beam . . . amidst the horror and consternation of an event so fearful, bricks and tiles still falling – doors, windows, shutters rattling in the storm . . .'[29] The graphic depiction of the collapse of an

---

20 Ibid., iv, 172.   **21** Ibid., 70.   **22** Ibid., ii, 212.   **23** Breandán Ó hEithir, *A pocket history of Ireland* (Dublin, 1996), pp 34–5.   **24** R.F. Foster. 'Ascendancy and Union', in R.F. Foster (ed.), *The Oxford illustrated history of Ireland* (New York, 1996), pp 180–2.   **25** Robert Welch (ed.), *The Oxford companion to Irish literature* (Oxford, 1996), p. 403.   **26** Owenson, *The O'Briens and the O'Flaherty* , ii, 39.   **27** Julia M. Wright, 'National erotics and political theory in Morgan's *The O'Briens and the O'Flahertys'* in *European Romantic Review,* 15 (2004), pp 229–53.   **28** Owenson, *The O'Briens and the O'Flahertys,* iv, 257.   **29** Ibid., ii, 332.

imposing, redoubtable, and powerful family home and its inhabitants, all they are, all they have, all they stand for. Closer to home, to this novel, the doom of the Protestant Ascendancy hangs and falls with 'the fall of Arranmore House'.[30] And, later, association with O'Brien causes a similar catastrophe for the woman who has been his unknown guiding spirit throughout the novel, his soul-mate, scion of his family's once arch rivals, his cousin, Beavoin O'Flaherty. She loses the Abbey of Moycullen, a foundation of a new dispensation which she has begun for the sake of a new Ireland, when it similarly collapses in fire and destruction after he visits.[31] In some ways hero O'Brien is not the saviour, but the destroyer of things Irish.

As a fugitive, O'Brien, who cannot save himself much less anyone else, is therefore estranged from his land, but potential sources of sanctuary loom, and as the novel approaches them in his flight, the reader encounters moments of the affirmation of the landscape that were so apparent in Edgeworth's novels, and in *The Wild Irish Girl*. We read: 'The mountains, the lakes, the Abbey, all the sublime objects, on which his senses had dwelt in the dim, mysterious light of a waning moon, and under the influence of a dreaming fancy, were now spread before him, in the full reality of form and colour.'[32] Burkean sublime is therefore available, but muted, hushed by political ferment and inhuman injustice and oppression, and it will not prevail against the forces rampant in the novel. Eluding his pursuers, O'Brien finds occasional temporary refuges, once in a familial shelter with his elderly maiden aunts,[33] and once in a haven with one of two secluded religious orders depicted in the novel. I have already mentioned the Abbey of Moycullen for women, described as 'a confraternity of no particular religious order',[34] and there is another 'confraternity'[35] for men, where O'Brien is himself nursed back to health at one low point in his manifold getaways.[36] This is a place 'known only by the good they did; for they were charitable and almsgiving, and being of all professions, they applied their skill and acquirements to relieve the various ills to which the unaccommodated wretchedness of the Irish peasant stands every where exposed'.[37] In other words, the brothers, like the women of Moycullen, undertake good works, serving the community, ministering to the afflicted of which, clearly, is Ireland itself. Both Moycullen and the men's foundation are isolated; the Abbess even likens hers to a 'desert',[38] a significant word in Celtic religious orders connoting retreat from the hurly-burly to a pilgrimage destination.[39] Interestingly, Owenson identifies an actual location for the men's foundation, a rebuilt Abbey of Cong, which inspires a rare landscape rapture: 'the ruins of its ancient abbey, that bathes its delicate reflections of gable and tower in the beautiful river, which runs in liquid silver beneath its walls ... [a] magnificent monastery ... one of the most beautiful of the ecclesiastical establishments in the island of the Saints'.[40] But like his aunts' home, this site affords only transient solace for the man on the run. These are oases of sanctuary, but they cannot, finally, save the country.

30 Ibid., iii, 188.   **31** Ibid., iv, 302–3.   **32** Ibid., p. 275.   **33** Ibid., iii, 3–4.   **34** Ibid., iv, 208.   **35** Ibid., iii, 201–2.   **36** Ibid., p. 206.   **37** Ibid., p. 198.   **38** Ibid., iv, 265.   **39** Marcus Losack, 'The Bible, the desert and the Celtic tradition', in Padraigín Clancy (ed.), *Celtic threads: exploring the wisdom of our heritage* (Dublin, 1999), pp 56–8.   **40** Owenson, *The*

The sisterhood, under the direction of the Abbess of Moycullen, falls, as we have seen, though not before Owenson has tried to uphold it as a kind of religious compromise for Ireland similar to the interfaith marriage at the end of *The Wild Irish Girl*, although that was when she was feeling more optimistic about the fate of her land. Here, the O'Flaherty heir declares, '*I will live in Ireland*'[41] and the italics of the original indicate how profound her connection to the land is, even as she urges O'Brien, 'for your sake, for both our sakes, you must leave this country'.[42] However, he is equally adamant to stay and for once face his accusers and persecutors, which he does, and which leads to his conviction.[43] However, with Beavoin's connivance, he flees, and the novel ends with both of them in exile and married. Thus, salutary life is possible only away from the land of Ireland, and the country remains unredeemed. *The O'Briens and the O'Flahertys* ends, then, with a reconciliation of the feuding families, but their disaffection from the land is complete. Where sublimity, and unity and transcendence once beckoned, now all that is left in Ireland is sundered and alienated. Not until the political and religious differences are resolved can the spirit of the land be rediscovered and bestow the sublimity its landscapes, its earth and water and sky, pledge.

O'Briens and the O'Flahertys, iii, 191–192.   **41** Ibid., iv, 270.   **42** Ibid., p. 267.   **43** Ibid., p. 326.

Revolutionary landscapes: the picturesque, Salvator Rosa and *The Wild Irish Girl*

SUSAN EGENOLF

In describing the Irish landscape, Horatio M——, later Mortimer, the hero of Sydney Owenson's *The Wild Irish Girl: A National Tale* (1806), asserts:

> To him who derives gratification from the embellished labours of art, rather than the simple but sublime operations of nature, *Irish* scenery will afford little interest; but the bold features of its varying landscape, the stupendous attitude of its 'cloud-capt' mountains, the impervious gloom of its deep embossed glens, the savage desolation of its uncultivated heaths, and boundless bogs, with those rich veins of picturesque champagne, thrown at intervals into gay expansion by the hand of nature, awaken in the mind of the poetic or pictoral traveller, all the pleasures of tasteful enjoyment, all the sublime emotions of rapt imagination.[1]

This passage is striking because even though the 'embellished labours of art' appear to have been demoted at the beginning of the passage as the pleasures of persons with limited sensibility, Horatio's description is greatly indebted to the discourse of art. Owenson's hero participates in the practice encouraged by eighteenth-century guidebooks and authors such as William Gilpin, Richard Payne Knight and Uvedale Price of contemplating a landscape as if it were a landscape painting. Horatio makes this practice explicit as his description continues: 'And if the glowing fancy of Claude Loraine [*sic*] would have dwelt enraptured on the paradisial charms of the English landscape, the superior genius of Salvator Rosa would have reposed its eagle wing amidst those scenes of mysterious sublimity, with which the wildly magnificent landscape of Ireland abounds. But the liberality of nature appears to me to be here but frugally assisted by the donations of art.'[2] Although the pages of *The Wild Irish Girl* are filled with descriptions of this untamed 'natural' landscape, the descriptions themselves frequently draw upon the rhetoric of eighteenth- and early-nineteenth-century aesthetics of landscape painting and gardening, thus familiarizing and codifying the wildness of Ireland for Owenson's British readers. While the ruins and aestheticized landscapes of *The Wild Irish Girl* reassure British readers of native Irish impotence, of a civilization to be admired but not feared, the use of Salvator Rosa, I wish to argue,

---

1 Sydney Owenson, *The Wild Irish Girl*, ed. Kathryn Kirkpatrick (Oxford and New York, 1999), p. 18.   2 Ibid., p. 18.

creates tension between imperial nostalgia and potential insurgency. Evidence from Owenson's later writings, especially *Patriotic Sketches of Ireland* (1807) and *The Life and Times of Salvator Rosa* (1824), shows that Owenson drew upon picturesque conventions, handling them with subtle irony, and by means of Rosa, known to her as a revolutionary, created a subversive aesthetic subtext in *The Wild Irish Girl*.

The ending of Owenson's first 'National Tale' has long posed a problem for critics because the marriage of the wild Irish girl, Glorvina, to Horatio, the son of the British family that usurped her family's ancestral lands, seems to undercut the many pages of detailed discussion promoting the cultural glories of Ireland. At the novel's end, Glorvina's father, the ancient Irish chieftain and Prince of Inismore, dies, leaving his daughter, his people and his land presumably to be absorbed by Horatio's British Ascendancy family. Unbeknownst to each other, Horatio and his father, Lord M——, have separately infiltrated the once mighty fortress of Inismore, which represents the last vestige of native Irish land in their extensive plantation. By taking on assumed identities, they are welcomed and quickly incorporated into the Inismore family; there is no resistance to their covert invasions. Given Owenson's contributions to the rise of Irish nationalism, critics have struggled to explain how the union of Glorvina and Horatio supports an Irish nationalist agenda. Clearly Horatio must earn union with Glorvina through the loss of his initial prejudice and his new understanding of the rich Irish traditions of arts, letters and sciences. Horatio's cultural reform mitigates the inherent disparities and inequalities of a union between colonizer and colonized. Robert Tracy reads the union, what he terms the 'Glorvina solution' in this and other Irish novels, as the 'intermarriage/assimilation of Irish and Anglo-Irish, of modern efficiency and ancient tradition, of legal right and traditional loyalty'.[3] Katie Trumpener argues that the marriage of Horatio and Glorvina becomes a prototype for the early nineteenth-century national tale 'with its allegorical presentation of the contrast, attraction, and union between disparate cultural worlds'.[4] For Mary Jean Corbett, this 'union of disparate cultural worlds' does the 'intercultural work of imaginatively constituting the domestic stability considered so crucial to national and colonial security'.[5] I would argue that the 'domestic stability' represented by the union of Horatio and Glorvina coexists uneasily with the iconography of the wild and picturesque Irish coast.[6] A fruitful approach to understanding

---

3 Robert Tracy, *The unappeasable host: studies in Irish identities* (Dublin, 1998), p. 31.   **4** Katie Trumpener, 'National character, nationalist plots: national tale and historical novel in the age of *Waverley*, 1806–1830', *ELH*, 60 (1993) 697.   **5** Mary Jean Corbett, *Allegories of union in Irish and English writing, 1790–1870* (Cambridge, 2000), p. 53.   **6** For two recent critics who also argue that the allegorical union may be less than harmonious, see Marie-Noelle Zeender, 'Resistance in *The Wild Irish Girl*', in *Cycnos*, 19:1 (2002), pp 65–75, and Heather Braun, 'The seductive masquerade of *The Wild Irish Girl*: disguising political fear in Sydney Owenson's national tale', in *Irish Studies Review*, 13:1 (2005), pp 33–43. Zeender argues that the novel is a 'challenge to the authorities' (65), and reads the behavior of Glorvina and the Prince as 'seditious' because 'it reflects the absolute contempt of the Irish for the colonial order imposed upon them' (69). Braun maintains that 'Glorvina's hybrid character reveals

the political themes, including resistance to colonial appropriation, of *The Wild Irish Girl* is a closer examination of the novel's aesthetic references.

Owenson came of age amidst a proliferation of essays attentive to the aesthetics of landscape. Edmund Burke's *A Philosophical Enquiry into the Origin of Our Ideas of the Sublime and Beautiful* was first published in 1757 and released in new editions well into the 1790s. Gilpin's *Observations relative chiefly to Picturesque Beauty* series began with his *Observations on the River Wye ... made in the Summer of 1770* (1782) and continued through several tours of Great Britain. Gilpin focused upon the relationship of the picturesque traveller to the landscape, providing detailed suggestions for the viewing of particular prospects, and for capturing a scene through sketching. Uvedale Price first formulated his *An Essay on the Picturesque, as Compared with the Sublime and the Beautiful* in 1794, eventually expanding it to a three-volume work filled with practical advice for 'improving real landscape' based in the study of pictures; he included such helpful tips as 'sheep are the best gardeners' because the 'bite of sheep' produces the desirable 'slight inequalities' in the turf 'which the scythe cannot imitate'.[7] In much the same fashion that Gilpin's and Price's work had taken on Burke's early treatise, Richard Payne Knight addressed his 1794 'The Landscape, a didactic poem' to Price; Price obliged Knight with a response. The premises and rebuttals expressed in these writings ensured that even the most casual reader would be familiar with descriptions of the landscape posed in terms of the sublime and the picturesque.

Owenson was an attentive reader of this new discourse, as evidenced by her use of the prominent theorists of the picturesque in her descriptions of Connaught scenery in *Patriotic Sketches*, published the year following *The Wild Irish Girl*. In her trek up the scenic mount Alt-bo, Owenson worked through her ideas of the Burkean sublime: 'if the source of the true sublime consists in that which excites ideas of pain and danger, and operates on the mind in a manner analogous to terror, the sublimest object I have ever beheld is the abyss at Coradun'.[8] Another hike produced the following vignette, where Owenson's description rehearses the characteristic elements of the beautiful, the sublime, and the picturesque:

> As we descended the mountain's brow, a little vally [*sic*] gradually opened between its steep acclivities, which still ascending with the elevation of the mountains, was still embosomed by its irregular and overhanging projections, while the streams which serpentined through it, seemed to expand as we proceeded along its banks, sometimes dashing wildly over those pieces of rock it had torn away in its steep descent, sometimes stealing its thin pellucid wave over broad flags of marble ... We frequently paused in the course of our

crucial ways in which an actual political moment can be fortified and obscured through the literary imagining of the appeals and dangers of a united Ireland' (33).   7 Uvedale Price, *Essays on the picturesque, as compared with the sublime and the beautiful*, 3 vols (London, 1810), iii, 171.   8 Owenson, *Patriotic sketches of Ireland, written in Connaught*, 2 vols (London, 1807), ii, 177–8.

> ramble from the weariness of the continued ascent; but more frequently to contemplate such scenes as included within a coup-d'œil, much of the beautiful and sublime of picturesque creation. The boundless ocean, the Alpine rock, the dreary heath, the luxurious vale, and many landscape traits incongruous to each other, seemed here happily united in one harmonious combination; while many a ruin which time had 'mouldered into beauty,' many a hut which necessity had hung upon the virid point of some tall cliff, charmed the fairy gaze of fancy, and awakened in the musing mind a train of associated ideas which shed an extraneous interest over every object on which the eye reposed.[9]

Here Owenson is obviously providing a visual pleasure for her readers using painting as both analogue and source. She surveys the 'irregular' outcroppings, the changeable water feature (which 'serpentined'), the scenic view, the ruin and the peasant huts, surmising that the variety and incongruity of these features form a picturesque whole. Though Owenson writes in *Patriotic Sketches* that she beheld 'numerous' such picturesque scenes in her 'native country', she also claims that these scenes were 'frequently concealed in those remote places which national observation has never visited, and to which foreign curiosity has never been pointed'.[10] As Owenson no doubt knew, however, the romantic ideal of the intrepid traveller was rapidly changing in Ireland with attention to both the urban and rural picturesque in such collections as James Malton's *A Picturesque and Descriptive View of the City of Dublin* (1799) and Thomas Sautell Roberts's *Illustrations of the Chief Cities, Rivers, and Picturesque Scenery of the Kingdom of Ireland*, a series of 'scenes' 'engraved in aquatint and published between 1795 and 1799'.[11] Malton's and Roberts's works provide a pictorial codification of scenes long deemed picturesque in Irish travel writing.

The Wild Irish Girl's epigraph is taken from Fazio Delli Uberti's 'Travels through Ireland in the 14th Century': 'This race of men, tho' savage they may seem, / This country, too, with many a mountain rough, / Yet are they sweet to him who tries and tastes them,'[12] and it invites us to couple our reading of the Irish people with our reading of the terrain. Owenson's topographical descriptions function to augment the ethnographic ones, and in this sense they follow conventions of imperial travel writing. Arthur Young's *A Tour of Ireland, 1776–1779* (1780), deemed the most judicious account of Irish life and culture by Owenson, and such prominent families as the Edgeworths, focuses explicitly on agriculture, landscape, and land use. Though Gilpin suggests that '[f]rom scenes indeed of the *picturesque kind* we exclude the appendages of tillage, and in general the works of men,'[13] descriptions of colonial landscapes rely

---

9 Ibid., ii, 190–2.   **10** Ibid., ii, 192.   **11** Brian P. Kennedy, 'The traditional Irish thatched house: image and reality, 1793–1993', in Adele M. Dalsimer (ed.), *Visualizing Ireland: national identity and the pictorial tradition* (Boston and London, 1993), pp 166–7.   **12** Fazio Delli Uberti, 'Travels through Ireland in the 14th century', as quoted in Owenson, *Wild Irish Girl*, n.p.   **13** William Gilpin, *Three essays: On picturesque beauty; On picturesque travel; and On sketching landscape*, 2nd ed. (London, 1794), p. iii.

heavily on an ethnographic reading of the state of a land's cultivation, or potential for improvement. In his study of the creation of the romance of the Scottish Highlands, Peter Womack argues: 'From Pope to Austen and Peacock, what happens to the appearance of the landowner's physical environment can function as the literary measure of his taste, wisdom and even mortality, because of an underlying consensus which refers all cultural values back, in the last analysis, to that of the land itself.'[14] Owenson makes this connection explicit when she shifts from the picturesque scene, quoted at length above, to the following observation: 'Notwithstanding the rough acclivities of which these mountains are composed, we found them cultivated to their summits.'[15] In a note, she adds, 'A cultivation so constantly formed on the summits of the highest mountains in Ireland, proves that native taste for agriculture, which to the modern Irish has been so unjustly denied, and of which the ancient left such irrefragable proofs'.[16] For Owenson, observing the landscape provides not only pleasure but insight.

The epistolary *Wild Irish Girl* begins with an exchange of letters between the prodigal Horatio and his father, the Earl of M——, but the rest of the novel (excepting the odd third-person conclusion) consists of a series of letters from Horatio to his friend J.D. Esquire, an Englishman who seems never to have set foot in Ireland.[17] When Horatio writes, in his opening letters of the novel, of his banishment from society and the pleasures of England to the 'savage' and 'semi-barbarous, semi-civilized' country of Ireland, he recollects a passage from the 'travels of *Moryson* through Ireland' where Moryson asserts that 'so late as the days of Elizabeth, an Irish chieftain and his family were frequently seen seated round their domestic fire in a state of perfect nudity'.[18] Horatio confesses that after encountering this detail in his boyhood reading, 'whenever the *Irish* were mentioned in my presence, an *Esquimaux* group circling round the fire which was to dress a dinner, or broil an enemy, was the image which presented itself to my mind'.[19] Such comparisons remove Ireland halfway around the world with images of canabalistic natives akin to sixteenth-century reports from the New World rather than portraying her as the sister nation to England that she had nominally become with the Union of 1800. Owenson imbues her young protagonist with such broad prejudices against the native Irish so as to quickly dispel them in the letters that follow from Ireland. Horatio's seeming conversion is shown to owe much to his visual pleasure.

As Horatio's 'packet' arrives in Ireland, he describes the bay of Dublin as 'one of

---

14 Peter Womack, *Improvement and romance: constructing the myth of the highlands* (London, 1989), p. 61. **15** Owenson, *Patriotic sketches*, ii, 193. **16** Ibid., ii, 194. **17** Ina Ferris suggests that the national tale as developed by Owenson expands upon the 'proto-ethnographic discourse of travel' to relocate the 'scene of cultural encounter', confounding the distinction between 'over here' and 'over there' in order to move the modern metropolitan subject/reader into a potentially 'transformative relation of proximity', in her 'Narrating cultural encounter: Lady Morgan and the Irish national tale', in *Nineteenth-Century Literature*, 51:3 (1996), 288. **18** Owenson, *Wild Irish Girl*, pp 10–13. **19** Ibid., p. 13.

the most splendid spectacles in the scene of picturesque creation I had ever beheld, or indeed ever conceived'. He notes that a 'foreigner on board the packet, compared the view to that which the bay of Naples affords', adding, 'I cannot judge of the justness of the comparison, though I am told one very general and common-place.'[20] Such a comparison had likely become 'common-place' because of the widely available images of the Bay of Naples. Owenson, in fact, lists a Salvator Rosa *View of the Bay of Naples* in her pictures by Rosa. The Italian overlay that Owenson constructs here runs throughout the novel, with Horatio requesting a 'box of Italian crayons' as one of the few provisions that he will take into exile, the aforementioned references to the painters of the Italian school, and Horatio calling the Lodge his father's '*Tusculum*' and the ancient caretaker there his '*Cicerone*' rather than guide.[21] This is all part of Owenson's relentless effort in the novel to connect the scenery and customs of Ireland to ancient Greek and Roman civilization, to a classical past, but the Italian references particularly mark Horatio's narrative.

Horatio augments his frequent classical references with repeated observations indebted to contemporary aesthetic discourse. After finding Dublin to be much more cosmopolitan than he had expected, Horatio sets out for the northwest coast of Connaught where the native Irish 'were separated by a provincial barrier from an intercourse with the rest of Ireland' and where Horatio supposes he will have the opportunity to observe the 'Irish character in all its *primeval* ferocity'.[22] Such ferocity is, however, repeatedly contained in the aestheticized descriptions of Connaught and of the Castle of Inismore, where the primary action of the novel transpires: near the end of a peninsula, 'wildly romantic beyond all description,' Horatio writes, 'arose a vast and grotesque pile of rocks, which at once formed the scite [*sic*] and fortifications of the noblest mass of ruins on which my eye ever rested'.[23] When Horatio moves closer to the Castle, he finds the half-ruined chapel 'strikingly picturesque', and after hearing and seeing mass, he exclaims, What a religion is this! ... What a captivating, what a *picturesque* faith!'[24] Carried away by his aesthetic pleasure, Horatio seems ready to deem anything he encounters 'picturesque,' but his application of the term to the Catholic faith merits some analysis. To term 'faith' picturesque is to make it static, to remove it from a world of active practice, to cast it as neutral. Horatio, clearly a Protestant, elides centuries of sectarian violence by neutralizing any 'real' power that the faith might have. Michael Charlesworth has explored just such an attitude in relation to religious ruins, particularly Rievaulx Abbey in Yorkshire. In examining various paintings and poems that cast the ruins as picturesque, he notes that this 'nostalgic attitude would not have been possible without the decline in the Jacobite threat'.[25] Such representations of the Abbey come into being, then, only after the decisive suppression of the Jacobite rebellion in the mid-eighteenth century.

---

20 Ibid., p. 14.   **21** Ibid., pp 11; 36.   **22** Ibid., p. 17.   **23** Ibid., p. 44.   **24** Ibid., pp 46; 50.   **25** Michael Charlesworth, 'The ruined abbey: picturesque and gothic values', in Stephen Copley and Peter Garside (eds), *The politics of the picturesque* (Cambridge, 1994), p. 69.

Likewise, Horatio's joy at discovering the half-ruined chapel at Inismore partakes of a certainty that this faith offers no threat to the Ascendancy.

As he traverses the Irish countryside, Horatio's venture in Ireland seems directed by Gilpin's suggestions 'On Picturesque Travel': 'The first source of amusement to the picturesque traveler, is the *pursuit* of his object – the expectation of new scenes continually opening, and arising to his view. We suppose the country to have been unexplored'.[26] The picturesque traveller as original explorer easily employs the rhetoric of the colonial enterprise; Horatio reports his purpose for visiting Ireland as being 'to *take* views, and *seize* some of the finest features of its landscapes'.[27] Horatio not only literally stands to inherit the land; he also enacts his colonial status through aesthetic appropriation. As Stephen Copley and Peter Garside argue, the 'discourse of the Picturesque intersects with and is shaped by the discourses of colonialism'.[28] And, as Anne Fogarty notes specifically about *The Wild Irish Girl*, 'The Gothic sublimity of the Castle of Inismore has as its absent cause the depredations of colonialism'.[29] The beautiful ruins that Horatio begins to covet here have their origin in the Cromwellian wars; the Lodge's caretaker tells Horatio that the Prince's 'family flourished ... until the Cromwellian wars broke out, and those same cold-hearted Presbyterians battered the fine *old ancient* castle of Inismore, and left it in the condition it now stands'.[30] We should not miss the irony, nor the diminutive, as Horatio muses: 'I raised my eyes to the Castle of Inismore, and sighed, and almost wished I had been born the Lord of these beautiful ruins, the Prince of this isolated *little* territory.'[31] Horatio's family holds the title to most of the surrounding land, except this 'little' peninsula still occupied by the Prince. Horatio's musings shift his perspective rapidly from Gilpin's traveller's gaze to Price's landholder's gaze.

Owenson endows Horatio with a sense of colonial entitlement that he affects through the metaphorical appropriation of the picturesque scenes, which quickly come to include the Lady Glorvina as well as the ruin. As Horatio scales the unstable ruins and secretly watches the Princess Glorvina playing her harp, he wishes that he could 'but realize the vivid tints of this enchanting picture'. And though perched precariously outside the window, he takes time to notice that 'at the back of her chair stood the grotesque figure of her antiquated nurse. O! the precious contrast. And yet it heightened, it finished the picture.'[32] Horatio's descriptions are readily seen to be taking part in contemporary aesthetic discussions of the picturesque. Indeed, Owenson's descriptions of Horatio's views of Ireland, whether landscapes or this intimate interior scene, specifically demonstrate his (and her) understanding of picturesque composition in terms of Gilpin's 'roughness' and 'contrast'; the nurse's form must be 'grotesque' in order to offer the contrast to Glorvina's perfect and

---

26 Gilpin, *Three essays*, p. 47.　**27** Owenson, *Wild Irish Girl*, p. 56; emphasis mine.　**28** Stephen Copley and Peter Garside, 'Introduction' in Copley and Garside (eds), *The politics of the picturesque*, p. 6.　**29** Anne Fogarty, 'Imperfect concord: spectres of history in the Irish novels of Maria Edgeworth and Lady Morgan', in Margaret Kelleher and James Murphy (eds), *Gender perspectives in nineteenth-century Ireland: public and private spheres* (Dublin, 1997), p. 126.　**30** Owenson, *Wild Irish Girl*, p. 38.　**31** Ibid., p. 52; emphasis mine.　**32** Ibid., p. 53.

smooth beauty. Gilpin writes that '[p]icturesque composition consists in uniting in one whole a variety of parts; and these parts can only be obtained from rough objects'; 'variety' and 'contrast' are 'equally necessary' in the artist's composition.[33] We are reminded that Gilpin observed that the 'regularity' of the 'gabel-ends' at Tintern Abbey 'hurt the eye' and 'disgust it by the vulgarity of their shape'; he suggested a 'mallet judiciously used (but who durst use it?) might be of service in fracturing some of them'.[34] Though Horatio does not carry a Claude-glass, the device popular among picturesque tourists for its ability to transform a landscape by reflecting a contained scene, Owenson portrays him as an individual who likewise self-consciously imagines his lived Irish experiences as framed pictures. Moments after Horatio's aesthetic critique of the interior scene of the castle, he loses his footing, so 'entranced' is he with the picture, and plummets to the rocks below.[35] Horatio's severe injuries from the fall necessitate his convalescence at the Castle of Inismore, though he is a stranger. Because his father and all of his ancestors are the enemies of the Prince of Inismore, Horatio assumes an alternative identity, fixing, not surprisingly, on 'that of an itinerant artist'.[36] Horatio's primary occupation as he recovers is to sketch the ruins of the Castle and tutor the Lady Glorvina in drawing. As he and the Prince discuss 'various views' and prospects that he should capture, the earlier mention of the landscape artists Lorrain and Rosa comes readily to mind.[37] By invoking these two artists and making her main character into a landscape painter, Owenson easily exploits the British enthusiasm for landscape in the fashion of seventeenth-century paintings, making the wildest regions of Ireland seem familiar. In his discussion of Georgian gardens, David C. Stuart stresses that the Italian landscape painters Nicolas Poussin, Caspar Dughet, Claude Lorrain, and Salvator Rosa were 'constantly invoked in discussions on landscape design until well into the nineteenth century'. Stuart adds that it 'became fashionable to allude to any landscape, whether Thames-side meadow or Alpine cliff, in terms of one or other of the painters'.[38] As has been well-documented, the fundamental relationship between the seventeenth-century Italian landscape painters and the English landscape was not simply one of recognition of forms, but of creation of those forms. Claude Lorrain's vision of Arcadia with pastoral landscapes and neo-classical structures was recreated in gardens throughout England by landscape architects such as Capability Brown and Sir Humphrey Repton (fig. 1).

The romantic landscape gardens in homage to Salvator Rosa followed (though there is much blurring in this chronology) with attention to cascades, grottos, hermitages, and ruins (fig. 2). Rose Macaulay describes Rosa, the 'fierce, ruin-minded, banditti-haunted Salvator,' as the artist 'who brought the savage world of rocks, ruins and brigandage into the general artistic consciousness'.[39]

The ruin, of course, features prominently in *The Wild Irish Girl* (fig. 3), yet

33 Gilpin, *Three essays*, pp 19–20.   **34** Gilpin, *Observations on the River Wye, and several parts of South Wales, &c. relative chiefly to picturesque beauty*, 2nd ed. (London, 1789), p. 47. **35** Owenson, *Wild Irish Girl*, p. 53.   **36** Ibid., p. 55.   **37** Ibid., p. 64.   **38** David C. Stuart, *Georgian gardens* (London, 1979), p. 28.   **39** Rose Macaulay, *Pleasure of ruins* (New York, 1953), pp 18–19.

1 Claude Lorrain. *View of Crescenza.* 1648–50. Oil on canvas; 15¼ x 22⅞ in (38.7 x 58.1 cm). The Annenberg Fund Inc. Gift, 1978 (1978. 205). Image © Metropolitan Museum of Art, New York City.

2 Salvator Rosa. *Bandits on a Rocky Coast.* c. 1656. Oil on canvas; 29½ x 39⅜ in. (74.9 x 100 cm). Charles B. Curtis Fund, 1934 (34. 137). Image © The Metropolitan Museum of Art, New York City.

3 William Bartlett. *Dunluce Castle.* c. 1841. Hand-colored engraving.
Collection of the author.

Owenson both exploits and complicates the idea of the ruin as an aesthetic object. When she first mentions the Castle of Inismore, for example, she includes a footnote (one of many) suggesting '[t]hose who have visited the Castle of Dunluce, near the Giants' Causeway, may, perhaps, have some of its striking features in this rude draught of the Castle of Inismore'.[40] However, such 'striking features' would have been quite familiar to her readers through Rosa's paintings, innumerable engravings of ruins, and their commodification as a desired feature of the English garden. James Howley has traced the 'earliest recorded proposal to use a ruined building as a garden ornament' to a 1709 letter from Sir John Vanbrugh to the duchess of Marlborough:

> In this he urges her to retain the ruined shell of Woodstock Manor as an eye-catcher to close a vista in the new park at Blenheim. Vanbrugh argued that buildings from the past can convey a stronger sense of history through association with their past occupants and reflection on the remarkable things which have been transacted in them. He continued to expound on the aesthetic and picturesque qualities of the ruin and ... suggests that the building would make, 'one of the most agreeable objects that the best of land-skip (sic) painters can invent'.[41]

40 Owenson, *Wild Irish Girl*, p. 45. **41** James Howley, *The follies and garden buildings of Ireland* (New Haven and London, 1993), p. 106.

Though the duchess of Marlborough thwarted Vanbrugh's plan by having the building demolished, existing ruins were successfully incorporated into garden schemes in England and Ireland in the decades immediately following.

By the mid-eighteenth century, plans appear with drawing designs for *newly* constructed, that is, created, ruins. In 1751, Sanderson Miller designed a mammoth ruin for the grounds of Wimpole Hall. Although Miller's design was not constructed for twenty years, his folly at Wimpole Hall became one of the most famous of the created ruins. In the decades that followed, the created ruins that proliferated in England and Ireland severely undercut the association of the ruin with a particularized past. The ruin became an ornament, a fetishized collectable, as structure or image. Ann Bermingham discusses the irony of the 'cult of the ruin', where the theoretical resistance of the picturesque to codification breaks down as the ruin becomes a standard feature that 'at once concedes the victory of nature over art and claims for art the power to transform waste into beauty'.[42] In this schema, the ruin's primary role is as aesthetic object, rather than as a historical signifier with a particularized past.

In *The Wild Irish Girl*, Owenson draws upon the ruin as an aesthetic object yet restores its relation to historical consciousness, employing the Prince and Horatio as advocates for conflicting interpretations of the ruin within the Irish context. The Prince of Inismore 'dwells with melancholy pleasure on the innumerable ruined palaces and abbeys which lie scattered amidst the richest scenes of this romantic province'.[43] Horatio, naively moved by the spectacle of the ruin, deems the Castle of Inismore, 'Grand even in desolation, and magnificent in decay'.[44] However, the Prince understands such picturesque ruins to signify great loss, lamenting, 'the splendid dwelling of princely grandeur, the awful asylum of monastic piety, are just mouldering into oblivion with the memory of those they once sheltered. The sons of little men triumph over those whose arm was strong in war, and whose voice breathed no impotent command; and the descendant of the mighty chieftain has nothing left to distinguish him from the son of a peasant, but the decaying ruins of his ancestors' castle.'[45] The Prince's comment reinvigorates the aestheticized ruins with political potency. Horatio's and the Prince's oppositional interpretations of Irish ruins foreground the contemporary critical debates regarding the aesthetic work that ruins perform. Anne Janowitz argues that the 'ruin serves as the visible guarantor of the antiquity of the nation, but as ivy climbs up and claims the stonework, it also binds culture to nature, presenting the nation under the aspect of nature, and so suggesting national permanence'.[46] In a process that solidified British ideals of nationhood, the poetry and paintings from the mid-eighteenth century onward that incorporated ruins engaged in an aestheticization whereby the 'violent and divisive upheavals that accompanied the Reformation and the Civil War, and which led directly to physical ruin of many abbeys, houses and castles, are seldom mentioned'.[47]

42 Ann Bermingham, *Landscape and ideology* (Berkeley, 1986), pp 84–5. **43** Owenson, *Wild Irish Girl*, p. 63. **44** Ibid., p. 44. **45** Ibid., p. 63. **46** Anne Janowitz, *England's ruins: poetic purpose and the national landscape* (Oxford, 1990), p. 54. **47** Sean Ryder, 'Ireland in ruins: the

However, as Sean Ryder compellingly argues such a move to aestheticize the ruin in Ireland was complicated by the fact that Ireland's history was still under negotiation: 'As a consequence, the Irish ruin was not simply an aesthetic feature, integrated into the landscape as a tranquil sign of natural process and order. Instead it tended to serve as a site of continuing historical and ideological activity.'[48] The disconnection Owenson features between Horatio and the Prince in their reading of the ruins reveals their differing perceptions of how negotiable the future of Ireland might be. Ina Ferris argues that the 'scene of colonial ruin, abrasive and knotted, moves destruction rather than 'calm decay' into the foreground ... reattaching the ruin to history and releasing more aggressive energies that impinge more heavily on the present'.[49]

Though the Prince does not realize it at the time, he is speaking to what he terms the 'son of a little man'. Horatio's family 'earned' their Irish lands 'by the sword' of their ancestor who murdered the Prince's ancestor in the Cromwellian wars.[50] For Horatio and Owenson's British readers, the ruins are most 'magnificent in decay' because they embody the parallel decay of the power of the native Irish chieftains. Though Owenson sets the original conflict between the families in a far-distant past, the fierceness of the Irish chieftain, like the Prince of Inismore, might have been represented more recently in one of the horrifying images of the Irish rebellion of 1798, or in one of the more than twenty narratives published in the five years immediately following the rebellion. Narratives such as Sir Richard Musgrave's *A Concise Account of the Material Events and Atrocities Which Occurred in the Late Rebellion* (1799) vividly recount what he terms the 'many outrages and barbarities' committed by 'sanguinary monsters'.[51] However, in the novel, the horror of the recent rebellion (though mentioned in a footnote and alluded to in Horatio's father's story)[52] seems to be contained through the constant presence of the picturesque ruin. The Prince is not to be feared; his body shares the state of deterioration of his castle: he moves 'with difficulty' and his 'colossal, but infirm frame' needs the support of his daughter even to walk.[53] Owenson writes that he 'like Milton's ruined angel, "Above the rest, / In shape and feature proudly eminent, / Stood like a tower"'.[54] Owenson's Miltonic

---

figure of the ruin in early nineteenth-century Irish poetry', in Glenn Hooper (ed.), *Landscape and empire, 1770–2000* (Aldershot and Burlington, VT, 2005), p. 80.   **48** Ibid., p. 81. **49** Ina Ferris, *The romantic national tale and the question of Ireland* (Cambridge, 2002), p. 110. **50** Owenson, *Wild Irish Girl*, p. 32.   **51** Sir Richard Musgrave, *A concise account of the material events and atrocities which occurred in the late rebellion*, 3rd ed. (Dublin, 1799), pp 35; 69. **52** In a lengthy footnote defending the charge of '*barbarity*' among the Irish, Owenson discusses the 1798 rebellion, particularly the '*atrocities*' at Wexford, where, she asserts, 'scarcely any feature of the original Irish character, or any trace of the Irish language is to be found' (*Wild Irish Girl*, p. 176). In other words, the most barbaric Irishmen are of British descent. For Owenson's discussion of Lord M——'s masquerade as Irish rebel, see *Wild Irish Girl*, pp 213–14.   **53** Owenson, *Wild Irish Girl*, p. 48.   **54** Ibid., p. 50. As Owenson likely knew, Edmund Burke included this particular passage from Milton in his *A philosophical enquiry into the origin of our ideas of the sublime and beautiful* (London, 1757), p. 48, introducing it with '[w]e don't any where meet a more sublime description than this justly celebrated one of Milton, wherein he gives the portrait of Satan with a dignity so suitable to the subject'.

reference casts the Prince as having fallen from power, while simultaneously completing the metaphor of his body as the 'ruined tower'. His adherence to ancient costume and customs make him a sort of endearing relic.

Though Horatio's first letter from the Castle of Inismore suggests he could be held there as 'prisoner of war, or taken up on suspicion of espionage, or to be offered as an appeasing sacrifice to the *manes* of the old Prince of Inismore,' no member of the Inismore household (or its surrounding environs) seems remotely to possess the potency to do him any injury.[55] There are no strong young men to mount resistance; not since the oarsmen in the Dublin harbour, described as 'progeny of the once formidable race of Irish giants,' has Horatio encountered any potentially dangerous masculine force.[56] The rebels of the images in circulation at the time of the publication of *The Wild Irish Girl* appear nowhere in the novel. Horatio and his father are rivals to each other; there is no insurgent threat.

Interestingly, the Prince does wear a sheathed dagger or '*skiene*' as part of his ancient costume, but it is discussed as an 'article of the dress'.[57] He reminisces about his 'boyish days' when he would 'contemplate these ruins' and 'strange stories of the feats of my ancestors' and dream of 'my arm wielding the spear in war'; he affirms, however, 'it was only a dream!'[58] The weapons of the novel consist of artifacts on display in the castle's great-hall, what Horatio terms a 'cabinet of national antiquities, and national curiosities'.[59] As the Prince schools Horatio on the ancient order of knights in Ireland, he displays the fine craftsmanship of the 'collar,' the 'salet' or helmet, the 'gorget' (for protecting the throat), a shield and a coat of mail worn by the 'ancestor who was murdered in this castle' (by Horatio's ancestor), defensive weapons all. In contrapoint to the Prince's displays, Horatio holds up a 'sword of curious workmanship,' a 'battle-axe,' and a 'beautiful spear,' all weapons of the aggressor.[60] The lone insurgent appearing in the text is Lord M——, who employs that disguise to gain admittance to the Castle, requesting sanctuary from the Prince. The only bloodshed occurs when the 'loose stones' of the ruin give way beneath Horatio's feet, resulting in a 'bleeding temple' and a 'dreadfully bruised and fractured' arm.[61] The threat comes not from the inhabitants, therefore, but from the ruin itself, and Horatio recalls that it was the 'contemplation' of those 'interesting ruins' which 'I had nearly purchased with my life'.[62] However, Horatio's fall, occurring shortly after the Miltonic reference to Lucifer, should be read as more than a stumble. Owenson suggests that we read Horatio's mediation of Ireland in terms of the picturesque with some irony, and she implies here some lurking danger in the ruins, in contemplating them as neutral aesthetic objects. Though insurgent violence seems muted and contained in the novel, the British role as aggressor and invader is remarkably present. The only death in the novel is the Prince's, precipitated by the revelation of Horatio's and his father's true identities. Though the Prince is described as infirm from his first appearance, Glorvina sees his death as far from natural, shrieking at Horatio and Lord M——, 'Which of you murdered my father?'[63]

---

55 Ibid., p. 44. **56** Ibid., p. 14. **57** Ibid., p. 48. **58** Ibid., p. 64. **59** Ibid., p. 102.
60 Ibid., pp 104–6. **61** Ibid., p. 53. **62** Ibid., p. 59. **63** Ibid, p. 242.

Sydney Owenson's self-conscious manipulations of the discourse of art, coupled with her later writings, demonstrate that she does not intend to contain the underlying claims of the Irish. In the Preface to her 1827 novel, *The O'Briens and the O'Flahertys*, she writes, 'To live in Ireland and to write for it, is to live and write *poignard sur la gorge*; for there is no country where it is less possible to be useful with impunity, or where the penalty on patriotism is levied with a more tyrannous exaction,' explicitly noting that her political writing began with *The Wild Irish Girl*, 'under the banners' of which, she says, 'I fleshed my maiden sword'.[64] *The Wild Irish Girl* becomes politically subversive with her decision to employ the rhetoric of the picturesque with ironic difference, and to cast the Irish landscape as that most likely to be represented by a Salvator Rosa painting. As Owenson well knew, Rosa was a revolutionary and his paintings hinted at that which was dark and troubling in the sublime landscapes. According to her preface to the first edition, Owenson was motivated in part to write the biography of Rosa because of the 'peculiar character of the man' rather than the 'extraordinary merits of the artist'.[65] In her 1855 preface, however, Owenson is more explicit: Rosa 'worked through his great vocation with a spirit of independence that never quailed, and with unflinching resistance to the persecutions of despotism . . . The story of Modern Italy writhing under foreign rule, he depicted in those groups of outlawed gentlemen and an outraged people, who, being denied all law, lived lawlessly.'[66] Though her factual accuracy is questionable, Owenson highlights Rosa's relations with banditti and his participation in the 1647 Neapolitan rebellion, an uprising lead by the young fisherman, Masaniello.[67] She quotes an Italian source that praised Rosa as 'one of Masaniello's best soldiers'.[68] Owenson stresses that Masaniello, a humble man of the people, effected a bloodless revolution, redressing the wrongs against the poor, and briefly establishing a republican government. Owenson clearly intends to draw a parallel between the Neapolitan political situation and the Irish one.

Owenson terms Rosa the 'poet of liberty' and imagines:

> Did Salvator live now, one might fancy him joining the ranks of the gallant defenders of national independence and civilisation; standing out, like one of his own bold figures, upon the heights of Balaklava, pencil in hand and revolver in belt, realising for the homage of posterity the grand battle raging below, till, borne away by his kindling sympathies, he flings down his pencil,

64 Sydney Owenson (Lady Morgan), *The O'Briens and the O'Flahertys: a national tale* (London, 1988), p. xv.   **65** Sydney Owenson (Lady Morgan), *The life and times of Salvator Rosa* (London, 1855), p. vii.   **66** Ibid., pp iii–iv.   **67** For contemporary scholarly accounts of Salvator Rosa see Jonathan Scott's *Salvator Rosa: his life and times* (New Haven, 1995) and James S. Patty's *Salvator Rosa in French literature: from the bizarre to the sublime* (Lexington, 2005). Though his title is clearly an homage to Owenson, Scott finds much of her discussion of Rosa to be fanciful. Patty attends to Owenson's influence on the nineteenth-century and contemporary reception of Rosa, with chapters entitled, 'Enter Lady Morgan' and 'Lady Morgan's Legacy'.   **68** Owenson, *Life and times*, p. 157.

and, plunging into the *mêlée*, meets a glorious death or shares a not less glorious triumph.[69]

In Rosa, I believe we have located a figure far more threatening than the aged Prince of Inismore. Though Owenson evokes the security of the aestheticized landscape, she destabilizes this seemingly neutralized landscape by introducing the painter who championed rebellion, thus suggesting the potential for Irish insurrection. Making the connection of Rosa to the Irish insurgency explicit in the 'United Irishmen' chapter of *The O'Briens and the O'Flahertys*, Owenson has her hero Murrogh O'Brien describe the assembled United Irishmen as 'ready grouped for the purpose of a well-sketched conspiracy . . . that recalled the '*grande quadro*' of Salvator's pride and glory'.[70]

In her own extended meditations on the picturesque landscape of Connaught, the same landscape where *The Wild Irish Girl* takes place, in *Patriotic Sketches* Owenson rarely loses sight of the humble individuals inhabiting the magnificent landscape. In her ninth sketch, she writes:

> I am at present residing in that part of Ireland where the association of thrashers first arose.[71] I am consequently surrounded by those who formed that association: a peasantry poor, laborious, vehement, and enterprising; capable of good or ill; in the extremes of both; left to the devious impulse of either; but oftener impelled by the hardest necessity to the latter . . . Punished with rigorous severity when acting wrong, but neglected, unnoticed, and unrecompensed when acting right; forming the last link in the chain of human society, and treated with contempt because unable to resist oppression.[72]

Owenson chooses to see these people; she understands the glorious and forbidding landscape of Connaught to be one of particular difficulty for the laborer. Owenson rereads the roofless peasant cabin (incorporated into the earlier picturesque sketch as part of the 'fairy gaze of fancy') and 'shuddering groups of literally naked children,' as victims of deprivation. In much the same way that she applauds Rosa's actions, Owenson praises the thrashers 'who daringly seized in their own hands the power of summary retribution, proportioned and appropriate as they conceived to their real or fancied grievances'.[73] For Owenson, then, the picturesque coast of western Ireland remains a point of negotiation, a place where the potential for insurgent activity lies unnoticed but radically present.

---

69 Ibid., p. iv.   **70** Owenson (Lady Morgan), *The O'Briens and the O'Flahertys*, pp 312–13.
71 The thrashers were a rural insurgent group akin to the '*white boys, hearts of steel, hearts of oak, break-of-day boys, right boys, defenders*' (Owenson, *Patriotic sketches*, 90). Like the other insurgent groups, the thrashers revolted on a local level against tithes and rents.   **72** Owenson, *Patriotic sketches*, p. 79.   **73** Ibid., p. 94.

The landscape for all – no penny-in-the-slot at the Giant's Causeway

IRENE FURLONG

The issue of the private ownership of and public access to the landscape, particularly in areas of outstanding scenic beauty, forms the core of this essay. It will examine the evolution of the tourist industry in Ireland in the nineteenth century, particularly the emergence of the Giant's Causeway as a tourist attraction and will focus on the controversy surrounding the plan by a development syndicate to enclose and charge admittance for entrance to the causeway in the 1890s. This dispute concentrated attention on the question of public and private ownership of the landscape in Ireland and abroad, at a time when the concept of making the landscape available to all classes was beginning to surface:

> Farewell, thou source of horror and delight –
> Thy smiling day, thy never-ending night;
> Thy wild Cathedrals, clad in awful gloom;
> Thy fairy regions, that for ever bloom;
> Thy awful scenes, magnificently hurled,
> To form the leading *wonder of the world*.[1]

Written in 1808, at a time when the Giant's Causeway was first becoming known as a tourist attraction, this poem sums up the effect it had in a nineteenth-century context that was concerned with all that was sublime and awe-inspiring in the natural world. However, the problem of access to this marvel in the last decade of the century would be just one of many similar predicaments with regard to public right of entry to landscapes of outstanding beauty. With the industrial development of the United Kingdom had come the unprecedented flight from the land as thousands of people flocked to take advantage of employment opportunities in mills and factories, leading to their incarceration in smoke-filled and unhealthy cities. This radical change in what had been a mainly agricultural country led in turn to a new appreciation of the value of the countryside as an escape from these centres of manufacturing, and would also tie in with the emerging Victorian obsession with the landscape as a locus for the romantic and sublime. However, the Parliamentary Enclosure acts passed between 1760 and 1830 had the effect of transforming what had

---

1 Patrick O'Kelly, *Poems on the Giant's Causeway and Killarney with other miscellanies* (Dublin, 1808), p. 1.

been communal land into private property in the interest of improving agricultural production. They also removed the right of passage across these lands for ordinary people. At the same time, the glorification of the landscape by writers and poets such as Sir Walter Scott in Scotland and William Wordsworth in the Lake District led to a fashion for visiting areas of scenic beauty, which in turn focussed attention on the importance of the conservation of and rights of public access to such areas. As early as 1810, Wordsworth described the Lake District as 'a sort of national property, in which every man has a right and interest who has an eye to perceive and a heart to enjoy'.[2] However, in 1815 the British parliament passed legislation that stated if two justices of the peace agreed 'that any public Highway, Bridleway or Footway is unnecessary, it shall and may be lawful by Order of such Justices, or any Two of them, to stop up and to sell and dispose of such unnecessary Highway, Bridleway or Footway'.[3] As apprehension grew over the question of public access, concerned individuals came together to form various organizations and societies devoted to the concept of the right of public access to private land. The Association for the Protection of Ancient Footpaths in the Vicinity of York was founded in 1824 as a direct result of the threat to footpaths and was followed in 1826 by the Manchester Association for the Preservation of Ancient Footpaths. The 'right to roam' movement had begun, and with the growth in popularity of rambling during the reign of Queen Victoria, many more associations came into being with the aim of enabling people to escape from the deplorable living conditions in the cities. In 1884 the National Footpaths Preservation Society was established to cater for the needs of the early ramblers clubs and in the same year, James Bryce MP introduced the first Bill for Freedom to Roam but failed to have it passed. The bill was reintroduced every year until 1914 and failed each time. In 1892 the West of Scotland Ramblers' Alliance was formed and two years later the Peak District and Northern Counties Footpaths Preservation Society came into being. Further afield, the world's first national park was established in 1872 at Yellowstone, in the United States, and the 1880s saw a campaign which culminated in a commission led by State Survey Director James T. Gardner and Frederick Law Olmsted which prepared a Special Report ... on the Preservation of the Scenery of Niagara Falls, at the direction of the New York state legislature.[4] This commission advocated state purchase, restoration and preservation through public ownership of the scenic lands surrounding Niagara Falls. Accompanied by a Memorial to the governor signed by more than a hundred prominent citizens, the document defined the direction of the public campaign to save the beauties of Niagara. In Boston, Charles Eliot, a landscape gardener, proposed the establishment of private conservation organisations with a view to preserving 'special bits of scenery...which possess uncommon beauty and more than usual refreshing power'.[5] The western world was awakening to the value of the rural landscape as an

2 http://www.bridgend.gov.uk accessed 7 October 2005. 3 http://www.ramblers.org.uk/ news/media/ramblers-history.html accessed 7 October 2005. 4 http://memory.loc.gov/ ammem/amrvhtml/conshome.html accessed 7 October 2005. 5 http://www.the-

antidote to the ills of urban life, but also to the necessity to protect areas of uncommon beauty for posterity.

Britain's first national conservation organisation, the Commons Preservation Society was formed in 1865, originally to fight for open spaces in London, but later was renamed the Open Spaces Society when its interests become national. The society's founders and early members included John Stuart Mill, Sir Robert Hunter, Octavia Hill and Lord Eversley, who as George Lefevre, was a Liberal MP and a junior minister at the Board of Trade. He held a variety of posts including Commissioner of Works and was responsible for opening Hampton Court Park, Kew Gardens and Regent's Park to the public. The society worked to preserve commons for the enjoyment of the public and was active in protecting the historic and important rights-of-way network through England and Wales. In 1829 Sir Thomas Maryon-Wilson was anxious to build on Hampstead Heath, making many unsuccessful attempts to get Parliament's permission to build on his land. After his death in 1868 his successor reached a compromise with the Society and Parliament to transfer all his rights as lord of the manor to the Metropolitan Board of Works, a major victory for the Commons Society. In 1871, a Bill was introduced with the Society's help whereby eight Conservators were appointed for the future preservation of the common. Olivia Hill was determined to expand the efforts of the society to include buildings and gardens of worth and she developed a long working relationship with Robert Hunter, solicitor to the Commons Preservation Society. Hardwicke Rawnsley had collected rents for Octavia Hill as a young man and by the 1880s he was fighting to preserve the Lake District from development. Together these three became the founders of the National Trust, although the property that led to its establishment was not a great house, or mountain, or stretch of coast. It was a garden, Sayes Court, created by the seventeenth century diarist John Evelyn, in the heart of Deptford, in east London. In 1884 Octavia Hill was approached by a descendant of Evelyn's, but found there was no organization with the necessary legal powers for holding the property for permanent preservation. She turned for advice to Hunter, who proposed the establishment of a land company for 'the protection of the public interests in the open spaces of the country'.[6] Octavia Hill wanted a short, expressive name for the new company, and suggested the 'Commons and Gardens Trust' which Hunter shortened to 'the National Trust'. Nevertheless, it took ten years and a succession of disappointments and obstructions before the Trust was properly launched. The first building purchased by the Trust was Alfriston Clergy House in Sussex, bought for £10 in 1896 and its commitment to great buildings was confirmed in 1900 when Robert Hunter negotiated the gift of Kanturk Castle, in Co. Cork in Ireland. This series of developments provides the context in which the controversy regarding the enclosure of the Giant's Causeway took place.

The earliest published mention of the Giant's Causeway appears to be in a letter

trustees.org/ pages/89_historical_origins.cfm accessed 24 October 2005. **6** http://www. nationaltrust.org.uk/ main/w-trust/w-thecharity/w-history/

from Sir Richard Bulkley of Dunlavin, in Co. Wicklow to Dr Lyster, which was published in 1693 by the Royal Society. After a personal visit the following year, Dr Samuel Foley, the bishop of Down and Connor, furnished some additional information to Bulkley. Along with a description which appears in Philosophical Transactions of the Royal Society, was an engraving with the title: 'A Draught of the Giant's Causeway which is near Bengore Head in the County of Antrim by Christopher Cole AD 1694'.[7] Sir Thomas Molyneaux who died in 1733, was the first to publish a detailed account of the Causeway and through his influence and advice the Royal Society had an engraving made entitled: 'A true Prospect of the Giant's Causeway near Bengore Head in the county of Antrim, by Edward Sandys AD 1696 at the expense of the Dublin Society'.[8] Baron Wainwright, an Irish judge, sent a description of his visit in September 1736 to Mrs Clayton, afterwards Lady Sundon, lady in waiting to Queen Caroline:

> The Causeway is composed of numberless pillars of stone, compacted and fitted together so that there are no interstices to let down even water, and yet that they are separate pillars is visible. No artist could lay the dies of mosaic work more close ... I must say this great wonder of nature is well worthy of all the pilgrimages that can be made to it.[9]

A Miss Susanna Drury painted two pictures of the scene in 1740, which were subsequently engraved by Vivares, and published by Boydell in 1777. However, it is generally accepted that it was the Revd Dr Hamilton who first called general attention to the wonders of the Giant's Causeway by his 'Letters concerning the Northern Coast' published in 1786. At the same time as the Causeway grew in repute as a scenic attraction, more travel guides were being written about Ireland and Philip Dixon Hardy, writing in 1830, gives a typical description of its appeal:

> From the little hills ... the first view of the causeway is obtained; and a more sublime, imposing and beautiful scene could not by any possibility be imagined by the most enthusiastic mind, than that which now bursts upon the sight – an immense and magnificent bay, indented by a number of caves and headlands, which rise from a height of 350 to 400 ft above the level of the sea, presenting at all points a variety of the most magnificent and interesting views, as if nature and art had united their energies to form one truly grand and splendid picture.[10]

Dixon also spoke of the legend of how the Causeway came by its name, recounting what he called 'the hypothesis current among the vulgar' that the Giant's Causeway

---

7 Robert m'Cahan, 'The Giant's Causeway and Dunluce Castle' (Coleraine: Northern Constitution, n.d.), p. 1.   8 Ibid.   9 Robert m'Cahan, *The Giant's Causeway and Dunluce Castle* (Coleraine, n.d.), p. 1.   10 Philip Dixon Hardy, *The northern tourist, or stranger's guide to the north and north west of Ireland* (Dublin, 1830) p. 309.

I Vivares after Drury, 'The East Prospect of the Giants Causeway in the
county of Antrim in the Kingdom of Ireland', engraving c. 1740.

and Fingal's Cave, in the island of Staffa, were the extremities of an immense bridge which formerly extended between these two points, constructed by Fionn Mac Cumhaill to facilitate his progress in a war undertaken against the natives of the opposite coast.

However, the officers of the Ordnance Survey, collecting information in the 1830s, took a more prosaic view of the phenomenon. Lieutenant Thomas Hore, writing in August 1830, was unmoved by its grandeur:

> The celebrated Giant's Causeway, which consists of three piers of basaltic pillars, has the general appearance of a quay projecting from the base of a very steep cliff 500 or 600 feet into the sea. These pillars are irregular prisms of from 3 to 8 sides; the square, pentagon, hexagon and heptagon being the most common and standing in close contrast with each other ... they stand 40 ft across the low water level.[11]

Moreover, Hore was quite critical of those in the area who worked as guides at the Causeway during the summer:

> Idleness prevails to a great extent owing to the nature of their usual occupation, which, through sometimes very profitable, is nonetheless very

11 *Ordnance Survey memoirs – parishes of County Antrim, vol. 16, 1830–35, 1837–8* (Belfast, 1992) p. 36.

precarious, viz., acting as guides to the great variety of strangers visiting the great national curiosity. Besides this, they usually occupy their time during the season fishing and collecting seaweed for manure or kelp ... On the approach, however, of a set of visitors, they generally quit their occupations, even though they may be successful ones, to surround the strangers, upon whom they often force their services as guides.[12]

A later survey, carried out in 1835 by James Boyle, was more enthusiastic stating that 'on the western wide of this coast is the celebrated Giant's Causeway, one of the wonders of the world and the greatest natural curiosity in Ireland'. He was also more forthcoming on the work of the guides there:

> There is scarcely a spot at the Causeway to which the guides, to suit their own purposes and enhance their importance, have not affixed some name. In such a place, where there is so much variety and form and shape, nothing, however unimportant, has escaped a christening, and an attempt to describe or enumerate all these names or places would, instead of conveying an idea, only lead to confusion, besides being a repetition of what has appeared in the numberless guidebooks.[13]

However, he did not consider working as a guide to be any great boon to the people concerned: 'they are among the most indolent and improvident, as the money they then earn, though sufficient to support them through the winter, is spent before it commences'.[14] Boyle also had practical advice for those wishing to see the causeway to best advantage:

> It is in the neighbouring coast, particularly in the bays enumerated, that scenery, and that too of the most sublime and magnificent description is to be found. Instead of creeping down on the Causeway by degrees and in that manner losing all the imposing effect of its grandeur, a person visiting the Causeway for the first time should take a boat and, commencing at the Black Rock, go round the entire coast to Bengore, visiting on his way the several bays and ports. In this manner of viewing ... the most senseless, apathetic person cannot fail to be struck with its sublimity. Let the tourist then examine the curious minute detail of the causeways. Their extreme perfection, exactness and regularity must astonish the most uneducated and supply an extended field for the theories of the scientific. One hurried visit ... gives but a confused and imperfect idea of it. It will bear examination and investigation, and every succeeding visit will disclose new wonders and excite the amazement and attraction of those who were before uninterested and careless.[15]

12 Ibid.   **13** Ibid., *Memoir by James Boyle, August 1835, with notes and corrections by R.K. Dawson*, p. 43.   **14** Ibid.   **15** Ibid.

By the mid 1830s Bushmills, the nearest town to the Causeway, boasted a hotel and two small inns. The hotel was built by Sir Francis Macnaghten, a local landowner, stood three storeys high and could accommodate eighteen persons. Boyle found the charges at all the hotels very reasonable and concluded that the numbers who visited the town on their way to the Giant's Causeway contributed not only to the support of the hotel keepers, but also to that of the dealers and guides. [16] Families were in the habit of coming to the neighbouring coast for bathing during the summer months. Furthermore, it was evident that the Causeway provided the only source of entertainment for local residents:

> The people, though they are fond of it, have no regular amusements. There are no places of public amusement except the Giant's Causeway and numberless pleasure parties are daily made there from all parts of the country during the summer months. A fair (exclusively for amusement) is held at the Causeway on the 12th August, and it is anxiously looked forward to by the inhabitants of the surrounding country, who flock to it from even distant parts, and there is no part of Ireland where so great an assemblage of well-dressed country people may be seen. Dancing, strolling about the rocks and cliffs, and eating and drinking in the tents form the amusements of the day. [17]

The construction of the Antrim Coast Road between 1832 and 1842 greatly improved access to the causeway, and enabled many more visitors to go there. William Makepeace Thackeray, who went in 1845, was greatly impressed but not in a favourable way. He found the solitude 'awful' and the landscape peculiarly eerie: 'it looks like the beginning of the world somehow; the sea looks older than in other places, the hills and rocks strange'. He added rather dramatically: 'When the world was moulded and fashioned out of formless chaos, this must have been the bit over – a remnant of chaos!' [18] As for the guides, a booklet issued by the Imperial Hotel in Belfast in 1852 confirmed earlier perceptions of them as a nuisance:

> Let me, before leaving the causeway, express an honest indignation at, and abhorrence of, the obscene crowd of guides and boatmen, who regardless alike of entreaties and threats, continued to dodge our steps and mar our pleasure, until we ascended from their harpies' cave. These guides are indeed a peculiar plague of the causeway, for they waylay you miles before you reach the final objects of your journey, and well nigh overwhelm you with proffers of all sorts of information, as well as books and views of nearly every spot within leagues, as verbal dissertations on the geology and all other attributes of the neighbourhood. [19]

16 Ibid., p. 45.   17 Ibid., p. 47.   18 J. E. Mullin, *The Causeway coast* (Coleraine, 1974), p. 39.   19 *The Irish tourist's illustrated handbook for visitors to Ireland in 1852* (London, 1852), p. 156.

Nevertheless, Dr Thomas De Witt Talmage, a charismatic and celebrated American preacher who made several trips to Europe in the second half of the nineteenth century, was so carried away by the inspirational aspect of the landscape and its undoubted divine formation by the Creator that he proclaimed:

> A man is a fool who can look at these rocks and not realise that the world had a design and a Designer. Before you die, you must see the Giant's Causeway . . . there is nothing in the world like the Giant's Causeway. Ireland might well have been built if for nothing but to present the Giant's Causeway. It lifts us to the sublimities. It will be the last pillar of earth to crumble.[20]

As the Revd Dr Talmage was estimated to have millions of readers of his sermons and other works in the United States, this was an undoubted boost to the promotion of the Causeway there, but the greatest problem for many potential visitors to Ireland was the organisation of their trip and this was solved by the emergence of arguably the most vital ingredient in tourism traffic, the travel agent. In 1818 a Mr Emery of Charing Cross in London began organizing fourteen-day coach tours of Switzerland[21] and he was followed in 1841 by Thomas Cook who also organised excursions and who began operations in Ireland in 1849, taking a group of travellers from the Potteries to Dublin. In 1852 Cook introduced his short excursions and longer tours to Ireland, writing enthusiastically: 'From Derby to Dublin and back for 13s.! is an astounding announcement; and the artizan [*sic*] and mechanic classes may now regale their spirits with the pleasurable libations of travel'.[22] The following year he took thousands to the Dublin Exhibition, part of an effort to stimulate industry and to revive the Irish economy after the famine and he later conducted a number of parties to Ireland, filling two special trains with about 1,500 people in 1856.[23] His son, John Mason Cook, opened the first Cook office in Dublin in 1874[24] and by 1888 Cook was advertising tours in Ireland by rail, steamer and coach. In 1895 his first package tour from the United States arrived in Killarney and Glengarriff and offices were opened in Belfast, Cork and Queenstown.[25]

Ireland was slowly awakening to the economic potential of tourism, as railway companies penetrated to the furthest reaches of the island and many of the gentry associated with those companies realised the potential of their own estates. Irish publishing interests began to print guidebooks, handbooks and maps, but progress was slow. It must be borne in mind that Irish tourism development was hampered by a number of disadvantages, in addition to its isolated situation on the periphery of Europe. Along with its almost total dependence on visitors from abroad and the relative absence of well-known attractions, Ireland also suffered from deficiencies of accommodation, amenities and transport facilities, along with an image of lawlessness

---

20 Ulster Tourist Development Association, *Ulster Guide* (Belfast, 1928), p. 78.   **21** Piers Brendon, *Thomas Cook – 150 years of popular tourism* (London, 1991), p. 8.   **22** Ibid., p. 64.   **23** Ibid.   **24** Ibid., p. 168.   **25** Ibid., p. 248.

and political unrest. The lack of a literary figure to romanticise the Irish landscape as Scott and Wordsworth had done respectively for Scotland and the Lake District was a recurring theme in the debate on what was necessary to attract more tourist traffic to Ireland in the late nineteenth century. Unfortunately, the image of Ireland portrayed in the novels of Maria Edgeworth, a figure of comparative stature whose works had served as an inspiration to Scott, was not an alluring one. As Nenadic argues: 'If images of Scotland stressed the absence of people – or people located at a romantic distance – images of Ireland ... invariably evoked the "teeming millions", the clamouring and unruly masses, and hordes of beggars.'[26] While the 'teeming millions' of the pre-famine era had dissipated, the presence of clamouring and unruly beggars was a constant theme in travel literature on Ireland, and along with fears of disturbance on political grounds, constituted a major public relations problem for those promoting tourism. However, Anthony Trollope, who lived at Whiteabbey on the Antrim Coast, wrote encouragingly to a friend in England in 1854: 'Tho the north of Ireland is not the choicest permanent residence, it has some charms for the tourist – and should you take my advise [*sic*] and visit there, I beg to offer myself as your host and guide.'[27]

By the 1890s, great strides had been made to develop the area around the causeway as a tourism district. The first hydroelectric train in the world, known as the Portrush Tramway was built by William A. Traill, a local engineer who worked for the Northern Counties railway. It ran the seven miles from Portrush to Bushmills, and was opened by the lord lieutenant, Earl Spencer, in 1883.[28] Two years later it was extended to the Causeway and took tourists there from Portrush every half-hour during the summer.[29] Edgar Flinn wrote enthusiastically in his 1895 book on Irish resorts:

> The line to the causeway skirts the coast nearly the whole way, and some magnificent views are obtained in the course of the journey ... At the causeway there is remarkably good hotel accommodation, the Causeway Hotel being well situated and very comfortable, and affording splendid sea views. To those requiring a clear, bracing and dry climate, a most healthful and agreeable holiday can be spent here.[30]

Interestingly, this novel undertaking was seen by one London newspaper as Cockneyfying the Causeway,[31] but another British journal was quite enthusiastic about the development of easier access to that particular part of the island:

26 Stana Nenadic, 'Land, the landed and relationships with England: literature and perception, 1760–1830' in S.J. Connolly, R.A. Houston and R.J. Morris (eds), *Conflict, identity and economic development* (Preston, 1995), p. 159. 27 Ernest Sandford, *Discover Northern Ireland* (Belfast, 1976), p. 25. 28 J. McClelland Martin, *Guide to Belfast, Northern Counties Railway, Giant's Causeway and the Antrim Coast* (Belfast, 1895), p. 69. 29 Ibid., p. 92. 30 D. Edgar Flinn, *Irish health resorts & watering places*, 2nd ed. (Dublin, 1895), p. 96. 31 Thomas Macknight, *Ulster as it is* (London, 1896), p. 42.

2 Tourist and souvenir sellers at the Giant's Causeway, Co. Antrim.
Image courtesy of the National Library of Ireland.

Ireland has of late years obtained a notoriety – unenviable, no doubt – which has done much to frighten away tourists from its shores; but when it is remembered that the north of Ireland differs materially from the south and west – that its inhabitants are law-abiding, quiet, and industrious; and that while possibly the ready wit of the Celtic character is less often met with yet the sterling, honest characteristics of the English and Scottish element more largely predominate. Although situated at the extreme north of Ireland, the Giant's Causeway is by no means difficult of access, and is practically as near to the metropolis as are many of the health resorts which have not now the charm of novelty they once possessed.[32]

Meanwhile, due to the indefatigable efforts of an English-born entrepreneur, F.W. Crossley, the first Irish Tourist Association (ITA) was formed in 1884, uniting the Anglo-Irish gentry, the railway and steamship companies, accommodation providers and other commercial concerns that stood to benefit from the tourist traffic. By 1896, the tourist association was spreading its wings around the country and an Ulster branch was formed at a public meeting on 13 April 1896 in Belfast, chaired by the lord mayor, W.J. Pirrie. Held in the council chamber of the Town Hall, the meeting

32 *Journal of British and Foreign Health Resorts*, 7 (Manchester, July 1890), p.69

attracted Dublin ITA council members such as Judge Boyd, V.B. Dillon, W. Holder and the ubiquitous Crossley. Northern attendance included Lord Londonderry, Seaton F. Milligan, vice-president of the Society of Antiquaries of Ireland, and representatives of the transport companies, hotel proprietors and solicitors.[33]

The fledgling body soon found itself with a cause to champion. On 2 July the *Belfast Newsletter* reported, to the great alarm of many, including the Ballymena and Portrush town commissioners, that a syndicate called the Giant's Causeway Company had purchased the rights of the lessee at the Giant's Causeway 'as a private speculation' and were proposing to charge admission.[34] Railings and a tollgate were being erected and all paths, roads and ways to and around the Causeway would be closed to the public. The syndicate had been registered as a limited liability company at Londonderry on 6 June 1896. Though the driving force appears to have been Hugh Lecky, the local landowner of the land around the causeway, the original seven subscribers consisted of a group of lawyers and merchants from Coleraine and Dublin. The syndicate had substantial profits in mind, anticipating takings of £5,000 a year which at 6*d*. a head or £1 for 20 people implied a figure of 100,000 visitors.

The executive council of the Irish Tourist Association met in Dublin on 3 July and carried a motion deploring the proposal, and at its prompting the Belfast branch held a special meeting on 7 July with Pirrie in the chair.[35] Crossley drew attention to the terms of the Dublin motion, which stated that 'the enclosure of the Giant's Causeway would be a serious injury to the development of the tourist trade in Ireland, and should be resisted by every possible means'. He expanded on this to cries of 'hear, hear':

> When the English people were coming to the country in larger numbers, it would be folly for them on this side of the water to do anything that would give the English tourist or the American tourist the idea that they were trying to fleece them ... if that syndicate succeeded in placing barbed wire around the Causeway, the probability was that soon every cross, round tower, and ruin in the country, and ultimately the country itself, would be enclosed by barriers, and so the tourist invasion of Ireland which they all desired, and which they trusted would weld the two countries closer in bonds of fellowship, would be prevented.[36]

It was decided to form a Giant's Causeway Defence Committee, and to act with other committees formed for the same purpose in several northern towns, which were determined to resist all attempts to interfere with the rights of the public in and around the Causeway, which had been fully exercised without let or hindrance for many generations. Crossley proposed the establishment of a shilling fund and it was also agreed to write to *The Times*, as both the Irish and English press had given much publicity to the case.

33 *Irish Tourist*, 3:2 (Dublin, 1896), 37. **34** *Belfast Newsletter*, 2 July 1896. **35** *Weekly Northern Whig*, 11 July 1896. **36** *Irish Tourist*, 3:3 (1896), 53.

The matter was raised in the House of Commons by Mr MacAleese MP, but as there was no public right of way, the crown declined to intervene.[37] Further questions were asked of the Board of Trade, and it was confirmed that the crown did own the foreshore and the adjoining seabed, and that no barrier could be placed on crown lands. Indignation meetings were held at Ballymoney and Portrush over the 'seizure of the Causeway', and local people co-opted onto the defence committee, of which Seaton Milligan was elected secretary. There was much hostile comment in the Belfast press: James Thomson denounced the idea of 'handing over the Causeway to a band of money grabbers'. A letter from F.N. Cooke defending the company was published in the *Belfast Newsletter*, saying that the intention was to use the nominal dues to improve the entrance and construct a much superior walk to benefit every visitor to the causeway.[38]

On 17 July the Giant's Causeway Defence Fund was established and Sir William McCammond appointed honorary treasurer. During the autumn of 1896 it emerged that the syndicate company had placed two men at the Causeway to warn visitors that they were trespassing on private property, and that they had chosen three visitors to test their claim to the Causeway by an action in the court of law. A writ was served on these three, and the Defence Committee, at a meeting in the Town Hall, Belfast on 17 October 1896 resolved to undertake their defence, as it was felt that if the test cases were allowed to go by default, the right of free access to the Causeway would be lost for ever.

The trial began in the vice-chancellor's court on 18 March 1897 and went on for some days. Thirty-four witnesses were examined, and the vice-chancellor delivered his verdict on 29 April 1897. Despite conceding that the evidence had established that during living memory the Causeway had been open without interruption from the owners to all persons without distinction, he gave judgement in favour of the syndicate. His view was that a public way must lead from one public place to another, and he based his decision on that view. The committee felt that this blow was 'not only fatal to the rights of way locally, but also to such rights throughout the United Kingdom'[39] and resolved to appeal the judgement.

On 22 November 1897, the case opened in the Court of Appeal in Dublin, before the lord chancellor and three lord justices and on 14 January 1898, a judgement was delivered varying the original in that the public could continue to use 'that part of the road from Dervock to the sea', and also that the costs of the attorney-general which had been paid by the defence committee in the original case, were to be refunded to them, and that each of the parties should pay their own costs for the appeal. The lord chancellor's opinion was that any place to which the public resorted for some determinate purpose answered the definition of a public place, and that any

37 *Weekly Northern Whig*, 4 July 1896. **38** *Belfast Newsletter*, 8 July 1896. **39** *The Defence of the Giant's Causeway*, reprinted from the *Belfast Newsletter*, 22 March 1898 (Belfast: 1898), p. 4.

point on the seashore to which the public resorted might be a public way, even if it
ended in a cul-de-sac. He further said: 'It may be in law the owners might refuse at
the end of the road to let them leave it and wander over the Causeway, but they
cannot prevent it from being a public national sight in legend and history; no unfit-
ting terminus to any road'.[40]

The defence committee celebrated this achievement but had an enormous
problem with the payment of the costs involved in the actions, which amounted to
about £1,850. Only about £400 had been paid, and it was now felt that the public,
on whose behalf the action had been taken, should pay the remainder. Some monies
had been received from England as a result of the efforts of Henry Allnutt, secretary
of the National Footpath Preservation Society in London, who had distributed thousands of leaflets paid for by the duke of Westminster, president of the society,
appealing for funds. In addition, the Giant's Causeway Tramway Company had
commended the committee's actions in its annual report: 'your directors consider that
the influential committee which took charge of the public rights have good cause to
congratulate themselves on the result' and had contributed the sum of £50.[41]
Speaking at a meeting held to discuss means of raising the sum needed, views were
expressed regarding the importance of trying to preserve to the public and their
descendants 'free access in all times to that grotto of nature, with all its unique formations of rock, its majestic headlands, and its spirit-soothing bays and amphitheatres'.[42]
It was felt that the Causeway belonged to no special locality or special nation and
should be regarded as the Lakes of Killarney and other beautiful places, as a possession belonging to the whole world, as its magnificent scenery had been given to
humanity as something to elevate humanity, and belonged to every man, woman and
child on the face of the earth. These were interesting views coming from the higher
classes at a time when land ownership was itself a very contentious subject in the
country.

Seaton Milligan gave a lecture entitled 'Ireland as a Tourist Resort' under the
auspices of the Belfast Natural History and Philosophical Society on 4 September
1898 to raise funds to defray the costs. The lord mayor, James Henderson, declared
that there was no subject that interested him more and introduced Milligan as
someone who had done a great deal to popularize Ireland as a tourist resort. Milligan
declared that the second object of his lecture was to develop the tourist traffic in
Ireland. He had selected this theme because of its importance to the country and
particularly to the Congested Districts, referring to the role of the light railways in
opening up Donegal, Connemara, and Kerry. Milligan also alluded to the absence of
the royal family as being a decisive factor in the lack of visitors to the country:[43] The
lecture was accompanied by 150 lanternslides of Irish scenery and antiquities. John
Workman MP proposed a vote of thanks and William Gray, seconding the motion,

40 Ibid., p. 5.   **41** Seaton F. Milligan, *Ireland as a tourist resort, with notes and illustrations of its
scenic beauties* (Belfast: 1898), p. 2.   **42** Ibid., p. 4.   **43** Ibid.

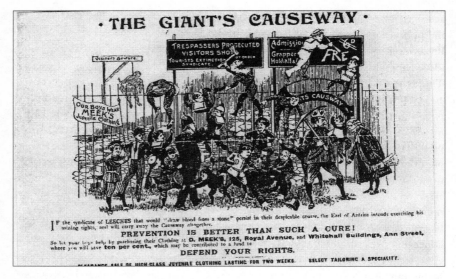

3 Antrim Papers, D/2977/2/13/3. Courtesy of Deputy Keeper of
the Records, Public Record Office of Northern Ireland.

said that Mr Milligan was one of a few who were endeavouring to protect the beauties of natural scenery, and to prevent their splendid country being marred by a
penny-in-the-slot system. However, Milligan, in reply said that when the actual
fighting came, two-thirds of the committee absented themselves and offered very
little financial help and but for Sir William McCammond, the defence would have
broken down.

Nevertheless, despite the efforts of the defence committee, the Syndicate was
victorious and early in 1898 the Giant's Causeway was railed in. The syndicate made
many improvements, including a path about a mile long around the bays but visitors
could still get a general view of the causeway from outside the enclosure or from the
top of the cliffs.[44] Although some visitors continued to complain about having to pay
for entry, many admitted that the syndicate had improved access to the causeway.
However, when Stephen Gwynn cycled there in 1899 he was not pleased to have to
pay sixpence for admission, finding it 'an innovation … which every good Irishman
resents'.[45] During the course of the twentieth century, there were more problems in
store for the site, but it was eventually given to the National Trust in the 1960s and
in 1986 Moyle District Council built a visitor centre. Nevertheless, the controversy
surrounding the events of the 1890s was very germane to the subject of the preservation of the landscape for posterity in the nineteenth century and that of public

44 Martin, *Guide to Belfast, Northern Counties railway, Giant's Causeway and the Antrim Coast*
(Belfast: W. & G. Baird, 1899), p. 71.   **45** Stephen Gwynn, *Highways and byways in Donegal
and Antrim* (London, 1899), p. 89.

access to it, and it took many years before the concept of opening large rural areas to the public became widely accepted in the British Isles. In 1912, the Society for the Promotion of Nature Reserves was founded by Charles Rothschild, with the aim of identifying places in need of protection and transferring them to the National Trust. The Forestry Commission was created in 1919 to restore British woodlands, as 400,000 acres had been felled during the Great War, and the Law of Property Act passed in 1925 gave the public the right of access 'for air and exercise' to commons in urban areas in England and Wales. In the Republic of Ireland, An Taisce, a prescribed body under the Planning Acts, was established in 1948 with the aim of preserving Ireland's natural, built and social environment. Although it is independent from the state government, local authorities are obliged to consult An Taisce on a vast array of development proposals and it seeks to educate, inform, and lead public opinion on the environment; to advocate and influence policy; and to manage heritage properties. Despite these developments, however, controversies such as that concerning the enclosure of the Giant's Causeway continue to surface, and that episode in the history of preservation and public access to landscapes of particular scenic value can be seen to have set a significant precedent in the Ireland of the late nineteenth century.

Land and landscape in the fiction of Somerville and Ross

ANDREW J. GARAVEL SJ

The novels and short stories of Somerville and Ross are replete with brief but vivid renderings of the Irish countryside, 'landscape after landscape of West Cork impeccably sketched in a hundred words,' as Lennox Robinson says of the *Irish R.M.* stories.[1] Indeed, the landscape descriptions are remarkable not only for their number but their compact richness, as seen in this passage from 'Great Uncle-McCarthy,' the first of the stories:

> Certainly the view from the roof was worth coming up to look at. It was rough, heathery country on one side, with a string of little blue lakes running like a turquoise necklet round the base of a firry hill, and patches of pale green pasture were set amid the rocks and heather. A silvery flash behind the undulations of the hills told where the Atlantic lay in immense plains of sunlight. I turned to survey with an owner's eye my own grey woods and straggling plantations of larch.[2]

Note how the ocean is concealed from sight by the waves – 'undulations' – of the land. The painterly quality of many of the landscapes to which Robinson alludes reflects Somerville's parallel career: a professional illustrator from the age of sixteen, she studied art in London, Paris and Dusseldorf, provided drawings for the *Irish R.M.* stories and other Somerville and Ross books in her middle years and, later in life, successfully exhibited her paintings in London and New York.[3] In the catalogue for a 1920 London show, her cousin, Ethel Coghill Penrose, makes a connection between the art work and the writings of Somerville and Ross, noting that viewers 'will recognize landscapes they have known long since in another medium; the wild outline, the glowing colour, the haunting melancholy of this corner of Ireland'.[4] Somerville would sometimes make a preliminary sketch of a scene in charcoal or pencil, and within the contours of the lakes and hills, she would insert the name of the colour to be applied to the eventual painting, so that, for example, the nearer fields are labeled 'gold,' the hills beyond 'green-blue' and the distant mountains 'purple-blue, fading to grey-blue'.[5]

---

[1] Lennox Robinson, 'Preface' in Geraldine Cummins, *Dr. E. OE. Somerville: a biography* (London, 1952), p. xi.   [2] E. OE. Somerville and Martin Ross, 'Great Uncle McCarthy' in *The Irish R.M. complete* (London, 1962), p. 19.   [3] Gifford Lewis, *Edith Somerville: a biography* (Dublin, 2005), p. 35.   [4] Ibid., p. 304.   [5] Gifford Lewis, *Somerville and Ross: the world of the*

In a sense, the collaborators attempt something similar in their prose depictions of the landscapes of Edith Somerville's West Cork and Violet Martin's County Galway. The elements of the scene are arranged with great deliberation, and at times the authors strain against the limitations of language, much as a painter experiments with the colors on her palette to achieve a precise shade, as here in *The Real Charlotte* (1894):

> They had ridden at first under a pale green arch of road-side trees, with fields on either side full of buttercups and dog-daisies, a land of pasture and sleek cattle, and neat stone walls. But in the second or third mile the face of the country changed. The blue lake that had lain in the distance like a long slab of lapis lazuli, was within two fields of them now, moving drowsily in and out of the rocks, and over the coarse gravel of its shore. The trees had dwindled to ragged hazel and thorn bushes; the fat cows of the comfortable farms round Lismoyle were replaced by lean, dishevelled goats, and shelves and flags of gray limestone began to contest the right of the soil with the thin grass and the wiry brushwood. We have said gray limestone, but that hardworked adjective cannot at all express the cold, pure blueness that these boulders take, under the sky of summer. Some word must yet be coined in which neither blue nor lilac shall have the supremacy, and in which the steely purple of a pigeon's breast shall not be forgotten.[6]

This is the countryside of the Martins on the shores of Lough Corrib (as a prominent Irish naturalist describes it, 'The western side of the lake from Moycullen to Oughterard fringes strange country – a flat limestone tract, with stretches of bare pavement . . . and dense scrub mainly of Hazel . . .').[7] But, typically for Somerville and Ross, this passage from *The Real Charlotte* is not merely an exercise in verisimilitude. Rather, the landscape serves to underscore the mood, as the change from 'sleek', 'neat' surroundings to those that are 'ragged', 'dishevelled' and 'thin' prepares the reader for what lies a mile down the road: the elderly and eccentric Julia Duffy's decaying house and farm, which has, like its mistress, gone 'from bad to worse', but has 'still about it some air of the older days when [her] grandfather was all but a gentleman . . . The tall sycamores that bordered the cart track were witnesses to the time when it had been an avenue, and the lawn-like field was yellow in the springtime with the daffodils of a former civilisation.'[8]

Such attention to landscape is not surprising, since both cousins were intimately connected to the land, not only as sportswomen but as managers of their respective family estates: Somerville, for example, had the primary responsibility for the running

Irish R.M. (London, 1985), p. 106. **6** E. OE. Somerville and Martin Ross, *The Real Charlotte*, ed. Virginia Beards (New Brunswick, NJ, 1986), pp 31–2. **7** Robert Lloyd Praeger, *The way that I went: an Irishman in Ireland* (Dublin, 1937), p. 209. **8** Somerville and Ross, *The Real Charlotte*, pp 34–5.

of Drishane for fifty years, from the time of her father's death in 1895 until her
nephew's return from the Second World War in 1945 (at which time she was eighty-
seven years old). One of the reasons the pair began to write was a desire to contribute
to the upkeep of these houses and lands in the increasingly straitened circumstances
their families inherited from the 1880s onwards. That the descriptions of the land
were written by women who had experience of caring for it, of managing farms and
raising livestock, and who also knew its wild places, is borne out time and again: 'It
was a curious wood – very old, judging by its scattered knots of hoary, weather-
twisted pine trees; very young, judging by the growth of ash saplings and slender
larches that made dense every inch of space except where rides had been cut through
them for the woodcock shooting.'[9]

The predominance of landscape throughout their fiction indicates that for
Somerville and Ross, as for many Irish writers, the land is not only a dominant
theme, but a pervasive presence. We are continually reminded that this is a world
where people live in an intimate relationship with the land, a relationship not
conceived in terms of abstractions, but as an inherent affiliation with a particular
place. A character's identity is to a great extent determined because she has been born
and brought up and has lived her life in this place, on this land, and not elsewhere –
the sort of attachment to a particular locale Elizabeth Bowen describes as being
'bound up not only in the sensation and business of living but in the exact sensation
of living *here*'.[10] Indeed, if a character is somehow separated from her native ground,
the results are sometimes fatal, as if life, or one's sense of self, were insupportable
anywhere else (like Julia Duffy in *The Real Charlotte*, who is driven out of her ancestral home and thence to madness and death by the title character).

This strong connection between place and people is emphasized by the writers'
frequent appropriation of actual places: the settings of the novels and short stories
(with few exceptions, such as *Mount Music*) are typical of the environs of Ross, the
Martin estate, or of the Somervilles' Castletownshend. Sometimes elements of both
are present in the same work, yet these places always retain their integrity. The
writer's relation to place is taken up by Seamus Heaney in speaking of the work of
Patrick Kavanagh: 'all of the early Monaghan poetry gives the place credit for
existing, assists at its real topographical presence, dwells upon it and accepts it as the
definitive locus of the given world ... The horizons of the little fields and hills,
whether they are gloomy and constricting or radiant and enhancing, are sensed as the
horizons of consciousness.'[11] Later, in Dublin, Kavanagh establishes a poetic identity
less dependent on the scenes of his youth; Somerville and Ross, however, never move
beyond the first stage Heaney posits: the horizons of their imaginations are largely
determined by place. They lived almost all their lives in their home places, and in
their fiction, too, they never leave home, so to speak.[12] It is likely they felt unable to

9 Ibid., p. 120.   10 Elizabeth Bowen, *Bowen's Court* (New York, 1942), p. 20.   11 Seamus
Heaney, *The government of the tongue: selected prose, 1978–1987* (New York, 1990), pp 4–5.
12 Violet Martin was to leave Ross after her mother's death in 1906, but spent the last nine

do so, either actually or imaginatively. Both cousins laboured and sacrificed to save the family estates, and both possessed a strong sense of familial duty, even though they at times felt the attraction of a more independent mode of life and work. A letter from Edith to Violet indicates how they had to subordinate their own wishes to the demands placed upon them: 'I don't look forward to going home. I suppose it would be too selfish for you and me to hike off somewhere to work and peace. It *would* be too selfish – say no more and let us shut our eyes to the "vision splendid"'.[13]

Throughout most of their lifetimes the cousins' hold on these places was under intense political and economic pressure as the feudal Ireland into which they had been born was largely in retreat.[14] But as their grip on the land was loosened, and even came to be accepted as inevitable, the land's possession of *them*, if anything, grew stronger. Geraldine Cummins, Somerville's biographer, recalled that her friend regarded Castletownshend with the sort of reverence a devout Jew might have for the holy places of Jerusalem, noting that we find in the books a 'passion for land, for the honour of the great house' that is 'of a kind industrialized people might not understand'.[15] As John Wilson Foster observes:

> The Irish are possessed by place ... In its preoccupation with place as an unseverable aspect of self, Irish fiction is a descendant of the Irish mythic tale. Certainly 'setting' is an inadequate word to describe the attention Irish writers lavish upon geographic location and topography. As in the case of poets ('An ancestor was rector there') and mythmakers, the fiction writer's preoccupation with place is a preoccupation with the past without which Irish selfhood is apparently inconceivable. The past is constantly made contemporary through an obsession with remembered place.[16]

For Somerville and Ross, their home places are themselves 'an unseverable aspect of self,' and thus they never develop the kind of detachment necessary for what Heaney elsewhere calls 'a domineering rather than a grateful relation to place', in which the writer 'create[s] a country of the mind rather than the other way round'.[17]

It is instead a relation to place closer to what George Eliot calls the 'homescene' of one's early imagination that is characteristic of Somerville and Ross, who write as they do because they have spent their lives in, and have had their imaginations formed by specific places, by these beautiful countrysides and remote houses. As Elizabeth Bowen observes:

years of her life at Drishane.   **13** E. OE. Somerville, Letter to Violet Martin, March 7, 1897, quoted in Lewis, *Somerville and Ross*, p. 182.   **14** The year of Edith Somerville's birth, for example, saw the founding of the Irish Republican Brotherhood; that of her death marked the declaration of the Republic of Ireland, the severing of the last link with the United Kingdom. See T.W. Moody and F.X. Martin, *The course of Irish history*, 2nd ed. (Niwot, CO, 1994), pp 450; 464.   **15** Cummins, *Dr E. OE. Somerville*, p. 43.   **16** John Wilson Foster, 'The geography of Irish fiction', in Patrick Rafroidi and Maurice Harmon (eds), *The Irish novel in our time* (Lille, France, 1977), pp 89–90.   **17** Seamus Heaney, *The place of writing* (Emory Studies in Humanities no. 1) (Atlanta, GA, 1989), p. 21.

> The influence of environment is the most lasting ... [and] operates deepest
> down ... [T]he majority [of writers] are haunted by the shadowy, half-
> remembered landscape of early days: impressions and feelings formed there
> and then underlie language, dictate choices of imagery. In writing, what is
> poetically spontaneous, what is most inimitably individual, has this source –
> the writer carries about in him an inner environment which is constant;
> though which also, as time goes on, tends to become more and more subjec-
> tive.[18]

As noted above, this is a development that Somerville and Ross do not undergo.

Though the places may be renamed and rearranged, and while the works venture
beyond mere description of the locales, we are always aware of these sites not just as
'space', but as fields and hills and shores. And even with all the attention the writers
pay to the appearance of a place, the reader is continually reminded that it is more
than a landscape, it is land from which trees and crops grow, and on which people
and animals live. The turf is cut, the streams are fished, and the fields are planted in
spring, harvested in autumn, and hunted over in winter. They are physical realities
that are indisputably *there*, setting the limits of action and of consciousness.

The constant awareness of the land on the part of authors, characters and reader
and the meticulous care with which the landscapes are rendered, underscore the fact
that, despite the importance of houses (a common attribute of 'Big House' fiction),
much of what happens in these books – and not just in the hunting stories – takes
place in the out-of-doors, which is a continual presence, even when the focus shifts
to interior scenes. In *The Real Charlotte*, for example, the land agent Roddy Lambert's
fascination with the newly-arrived Francie Fitzgerald (and his dissatisfaction with his
wife, Lucy, who has an abhorrence of fresh air) is reflected in the lovely countryside
insinuating itself into the unattractive interior of his house:

> An unshaded lamp was on the table, its ugly glare conflicting with the soft
> remnants of June twilight that stole in between the half-drawn curtains ...
>
> [Lambert] read his paper for a short time, while the subdued duet of
> snoring [of his wife and her dog] came continuously from the chair opposite
> ... Lambert threw down his paper as if an idea had occurred to him. He got
> up and went over to the window, and putting aside the curtains, looked out
> into the twilight of the June evening. The world outside was still awake, and
> the air was tender with the remembrance of the long day of sunshine and
> heat; a thrush was singing loudly down by the seringa bush at the end of the
> garden; the cattle were browsing and breathing audibly in the field beyond ...
> It seemed to Lambert much earlier than he had thought, and as he stood
> there, the invitation of the summer evening began to appeal to him with

18 Elizabeth Bowen, *Seven winters: memories of a Dublin childhood & afterthoughts: pieces on
writing* (New York, 1962), pp 79–80.

seductive force; the quiet fields lay grey and mysterious under the pale western glow, and his eye traveled several times across them to a distant dark blot – the clump of trees and evergreens in which Tally Ho Lodge [where Francie resides] lay buried.

He turned from the window at last, and coming back into the lamplit room, surveyed it and its unconscious occupants with a feeling of intolerance for their unlovely slumber. His next step was the almost unprecedented one of changing his slippers for boots, and in a few minutes he had left the house.[19]

Often there do not seem to be clear lines of demarcation between indoors and outdoors. The front door is generally wide open during the day, save in the wildest weather (an authentic detail of 'big house' life). The characters, even when they are indoors, spend a good deal of time looking at, thinking of, or talking about the surrounding country. In the first Somerville and Ross novel, *An Irish Cousin* (1889), the narrator, Theodora Sarsfield, is seen as trustworthy in part because she immediately asserts her 'dislike of [her] gaunt apartment' at Durrus, the seat of her cousins in County Cork, but is then so taken with the view that she leans out her window to see as much as she can.[20] The few who ignore the outdoors are seen as out of touch, like Lucy Lambert and the effete Christopher Dysart in *The Real Charlotte*, or misguided, like Shibby Pindy in *The Big House of Inver*, who attempts to restore the family's former splendor by scrimping and saving to fill the house with gimcrack furniture: 'Sitting in one of the wide windows though she was, with as fair a view of sea and sands on the one hand, and of sunny grass lands and woods, and distant mountains, on the other, as Ireland could show, Miss Pindy's face was turned inwards towards the room, and her eyes, fixed upon an atrophied Chesterfield sofa, had in them a lover's ardour'.[21]

To the modern urban sensibility at least, animals appear to have a nearly free run of these houses:

> A couple of young horses outside the windows tore at the matted creepers on the walls, or thrust faces that were half-shy, half-impudent, into the room. Portly pigeons waddled to and fro on the broad window-sill, sometimes flying in to perch on the picture-frames, while they kept up incessantly a hoarse and pompous cooing.[22]

This permeability between the natural and man-made environments is part of a remarkable element in the work of Somerville and Ross: the persistent sense that

19 Somerville and Ross, *The Real Charlotte*, pp 23; 26–27. **20** E. OE. Somerville and Martin Ross, *An Irish Cousin*, rev. ed. (London, 1922), pp 18; 32. **21** E. OE. Somerville and Martin Ross, *The Big House of Inver* (Garden City, NY, 1925), p. 52. **22** 'Philippa's Foxhunt', in Somerville and Ross, *The Irish R.M. complete*, p. 90.

humans and animals live in an inextricable relationship with each other and with the land; that they are, in fact, part of the land on which they live. In order to convey that a place and the creatures that live there are parts of a unity, the boundaries between them are, to one degree or another, obscured. All the elements of a given place – land, weather, people, animals, and even inanimate objects – may be associated with one another: the authors speak of inorganic things as if they were living, and features of the land are at times endowed with human qualities;[23] animals can be quite as idiosyncratic as their owners, while people are portrayed in animal terms. In *Mount Music*, for example, Dr Mangan, a large, slow, dignified man, is several times compared to an elephant; in the same novel Major Talbot-Lowry and his fellow landlords are called 'Pterodactyli' in light of their declining fortunes, while in *An Enthusiast*, the deteriorating position of the Anglo-Irish gentry is expressed by invoking the animal with which they are most closely associated: 'The position of the landless landlord is now a familiar one. As young horses of this generation [1921] accept with calm the bicycles and motors to which their parents died unreconciled, so did Daniel Henry Palliser step into the shoes that had caused acute suffering to his father, and find them endurable'.[24] In *The Real Charlotte*, the dull and timorous Lucy Lambert is regularly referred to by the narrator as 'the turkey hen', 'whose feathers were constitutionally incapable of remaining erect for any length of time'.[25] Charlotte Mullen, who feels constrained from revealing 'the real Charlotte', is likened to 'some amphibious thing, whose strong, darting course under the water is only marked by a bubble or two, and it required almost an animal instinct to note them'.[26] When her *sang-froid* is finally violated by Lambert's rejection, she 'moan[s] like some furious feline creature' and calls her false lover 'the cur, the double-dyed cur!'[27] In contrast, 'the timid hare' is the appellation given to the two ineffectual young landlords, Christopher Dysart and – twenty-seven years later – Dan Palliser.

On the other hand, animals can have an almost human degree of consciousness. The narrative is sometimes seen from an animal's point of view, as when several generations of the history of Tally Ho Lodge in *The Real Charlotte* are observed by the family cockatoo; in Chapter XII of the same work, the action is seen as much from the standpoint of animals as that of humans: dogs, birds and even fish are given their perspectives on the picnic expedition to an island in Lough Moyle. The gulf between species is sometimes bridged in startling ways: 'Peggy [a cocker spaniel] had belonged to Colonel Palliser, and since his death had fallen into somnolent widowhood ...'[28] Further boundaries are crossed when we are told that Charlotte's favorite cat is 'the patriarchal Susan': evicted from the spare bedroom, he 'went away by himself, and ... thought unutterable things', as if he were only prevented from giving voice to his plaint by the gravity of the matter.[29] The line between human and animal seems thoroughly blurred in a passage in which a dog, frightened by the sight of the

23 For example, a clock strikes the hour in a 'gentlemanlike voice' (*The Real Charlotte*, 26).
24 Somerville and Ross, *An Enthusiast* (London, 1921), pp 3–4.   25 Somerville and Ross, *The Real Charlotte*, p. 24.   26 Ibid., p. 222.   27 Ibid., p. 229.   28 Somerville and Ross, *An Enthusiast*, p. 50.   29 Somerville and Ross, *The Real Charlotte*, p. 16.

clergyman in his surplice, disturbs a church service by barking loudly. Afterwards, a parishioner comments: "'I wouldn't have that dog's conscience for a good deal," said Mrs. Gascogne as she came downstairs. "In fact, I am beginning to think that the only people who get everything they want are the people who have no consciences at all."'[30]

Human characters at times seem to (or wish to) disappear, either wholly or partially, into the landscape;[31] the land or the weather can be described in social or domestic terms, or personified as having agency or volition. Through this technique, we are given 'humanized space',[32] the sense that the people who have lived on the land have impressed themselves and their history upon it, but that the land has left its marks upon them also. The American novelist and essayist Wendell Berry speaks of the affiliation between the land and the creatures living on it:

> The concept of country, homeland, dwelling place becomes simplified as 'the environment' – that is, what surrounds us. Once we see our place, our part of the world, as *surrounding* us, we have already made a profound division between it and ourselves. We have given up the understanding – dropped it out of our language and so out of our thought – that we and our country create one another, depend on one another, are literally part of one another, that our land passes in and out of our bodies just as our bodies pass in and out of our land; that as we and our land are part of one another, so all who are living as neighbors here, human and plant and animal, are part of one another, and so cannot possibly flourish alone; that, therefore, our culture must be our response to our place, our culture and our place are images of each other and inseparable from each other.[33]

For Somerville and Ross, far more than for most writers, culture and place are indeed inseparable. The writers frequently present their connection to the land in the explicitly physical sense that Berry suggests: they belong to it because they and their ancestors have lived on it, eating its food and drinking its water; the land is literally in their bones. As Edith Somerville notes in a letter to one of her brothers, who, during 'the Troubles', wished to disavow his Irish connection: 'My family has eaten Irish food and shared Irish life for nearly three hundred years, and if that doesn't make me Irish I might as well say I was Scotch, or Norman, or Pre-Diluvian!'[34] To be connected to the land is, in a sense, the greatest virtue in these works. Like Flurry Knox riding to hounds, all of the sympathetic characters know their places: 'going as a man goes who knows his country, who knows his horse, and whose heart is wholly

30 Ibid., p. 100. **31** Christopher Dysart, wishing to be left alone, 'shrank lower behind a mossy stone, and wildly hoped that his unconcealable white flannels might be mistaken for the stem of a fallen birch'; in Somerville and Ross, *The Real Charlotte*, p. 71. **32** Yi-Fu Tuan, *Space and place: the perspective of experience* (Minneapolis, 1977), p. 54. **33** Wendell Berry, *The unsettling of America: culture and agriculture* (San Francisco, 1977), p. 22. **34** Quoted in Lewis, *Edith Somerville*, pp 164–5.

and absolutely in the right place'.[35] Apart from the authors' passion for fox-hunting, its prominence in the stories is not accidental, as only those who 'know [their own] country' can be proficient at it. On the other hand, those who are not connected to a particular place are generally seen as malign in the novels (like Donovan, the publican and Land League agitator in *Naboth's Vineyard*), or as faintly ridiculous in the short stories (like the gullible cabinet secretary Leigh Kelway, 'collecting statistics ... on various points connected with the Liquor Question in Ireland,' in 'Lisheen Races, Second-hand').[36] The exception seems to be Major Sinclair Yeates, the 'Irish R.M.,' and the stories as a whole can be read as his coming to know and appreciate the land and the people to whom he is at first a stranger.

The experience of both Anglo-Irish and 'mere' Irish on the land is presented in these works as an organic process in which social relations are naturalized and the 'rough edges' of history are made smooth: thus 'place' in these works is continually privileged over 'time'. Traces of the Ascendancy are actually inscribed on the land, which has been to a certain extent domesticated by the Anglo-Irish, as in 'the great flat boulder that had for generations been the table for shooting lunches'.[37] In another passage in the same story, the life of the family that has lived on the land parallels that of the flora that has grown there: 'The big rhododendron was one of the glories of Aussolas [Castle]. Its original progenitor had been planted by Flurry's great-grandmother, and now, after a century of unchecked licence, it and its descendants ran riot among the pine stems on the hillside above the lake, and, in June, clothed a precipitous half-acre with infinite varieties of pale mysterious mauve'. A moment later, Major Yeates continues the correlation between the two by noting their related colors: 'From the exalted station that had been given me on the brow of the hill, I looked down ... between the trunks of the pine-trees, and saw, instead of mysterious mauve blossoms, the defiant purple of Mrs. Knox's bonnet.'[38]

In a non-fiction account of life at Ross before the days of the Land League, Violet Martin depicts relations between 'master' and tenants as part of the natural order, taking place in a (literal) atmosphere of mutual trust:

> The quietness of untroubled centuries lay like a spell on Connemara...the old ways of life were unquestioned at Ross, and my father [James Martin] went and came among his people in an intimacy as native as the soft air they breathed. On the crowded estate the old routine of potato planting and turf cutting was pursued tranquilly; the people intermarried and subdivided their holdings; few could read, and many could not speak English. All were known to the Master, and he was known and understood by them, as the old Galway people knew and understood; and the subdivisions of the land were permitted, and the arrears of rent were given time, or taken in boat-loads of

35 'Philippa's Fox-hunt,' in Somerville and Ross, *The Irish R.M. complete*, p. 88.   **36** 'Lisheen Races, Second-hand', ibid., p. 70.   **37** 'The Man that Came to Buy Apples', ibid., p. 212. **38** Ibid., p. 211, p. 212.

turf, or worked off by day-labour, and eviction was unheard of. It was give and take, with the personal element always warm in it: as a system it was probably quite uneconomic, but the hand of affection held it together, and the tradition of centuries was at its back.[39]

However, as a number of texts acknowledge, such 'natural' tranquility had been swept away by more recent developments. In *An Enthusiast,* the reforming landlord Dan Palliser finds that, despite his good intentions, there is no place for him in the Ireland of the early 1920s; and even in one of the *Irish R.M.* stories, where conflict is generally subordinated, the company discusses a neighbour who has emigrated to South Africa: 'I suppose we'll all be going there soon ...Uncle says if Home Rule comes there won't be a fox or a Protestant left in Ireland in ten years' time; and he said, what's more, that if *he* had to choose it mightn't be the Protestants he'd keep!'[40] Images from the ongoing land struggle arise in various contexts. In *The Real Charlotte*, for example, published in 1894 but set shortly after the land agitations of the 1880s, the title character relates how she has bested 'Tom Casey, the land-leaguing plumber,' cornering him until he sings 'God save the Queen'; and another character tells Charlotte that 'if anyone could understand the Land Act I believe it would be you'.[41] Francie Fitzgerald, a Dublin 'jackeen', is an inexperienced rider, while her mount, '[t]he black mare was a lady of character, well-mannered but firm, and the mere sit of the saddle on her back told her that this was a case when it would be well to take matters into her own control; she accordingly dragged as much of the reins as she required from Francie's helpless hands, and ... [soon] had given her rider to understand that her position was that of a tenant at will'.[42] One of the goals of the 'Land Wars' of 1879–82 and 1886–87 was to stop the evictions of 'tenants at will': in 1879 Charles Stewart Parnell encouraged his followers 'to let the landlords see the tenancy intended to keep a 'firm grip' on their 'homesteads and lands'.[43] Several times in the novels a proposed course of action is called a 'plan of campaign,' which refers to one phase of the land reform struggle.[44] At times the landscape is described in terms of conflict:

> The look of the ordinary gorse covert is familiar to most people as a tidy enclosure of an acre or so, filled with low plants of well-educated gorse; not

---

39 E. OE. Somerville and Martin Ross, *Irish memories* (New York, 1925), p. 4.   **40** 'The Bosom of the McRorys', in Somerville and Ross, *The Irish R.M. complete*, p. 390.   **41** Somerville and Ross, *The Real Charlotte*, p. 13, p. 16.   **42** Ibid., p. 28. It is interesting to note here how an animal is not only anthropomorphised, but portrayed in a superior relation to her rider: the mare is in charge of the situation, and there is also the implication that the flirtatious Francie is *not* a 'lady of character'.   **43** Peter R. Newman, *Companion to Irish history, 1603–1921: from the submission of Tyrone to Partition* (Oxford, 1991), p. 105.   **44** Ibid., pp 162–3. 'The Plan of Campaign' was directed by the National Land League from 1886 to 1889 and involved the withholding of rents by tenants to promote 'peasant proprietorship and expropriation of the landlords'. The scheme was particularly active in Galway and Cork.

so many will be found who have experience of it as a rocky, sedgy wilderness, half a mile square, garrisoned with brigades of furze bushes, some of them higher than a horse's head, lean, strong, and cunning, like the foxes that breed in them, impenetrable, with their bristling spikes, as a hedge of bayonets.[45]

There is something here that runs throughout the stories, the portrayal of these places as wild, even uncouth, and unfamiliar 'to most people'; that is, to the authors' non-Irish readers, presumably more used to scenes that are 'tidy' and 'well-educated', not 'impenetrable', 'garrisoned with brigades' and 'bristling [with] spikes'. These landscapes are often, in effect, 'beyond the Pale,' and the rugged topography of West Carbery is presented as thoroughly un-English: 'It was not a nice hill to get down in a hurry, and I should think the chestnut horse dreams of it now, somewhere in the flat English Midlands, after he has overeaten himself on fat English oats'.[46]

The struggle to control the land – from which politics is never far removed – is a prominent concern in several texts. In the opening of *Naboth's Vineyard* (1891), the cousins' 'Land League' novel, we are given an image of the conquest of Ireland:

> Anyone who has glanced even cursorily at the map of Ireland, will have noticed how the south-west corner of it has suffered from being the furthest outpost of European resistance to the Atlantic. Winter after winter the fight between sea and rock has raged on, and now, after all these centuries of warfare, the ragged fringe of points and headlands, with long, winding inlets between them, look as though some hungry monster's sharp teeth had torn the soft, green land away, gnawing it out from between the uncompromising lines of rock that stand firm, indigestible and undefeated.
>
> Violent and unlovely though the usurping process may sound, the results, as is often the case, justify the usurper. Deep among the hills the sea has forced its way, and, in many quiet fiords, has settled itself down to country life, surrounded by all sweet inland sounds and sights, as serenely as if it had never tossed the *City of Rome* about like a shuttlecock ...
>
> Near the junction of the counties of Cork and Kerry there is one of these fiords, where everything has combined to help the sea in its masquerade of freshwater simplicity.[47]

Through a 'violent and unlovely ... usurping process' an outside element 'has forced its way' onto the shores of Ireland and 'torn the soft, green land away', and then, 'after all these centuries of warfare', has 'settled itself down to country life, surrounded by all sweet inland sounds and sights', so that 'the results, as is often the case, justify the usurper'. That this is intended, on one level at least, as an allegory of the English

45 'The Policy of the Closed Door', in Somerville and Ross, *The Irish R.M. complete*, p. 124.
46 'Major Apollo Riggs', ibid., p. 385.   47 E. OE. Somerville and Martin Ross, *Naboth's Vineyard* (London, 1891), pp 1–2.

conquest of Ireland is borne out by the presence of the same image in *An Enthusiast*, thirty years later, when the republican Eugene Cashen discourses on the history of England's brutal treatment of Ireland through 'successive "plantations" of soldier-settlers: 'They came ... like raging waves of the sea, foaming out their own shame!'[48] The corresponding process by which the usurpers lose control is expressed in *Mount Music* through the image of a river flowing out of the land and returning to the sea: 'the River Broadwater, a slow and lordly stream, that moved mightily down the wide valley ... and thence flowed onwards, broad and brimming, bearded with rushes, passing like a king, cloaked in the splendours of the sunset, to its suicide in the far-away Atlantic. The demesne of Mount Music lay along its banks . . .'[49] The text goes on to relate how the lordly Talbot-Lowrys lose control of Mount Music and end by leaving and crossing the sea to England. The other river bordering the estate, the Ownashee, is portrayed as a vassal of the Broadwater: 'a mountain stream, a tributary of the great river, that came storming down from the hills, and, in times of flood, snatching, like a border-reiver, at sheep, and pigs, and fowl, tossing its spoils in a tumble of racing waves into the wide waters of its chieftain'.[50] (Note that the vassal river has an Irish name, the liege an English one.)

In the main, the novels do not deal with the struggle for the land on the large scale, but as a very local issue, a matter of who will have possession of a given estate, farm or house. Many of the plots turn on this point and are structured by it. Yet, according to Somerville and Ross, it is only in the countryside that class antagonisms can hope to be resolved, since gentry and peasants supposedly have a bond in the fact that they both live on the same land. As Violet Martin asserts in a 1912 letter to Stephen Gwynn, a Redmondite MP: 'The people that I am most afraid of are the town politicians. I am not fond of anything about towns; they are full of second-hand thinking; they know nothing of raw material and the natural philosophy of the country people. As to caste, it is in the towns that the *vulgar* idea of caste is created. The country people believe in it strongly; they cling to a belief in what it should stand for of truth and honour – and there the best classes touch the peasant closely, and understand each other.'[51]

The cousins' relationship to the land can be seen as alternately celebratory or elegiac. Even though the *Irish R.M.* stories are ostensibly set in 'the present,' they largely depict an Ireland as it might have been, or as the authors remember it, on the Somerville and Martin estates before the days of the Land League: a pre-modern, semi-feudal world which, while not without its cruelty and violence, is still a scene where love of the land and mutual respect bind 'master and man' together. On the other hand, the novels often mourn the passing of the old way of life, presenting a decentered world where characters are isolated within the landscape as that organic process is violently cut short by the forces of modernity, so that the Big Houses,

---

48 Somerville and Ross, *An Enthusiast*, pp 120–1.   **49** Somerville and Ross, *Mount Music*, p. 12.   **50** Ibid.   **51** E. OE. Somerville and Martin Ross, *Irish Memories* (New York, 1925), p. 325.

'places that were once disseminators of light, of the humanities; centres of civilisation; places to which the poor people rushed, in any trouble, as to Cities of Refuge ... are now destroyed, become desolate, derelict'.[52] Like many of the actual big houses, those in the novels command the surrounding country, as their owners once did, but do no longer, and a significant number of the vistas described are from the point of view of the 'Big House'. In the tradition begun by Maria Edgeworth, the decline of the landowning class is represented by the fall, or the falling apart, of the gentry's houses. The importance of the land and the value placed on its ownership is reflected in the observation of Barry Sloan, who asserts '[t]he writers demonstrate that the question of Irish nationality was essentially one of who controlled and owned the land, for if there is any truth in the old adage that an Englishman's home is his castle, then its complement must be that an Irishman's plot of land is the measure of his identity. Thus references to the land and the landscape are a recurrent source of image and allusion to describe the state of the nation.'[53] And such is especially true of Somerville and Ross: the marks which the Anglo-Irish have made upon the land are now being erased. In 'The Pug-Nosed Fox', one of the *Irish R.M.* stories, we hear of a country house that has been bought by a nouveau-riche Dublin coal merchant, with its 'splendid beech-trees, servants of the old regime, preserving their dignity through the vicissitudes of the new'.[54] In another story, 'The Finger of Mrs Knox,' the aristocratic title character joins forces with one of her former tenants to defeat a middle-class publican who has bought up the land and is in the process of destroying it by cutting down a forest planted and nurtured for over eighty years by both landlord and tenant.

Throughout the novels the land and its loss, the big houses and their decline, are used to express one of the authors' overarching concerns: who will inherit the land of Ireland after the Anglo-Irish? As Wyndham's Act was being proposed in 1903 (allowing tenants to buy the land on which they worked at favorable rates and, under some circumstances, obliging landlords to sell), Somerville wrote to her brother Cameron: 'No doubt in ten or fifteen years there will simply be another lot of infinitely worse landlords to be dealt with'.[55] In *Mount Music*, Somerville and Ross look back to what is almost the last moment of Ascendancy power:

> [B]etween the eighties and nineties of the nineteenth century, the class known
> as Landed Gentry was still pre-eminent in Ireland. Tenants and tradesmen
> bowed down before them, with love sometimes, sometimes with hatred,

52 Ibid., pp 157–58.   **53** Barry Sloan, *The pioneers of Anglo-Irish fiction, 1800–1850* (Irish Literary Studies 21) (Gerrards Cross, Bucks, 1986), p. 244.   **54** 'The Pug-nosed Fox', in Somerville and Ross, *The Irish R.M. complete*, p. 182. The McRorys clearly lack the *noblesse* of the old gentry: '[O]ur cook, Mrs. Cadogan ... assured Philippa that wild pigs in America wouldn't be treated worse than what Mrs. McRory treated her servants'; pp 181–2.   **55** E. OE. Somerville, Letter to Cameron Somerville, January 27, 1903, quoted in Otto Rauchbauer, *The Edith OEnone Somerville archive in Drishane: a catalogue and evaluative essay* (Dublin, 1995), p. 203.

never with indifference. The newspapers of their districts recorded their enterprises in marriage, in birth, in death, copiously, and with a servile rapture of detail that, though it is not yet entirely withheld from their survivors [in 1920], is now bestowed with equal unction on those who, in many instances, have taken their places, geographically, if not their place, socially, in Irish every-day existence.[56]

The authors go on to assert, rather cautiously, that the Anglo-Irish domination of the land is part of 'a not wholly to be condemned past'.[57]

Of course, the loss of land by the gentry and its purchase by the small farmer or tradesman represents more than a mere transfer of property: the fact was that those who had once bowed down before the gentry were now going to take their places, geographically *and* socially. The various Land Acts, especially the Wyndham Act, brought about no less than a social revolution in Ireland, a revolution with which the Somervilles and Martins were, unsurprisingly, ill-at-ease. As one character notes in *Mount Music*, 'Ireland's a queer old place just now ... Everything's changing hands, and everyone's changing sides. You don't know what'll happen next!'[58] After Violet Martin's death in 1915, Somerville wrote that she felt as if the places she and her partner had known were fading away: 'The Ireland that Martin and I knew when we were children is fast leaving us; every day some landmark is wiped out ...'[59] It was, of course, the Anglo-Irish themselves who were disappearing from the land, at least in the role of those who had owned it, and in some sense had been responsible for it. The land remains, but the cousins recognized, however reluctantly, that the long associations their families had had with these places were not indelible. An anonymous eighteenth-century Irish poem asserts that yesterday the empires of Alexander and Caesar were turned to dust, today 'Tara is grass,' and the day might be coming when the traces of the English, too, will be erased from the land.[60] Seán O'Faoláin observes a similar phenomenon in his description of a place associated with the passing of the earlier aristocracy, Kinsale, where the old Gaelic order was defeated, not very many miles from Castletownshend, in 1601:

> Our history has seemed to fade from the land like old writing from parchment. Traditional memory is broken. Our monuments are finest when oldest,

---

56 Somerville and Ross, *Mount Music*, p. 11. The last line is fraught with snobbery, a vice of which the cousins have been accused. For example, Rauchbauer observes that Somerville 'could be very much *de haut en bas* to Roman Catholics whom she usually associated with a dogmatic and authoritarian hierarchy in Ireland, which would endanger the position of her class. But when it came to individual people, both in her immediate neighbourhood and among her social equals, she did settle for a *modus vivendi*'; (182).   57 Somerville and Ross, *Mount Music*, p. 11.   58 Ibid., p. 315.   59 Somerville and Ross, *Irish Memories*, p. 66. 60 'The world laid low, and the wind blew like a dust/Alexander, Caesar, and all their followers./Tara is grass; and look how it stands with Troy. And even the English – maybe they might die'; Anonymous, 'Epigram', in *The new Oxford book of Irish verse*, ed. and trans. Thomas Kinsella (Oxford, 1989), p. 218.

but then so old that their echoes have died away. The *pietas* which is so cherished and nourished in other countries, has here an inadequate number of actual moulds to hold it. National emotion is a wild sea-spray that evaporates like a religion without a ritual. We are moved by ghosts. Something powerful and precious hangs in the air that holds us like a succubus; but what it is we can hardly define because we have so few concrete things that express it.[61]

The land, then, can be seen as a kind of palimpsest upon which cultures, families, and individuals leave something of their own characters,[62] marks that are later scraped off, or allowed to fade over time.

Somerville and Ross were of the opinion that long familiarity with a place and its people is an invaluable asset for a writer, and it is clear that they expended a great deal of care and imagination in presenting, one might say in preserving, the character and the topography of the places they knew so well. In his work on the relations of literature and topography, J. Hillis Miller reminds us that the latter word has three distinct meanings. The oldest, now obsolete, 'a description in words of a place,' is closest to the word's etymology: from '*topos*, place' and '*graphein*, to write'; the significance then shifted to the practice of the graphic representation of a place by means of a map or chart. By extension, the now-prevalent meaning came into being: the features of the landscape themselves, 'the name for what is mapped, apparently without any reference to writing or other means of representation'.[63] The reverse of this process describes the career of Somerville and Ross: having begun with the places themselves, they end with descriptions on the printed page of the land and the creatures living upon it. The natural world is emphatically acknowledged in the works of Somerville and Ross. It can be argued that the struggle to hold onto their houses and lands, a struggle that consumed countless hours and incalculable effort over decades, dissipated the cousins' talents as writers.[64] Yet a great deal of the power of their fiction is rooted in the fact that these same places are, in a sense, characters in the novels and short stories, presences to which the human (and even animal) characters relate, and that much of the effect of these works comes from their being grounded in these vividly realized landscapes.

61 Seán O'Faoláin, *An Irish journey*, 1940, quoted in Patricia Craig (ed.), *The Oxford book of Ireland* (Oxford, 1998), p. 77. 62 A word that originally signified an instrument for inscribing marks on a surface, and later the marks themselves; *The compact edition of the Oxford English dictionary* (Oxford, 1971), i, 380. 63 J. Hillis Miller, *Topographies* (Stanford, CA, 1995), p. 3. 64 See, for example, Hilary Mitchell, 'Somerville and Ross: amateur to professional' in *Somerville and Ross: a symposium* (Belfast, 1968), pp 21–2.

'The cloven foot of communism': land agitation and issues of ownership in southern Irish loyalist propaganda

SIOBHÁN JONES

In loyalist press and propaganda of the nineteenth century, 'the land' was framed as an inherent ascendancy right, sanctioned by recourse to historically established precedents. While referring to ascendancy ownership as a prefixed historical truism, many within the loyalist press were reluctant to acknowledge the validity of counter-rhetoric on the part of nationalists. Nationalist allusions to the historical rights of 'the Irish' in relation to land ownership were deemed fictitious, and land legislation was often thought to extravagantly overindulge the peasant population. Journalism in England advocating tenant right was considered to guilelessly sanction nationalist 'fiction', and the loyalist press in Ireland assumed the role of undermining this sympathy by publishing the testimonies of tenants to the munificence and kindness of individual landlords, and private correspondence relating to the surreptitious payment of rent in opposition to the Land League. For loyalists, the land question was imagined as a vehicle which enabled nationalists to compound the efficacy of illegality by demanding, and receiving, concessions from the British government. Those in opposition to the nationalist movement insisted that exclusivity of knowledge on land issues belonged to the law-abiding population in the South of Ireland who lived amongst the agitators, and who could therefore report adequately on the 'groundless' nationalist claims of victimisation. Accounts of outrages and boycotting dominated the loyalist press – not merely to emphasise the besieged position of adherents to law and order, but to demonstrate to the British government that agitation debilitated the lives of the loyal only in the South and West of Ireland, and was thus beyond the experience of the Westminster legislator. Issues surrounding 'the land', and the erosion and subversion of ascendancy property rights, were integral to unionist political and propagandist campaigns after the establishment of the official unionist organisation (the Irish Loyal and Patriotic Union) in 1885.

With growing literacy and a discontinuation of newspaper tax in the 1860s, Ireland saw a rapid rise in the number of nationalist publications. The firmly established loyalist press observed this acceleration with unease, corresponding as it did with a heightened level of disorder and lawlessness, principally in Munster and Connacht. Nationalist publications of the late 1860s were condemned as 'fraught with treason', and Victorian loyalists tended to portray the 'Celtic' or 'Irish' character as highly susceptible to subversive ideals, particularly at the hands of the nationalist press. The lower orders, according to a pamphlet of 1867, 'are usually idle, excitable and have a natural taste for combinations against employers, and for conspiracies against every constituted authority ... they want tenant right as a stepping stone to get rid of the owners'.[1] Prior to the establishment of the Irish Loyal and Patriotic Union (ILPU), loyalist publications rarely displayed uniform anti-nationalism. Liberal journals, such as the *Irish Times*, tended to endorse limited concessions towards nationalists, while conservative loyalist contemporaries exhibited a more fervent form of anti-nationalism, and particularly, anti-Catholicism.[2] According to conservative newspapers, deference to Irish political demands occurred consistently at the expense of Irish loyalists – conservatives thus held that Catholic Emancipation, franchise reform, Church Disestablishment, and early land legislation should have marked the boundaries of concession towards 'the Irish'. Liberal 'Justice for Ireland' was considered to represent, not only injustice for Irish loyalists, but disruption for the tenets of the entire British empire. Measures of Gladstonian reparation relating to 'the land' were entirely desirable and justifiable in the eyes of the liberal loyalist press. The economic effects of absentee landlordism were deplored, but most also claimed to advocate (limited) tenant right, and recognized the urgent need to settle the land question in order to counteract disloyal and discontented elements.

Liberals pressed for a mutual understanding on the part of landlord and tenant that the interests and needs of the two classes should be brought into accord on a broad economic perspective. Tenants were urged to move away from indulging in religious animosity, or alluding to historical grievances in their approach to the land question. The press also advocated that every effort should be made on the part of landowners to cure Irish tenants of the 'delusion ... that men of their own class would prove better landlords than members of the aristocracy'.[3] The protection of property rights was long held to be the reserve of Protestant loyalists, and liberals anticipated that the ability of Catholics to purchase land would soon put paid to existing prejudices based on the coercive self-protecting Protestant. Indeed it was hoped that proprietary rights would supersede Catholic fraternalism, and that in exacting the 'utmost shilling' in rent, the Catholic landowner would soon disassociate himself from the nationalist zeal of his coreligionists – thus disarming the tenets of the wider nationalist movement.

Much hope was held for Gladstone's remedial land measure in 1870, but loyalist appraisal of Gladstonian measures relating to the Church and land indicated that nationalists *should*, as opposed to would, be satisfied with the legislation involved.

---

1 *Remarks on Ireland*, (anonymous, 1867), in 'Land' pamphlet collection, University College Cork.   2 In this text the term 'loyalist' is employed to denote the political and cultural 'separateness' expressed by the minority (and largely Protestant) population, which, until 1885, predated political Irish unionism: 'conservative' and 'liberal' loyalist are terms used to distinguish between the varying strands of loyalist identity (i.e. loyalist support, or lack thereof, for Catholic Emancipation, franchise reform etc.) existent in the nineteenth century prior to the emergence of the official unionist organization.   3 *Irish Times*, 23 September 1869.

Initially the Land Bill of 1870 was heralded as 'a great success'. Liberal loyalist news-papers noted that Ireland was gradually becoming more peaceful, contented and prosperous, and that only the 'extreme' section of agitators was unhappy with the bill. Fellow loyalists, though more conservative in outlook, did not share the enthusiasm of their liberal contemporaries. Most endorsed the view that absentee landlordism was injurious to Ireland, but also asserted that the rights of property were paramount, and that any coercive governmental transference of power from landlord to tenant should be resisted at all costs. The *Clonmel Chronicle* argued that political agitators had fanned the idea of tenant right into 'the utmost extravagance',[4] while other conser-vative newspapers held that Protestants and landowners had been alienated and disenfranchised without satisfying any of the demands of the so-called 'disaffected' classes. The *Cork Constitution* claimed that the concessions made by the propertied were 'unparalleled in the history of any nation', and that the legislation involved aimed at 'humiliating and injuring the loyal while flattering and pampering the disaf-fected'.[5]

Support for the Land Bill on the part of liberal loyalists was resented, not least when such support originated in England. The *Cork Constitution* reprinted corre-spondence from 'A Westmeath Landlord' to *The Times* after the English newspaper had highlighted tenant grievances through information relayed by a reporter in Ireland.[6] Irish loyalists often expressed resentment at the apparent inability of the average Englishman to appreciate the 'character' of the Irish, thus denying the right of English newspapers to speak authoritatively on the subject of Irish land issues at all. Sympathy for Irish tenants on the part of Englishmen was unwarranted, said the Westmeath Landlord, and English journalists sent to Ireland should appreciate that the Irish were 'the most communicative, but least truthful nation on earth'.[7]

As the 1870s progressed, loyalists were concerned that Home Rule principles had strayed into the hands of the radical or extreme section of nationalism. Tenant right began to underpin the principles of the Home Rule movement, leading the loyalist press to defend landlord rights in the face of increasing hostility from the nationalist press. Unease at Parnell's accession to leadership of the nationalist parliamentary party in 1877, along with the formation of the Land League in 1879, provoked much testi-mony in the loyalist press as to the kindness, goodness and 'munificent liberality' of most landlords. Reports of bad relations between landlord and tenant were dismissed as chapters of idle romance, and letters from tenants themselves appeared in which individuals thanked their landlords for unsolicited reduction in rents and acknowl-edged the 'kindness' of their characters. The press insisted that all landlords could not be castigated as evil, exacting despoilers, and that innuendos against landlords in the nationalist press should justify legal action if any harm came to the individual or to his agents.

Nationalist newspapers tended to claim that their loyalist contemporaries adopted

---

4 *Clonmel Chronicle*, 29 January 1870.   **5** *Cork Constitution*, 11 July 1870.   **6** Ibid., 18 May 1870.   **7** Ibid.

100 MURDERS.

THE hundred persons named below (including an old woman of 80 and a little girl of 4) were MURDERED in Ireland from agrarian and political motives during the period of Land League ascendency (1879-88).

1.	Bridget M'Collagh	Feb. 23rd, 1879
2.	James Miller	July 14th, 1879
3.	Michael Ball	Dec. 4th, 1879
4.	Edmund Brereton	Jan. 4th, 1880
5.	John Freeman	Jan. 16th, 1880
6.	Bernard Morris	Aug. 2nd, 1880
7.	Charles D. Boyd	Aug. 13th, 1880
8.	David Feerick	Aug. 14th, 1880
9.	Viscount Mountmorres	Sept. 25th, 1880
10.	Ryan Foley	Sept., 1880
11.	Michael Boylan	Sept. 30th, 1880
12.	Henry Wheeler	Nov. 12th, 1880
13.	Peter Mullen	Dec. 20th, 1880
14.	Patrick Dynan	Jan. 2nd, 1881
15.	Patrick Farrelly	Mar. 4th, 1881
16.	Patrick Lyden	April 23rd, 1881
17.	Martin Lyden	April 23rd, 1881
18.	Peter Dempsey	May 25th, 1881
19.	Mrs. Reilly	May, 1881
20.	— Lynch	July 18th, 1881
21.	Michael Moloney	Oct. 22nd, 1881
22.	Peter Doherty	Nov. 2nd, 1881
23.	Patrick Halloran	Nov. 12th, 1881
24.	Luke Dillon	Nov. 17th, 1881
25.	James Brennan	Dec. 13th, 1881
26.	Mrs. Croughan	Dec. 31st, 1881
27.	Joseph Huddy	Jan. 1st, 1882
28.	John Huddy	Jan. 1st, 1882
29.	— Hennessy	Jan. 20th, 1882
30.	Thomas Abram	Jan. 22nd, 1882
31.	John Lennane	Jan. 24th, 1882
32.	John Dillon	Feb. 20th, 1882
33.	Constable Kavanagh	Feb. 20th, 1882
34.	Patrick Freely	Feb. 24th, 1882
35.	— Connolly	Feb. 25th, 1882
36.	Michael Moroney	Feb. 26th, 1882
37.	Thomas Gibbons	Mar. 17th, 1882
38.	Peter Andrews	Mar. 19th, 1882
39.	Joseph M'Mahon	Mar. 28th, 1882
40.	A. E. Herbert	Mar. 30th, 1882
41.	Mrs. H. M. Smythe	April 2nd, 1882
42.	— Roache	April 17th, 1882
43.	John O'Keefe	April 30th, 1882
44.	Lord Frederick Cavendish	May 6th, 1882
45.	E. Burke	May 6th, 1882
46.	— Connors	May 12th, 1882
47.	— O'Donnell	May 22nd, 1882
48.	Cornelius Hickey	June 8th, 1882
49.	Henry East	June 8th, 1882
50.	Walter Bourke	June 8th, 1882
51.	Corporal Robt Wallace	June 8th, 1882
52.	John Duane	June, 1882
53.	Patrick Cahill	June 27th, 1882
54.	J. H. Blake	June 29th, 1882
55.	Teddy Ruane	June 29th, 1882
56.	John Kenny	July 4th, 1882
57.	Murty Fernane	July 9th, 1882
58.	— Connell	July 14th, 1882
59.	John Delougnty	July 19th, 1882
60.	Constable Ed. Browa	Aug. 12th, 1882
61.	John Joyce	Aug. 17th, 1882
62.	Bridget Joyce	Aug. 17th, 1882
63.	Michael Joyce	Aug. 17th, 1882
64.	Peggy Joyce	Aug. 17th, 1882
65.	Peggy Joyce (junior)	Aug. 17th, 1882
66.	John Leahy	Aug. 20th, 1882
67.	Thomas Hunt	Oct. 2nd, 1882
68.	Thomas Brown	Oct. 3rd, 1882
69.	Detective-Constable Cox	Nov. 25th, 1882
70.	John Sheridan	Jan. 2nd, 1883
71.	Constable Linton	July 24th, 1883
72.	Timothy Sullivan	Sept. 14th, 1883
73.	John Moylan	Sept. 15th, 1883
74.	Mr. Cretty	Sept. 27th, 1883
75.	James Spence	Oct. 14th, 1883
76.	Patrick Quinn	Oct. 27th, 1883
77.	— M'Mahon	Aug. 15th, 1884
78.	— Spillane	Nov. 14th, 1884
79.	John Rahen	Dec. 25th, 1884
80.	— Tonery	Dec. 29th, 1884
81.	Mr. Cashman	June 14th, 1885
82.	John Ryan	Sept. 13th, 1885
83.	Edmund Allen	Jan. 16th, 1886
84.	Daniel O'Brien	April 3rd, 1886
85.	Patrick Quigley	May 16th, 1886
86.	David Barry	May 29th, 1886
87.	Patrick Tangney	June 4th, 1886
88.	Patrick Flahive	Aug. 30th, 1886
89.	John Byers	Feb. 15th, 1887
90.	Cornelius Murphy	Feb. 20th, 1887
91.	Daniel Baker	April 10th, 1887
92.	John Connell	May 3rd, 1887
93.	Timothy Hurley	June 13th, 1887
94.	Hd.-Constable Whelehan	Sept. 11th, 1887
95.	Patrick Quirke	Nov. 8th, 1887
96.	James Fitzmaurice	Jan. 31st, 1888
97.	James Quinn	May 7th, 1888
98.	Peter M'Carthy	May 27th, 1888
99.	James Ruane	July 28th, 1888
100.	John Forhan	July 28th, 1888

N.B.—The list of Attempted Murders during the same period is, of course, much greater.

[96]

1 '100 murders' – Agrarian murders, Irish Unionist Alliance pamphlet, 1893.

a bigoted approach to the land question by glossing over the negative aspects of Irish landlordism, or by denying that reform should be undertaken by the British government. Several liberal loyalist newspapers denied this accusation, and asserted themselves to be proponents of just and properly administered tenant right. Some referred to the days of the Famine in an effort to redeem the character of the landlord class: 'A Lover of the Old Country' wrote to the *Clonmel Chronicle*, and stated that in times of famine, 'it has always been the lord of the soil who stood by poor Pat, and has given him aid and comfort, whereas now, as in previous times of want, the political agitators have not one of them put their hands in their own pockets'.[8]

Loyalist fears escalated with the murder of Lord Leitrim in 1878. As a landlord, nationalists considered the man to represent all that was unscrupulous in the stereotype of his creed, but it was nationalist reaction to his death that caused unease in the loyalist press. The *Carlow Sentinel* claimed that a section of the nationalist press had 'unceasingly assailed his memory and vilified his character, with the evident intention of excusing, if not condoning, the murder'.[9] Loyalists were alarmed by the idea that any murder, but particularly the murder of a Protestant peer, could be apparently 'justified' thus by nationalists. A number of loyalists made efforts to vindicate Lord Leitrim's memory, and to imply that a nationalist conspiracy existed to prevent his tenants from speaking favourably on the character of their murdered landlord, as such testimony would undermine the 'slanderous' accusations in the nationalist press. Loyalists believed that this nationalist propaganda adversely affected class relations countrywide, and it did not go unnoticed that Lord Leitrim's funeral had been disturbed by a city mob. The *Cork Constitution* noted that the Dublin nationalists who disrupted the funeral were entirely unconnected with the Donegal estate of the deceased, but having been fuelled by nationalist propaganda, the mob nonetheless lined the city streets to shout 'damned Protestant' after the funeral.[10]

Disquiet on the part of loyalists was reinforced by the official launch of the Land League in 1879. The League was condemned as representing 'the cloven foot of communism',[11] and of arising out of 'Fenianism and Irish-American journalism'.[12] *The Union* newspaper, published in Dublin, asserted that land agitation was the natural outcome of a legislation 'which has rewarded idleness and perjury, and has taught "the people" that agitation will pay them better than agriculture, that an ostentatious poverty is the sure road to wealth and comfort. The Irish tenant is told that he can become rich and happy by legislation, and not by labour'.[13] The editor of *The Union* – Philip Bagenal, a prominent southern unionist, solicitor and author – claimed that an intimate connection existed between Fenianism and land agitation. He consistently warned that the Land League represented the first ripple of socialism in Ireland, and that land and labour united aimed to wrest all power and privilege from the upper classes of the country.

8 *Clonmel Chronicle*, 14 April 1880. **9** *Carlow Sentinel*, 20 April 1878. **10** *Cork Constitution*, 15 April 1878. **11** *King's County Chronicle*, 29 November 1881. **12** *Argus* (Monaghan), 11 December 1880. **13** *The Union*, 5 February 1887.

Prior to the establishment of the Land League, liberal loyalists argued that the issue of tenant right should be remedied by a series of lawful measures beneficial to both landlord and tenant. Instead it appeared that the movement was justifying unlawful and 'communistic' means to assert tenant property rights. Even the liberal *Irish Times* was unnerved by the increase in land agitation, particularly as agitative directives seemed to imbue Parnell with dictatorial status in nationalist affairs. The *Irish Times* recognized the political aptitude of Parnell, and thought that his energies might be expended more effectively if his support was offered to the Land Commission. The newspaper denounced the 'Moral Coventry' speech in 1880, and maintained that the Land League was in existence not to enlighten legislators with a view to reform, but to 'coerce landlords and tenants alike to such a point that they will be prepared to endure any fate that may be in store for them'.[14]

The location of sustained land agitation did tend to bear upon the comment of the loyalist press. In Monaghan, the local *Argus* newspaper expressed gratitude that the Land League was predominant in the 'South and West', though the lack of initiative to found branches in the North was due, according to the newspaper, to the fact that a 'murderous and agitatory spirit' did not exist in that part of the country.[15] When coercive measures were introduced in 1881, the newspaper was particularly proud that the county of Monaghan had not incurred the attention of the authorities, and consequently, 'they refrain from placing us amongst the black sheep'.[16] The *Argus* maintained that a revolution of the kind envisaged by Land Leaguers could never succeed without the support of northern Protestant tenant farmers. Anti-nationalist analogies in this newspaper included references to the French Revolution with the *Argus* comparing the cries of the Land Leaguers with 'those jackal howls which rose from the scum of France gathered round the scaffold to see the heads of the bravest and noblest of that land fall into the basket of the guillotine'.[17]

While accounts of agrarian outrage and illegality increased, the conservative loyalist press maintained that the Catholic priesthood was openly supporting agitative actions. The *Ballyshannon Herald* of Donegal noted that priests in Clare stood by with composure as cries of 'Shoot him' were levelled against 'land-grabbers'. In fact the newspaper claimed that the priests listened to such cries 'with delight ... and silently gave assent to the cold-blooded measures'.[18] Unionist propaganda in later years recalled incidences of murder and outrage in a pamphlet entitled WHEN THE PRIESTS WERE SILENT!!'[19] – the title's punctuation representing unionist acknowledgment that their own propaganda relied heavily on the fact that priests were never silent, but that in the case of murder and outrage against unassuming citizens, the clergy made expedient exceptions. The direct, but more innocuous, involvement of priests in land affairs was resented equally – the *Dublin Daily Express* remarked that it was humiliating 'to every loyal man ... that a landlord should be obliged in the

---

14 *Irish Times*, 20 September 1880.   15 *Argus*, 2 July 1881.   16 Ibid.   17 Ibid., 22 November 1879.   18 *Ballyshannon Herald,* 25 September 1880.   19 Irish Unionist Alliance publications, seventh series (1893), leaflet n. 109.

presence of the police and the people, to have recourse to a priest in order to obtain his rents, which were fixed under the authority of the law'.[20] Hundreds of instances of clerical involvement with boycotting were published in pamphlet form by the Irish Unionist Alliance (which terminologically replaced the ILPU in 1891) and, as the tenant and Home Rule movements grew, disloyalty and Catholicism became inextricably linked in the eyes of many Protestant loyalists. The lack of support from northern Protestants was testimony enough, according to some, to the 'Catholic' nature of agrarian discontent. The *Ballyshannon Herald* characterized the land leaguers 'purely and simply [as] the Romish section of the population – a section which fills our jails and workhouses, entails enormous expense on the peaceable citizens, and forms the elements from whence emanates violence, outrage and crime'.[21] The *Herald* was a resolutely anti-Catholic journal, and claimed that the historical 'massacres of Irish Protestants' were 'undisguised religious movements on the part of the Romish priesthood and their followers ... the Land League has almost every feature of these past horrible transactions'.[22] In later years, unionists were anxious to discredit the assumption that Protestants were the primary victims of the boycotting system. Loyalist and unionist propaganda claimed to champion the cause of the 'ordinary' Roman Catholic by highlighting boycotting cases that were conveniently omitted from the nationalist press; simultaneously these cases could undermine nationalist religiosity by referring to intra-Catholic treachery. Reports alluding to the abject sectarianism existent amongst Catholics themselves appeared in every loyalist newspaper. *Notes from Ireland*, a propagandist journal published by the official unionist organisation, referred to many cases involving priestly collusion with the boycotting system. The journal also focused on the victimisation of young mothers, children, the elderly or infirm at the hands of boycotters who had grievances against only one (generally male) individual within a family. In the eyes of loyalists, this 'guilt by association' was utterly reprehensible, and resonated in the fact that landlords themselves were denounced as 'guilty' parties, simply by virtue of owning land.

Disturbances persisted throughout 1880, and the loyalist press made much effort to discredit nationalist legitimisation of continued land agitation. Twenty-three additional police stations were required in West Galway, yet locals were refusing to allow police to purchase supplies in the area. Provisions, therefore, were sent from Galway town, but were systematically destroyed by mobs before reaching the police stations. The unionist *Galway Express* sardonically remarked that wilful destruction of provisions and cattle 'by persons reported to be starving is rather strange ... while a public fund is being raised to keep people in the West from starving'.[23] The ostracism of Captain Boycott occurred in September of the same year, and though critical of the governmental apathy that had allowed the situation to deteriorate, the conservative loyalist press anticipated that much beneficial publicity could arise from the Boycott issue. Many loyalist newspapers set up subscription funds to aid Boycott, and by

20 *Dublin Daily Express*, 1 January 1886.   **21** *Ballyshannon Herald*, 27 May 1882.   **22** Ibid., 20 November 1880.   **23** *Galway Express*, 3 January 1880.

2 Illustration of Captain Boycott and his family getting in their harvest before the arrival of the troops, *The Graphic*, 29 Nov. 1880. Image courtesy of the National Library of Ireland.

November a relief expedition of Orange labourers had been organized. The Monaghan *Argus* was triumphant that it was Ulster volunteers who were called upon to counteract 'those bellowing monsters of communism'.[24] The English, said the newspaper, 'would see clearly what has been too long kept out of their view by the thunderers of the Vatican in the South and West – that the wealthy, the industrious, the anti-rebellion men of Ulster ... are ranged on the side of order and manliness'.[25]

The Boycott incident, and other anti-rent agitation, dismayed those landlords who believed that communistic elements were establishing troubling precedents in an otherwise peaceful country. A letter from a landlord, Erasmus D. Borrowes, to the *Kildare Observer* outlined that he had maintained good relations with his tenants in the days before the Land League, and that all had paid their rents honestly. He had recently received a threat upon his life with a drawing of a coffin and the words 'You are doomed, you oppressor' emblazoned on one side.[26] In the face of pro-tenant right journalism in Britain, landlords submitted copies of letters from Irish tenants who begged for rent notices (despite having paid in full) in order to keep up the appearance of non-payment publicly. A Co. Cork landlord sent a letter received from one of his tenants to the *Times* in London, which was subsequently reprinted in the *Cork Constitution*:

24 *Argus*, 13 November 1880.   **25** Ibid.   **26** *Kildare Observer*, 27 November 1880.

Dear Sir – My Self and My Family or not sleeping aney Night We or afraid
That our Hay & our Cattle Will Be Bunred We have Too Bad nebours They
all says That i have My Rent Paid i hope You Wont Refuse me in asking you
to send me a letter Calling for Rent The same as You or Dooning For The
Rest of Them[27]

The apparent inadequacies and hypocrisies of the Land League were thus docu-
mented in the loyalist press, but the bewilderment expressed by landlords often
characterised the general response of the landowning loyalist. This response tended
to centre on a denial of the need to redress the land system, as tenants were inclined
to passively submit to a landlord's rule in the historical absence of agitators. Also, by
highlighting individual cases where tenants were surreptitiously paying rent privately,
and acting the Land Leaguer publicly, attempts were made to discredit the whole
premise of land agitation. Tenants were often portrayed as submissive individuals,
whether to the landlord or to the League – publicly clamouring for war, but privately
requiring the reassurance of the landowning authority figure. That the aforementioned *Times* letter was printed verbatim suggests that many landowners were of the
belief that if Irish property rights were on trial, so too was the intelligence of those
clamouring for reform.

After several years of agitation, few liberal loyalists denied that further reform to
the land laws of Ireland was necessary. What was denied was that reform should be
sought by incendiary doctrines, indiscriminate denunciations of landlords, and the
accompanying outrage and agitation. The Land Act of 1881[28] represented a further
'boundary' in reformative legislation according to loyalists. The measures of the act
were opposed by some – the *Cork Constitution* claimed that the legislation was in
direct and 'ostentatious opposition to every principle of justice and economic
science', and had given tenant farmers 'the taste of blood which converts the tiger
into a man-eater'.[29] Liberal loyalist newspapers counselled the Land League to
submit to the laws of the Land Courts and to condemn further violence, but in the
absence of such acquiescence, rigorous governmental legal pressure was advised.
Many proposed that the integrity of the tenant farmer was to be sacrificed to further
the political agenda of self-serving nationalist politicians. Pressure to suppress Land
League activity after the introduction of the Land Act was based on the proposal that
nationalist politicians were unlikely to debase the value of the land question to
broader nationalist intentions by submitting to the provisions of any legislation. The
Irish Times stated that the tenant farmer was to be sacrificed 'in all that concerns his
welfare to force the English Government and people into such a position that they
will cut Ireland adrift and say to Mr Parnell or some other leader "Take the country,

---

27 *Cork Constitution*, 15 January 1886.   **28** The Land Act of 1881 legislated for a number of
Land League demands (including the 'Three F's), improved on land purchase provisions and
provided for the establishment of the Land Commission as a judicial arbitrator of rents.
29 Ibid., 18 October 1881.

and make of it what you will; we are sick of it."'[30] The loyalist press advised against the arrest of Parnell at the outset of the Land War; this advice arose from the suspicion that historically such action had proven to confer the status of martyrdom on nationalists. However, his arrest in 1881 was seen as a highly desirable reaction to the dictatorial agenda of the Land League. Parnell's 'no-rent manifesto', issued from Kilmainham Jail, was decried in the loyalist press as an illegal, unconstitutional and communistic document, which forced tenants into the position of orchestrating their own destruction. After the suppression of the Land League, Irish loyalists placed emphasis on the fact that their own section had advised coercive action for years – editorials expressed satisfaction that the government had at last been forced to take a form of action which seemingly undermined its liberalistic approach to Irish affairs.

However, the League's suppression did not deter outrage and agitation sufficiently in the eyes of loyalists. Boycotting, non-payment of rent and general 'sedition' continued to be reported in the press. Demands were made that the government adopt a policy to put an end to the National League and liberate the loyal of Ireland from 'the grinding and galling tyranny of the "League of Hell".'[31] Suggestions as to the nature of an adequate response varied. A letter to the *Dublin Daily Express* proposed that the non-payment of rent be combated by the 'planting' of English and Scottish farmers and discharged soldiers on landlord estates.[32] The correspondent suggested that the installation of British tenants could create strong bodies of local loyalists in existing nationalist areas. Other newspapers proposed that the *laissez-faire* attitude of the government towards the National League was an encouragement to crime – it was alleged that insufficient arrests were taking place, and that long delays occurred between the period of an arrest, and that of an actual trial. This perceived reluctance on the part of the government to reinforce laws against land agitation had led to the establishment of the Cork Defence Union (CDU) in 1885. The union had been set up by Lord Bandon, Viscount Doneraile and Arthur Smith-Barry, and claimed to be non-political and non-sectarian, its aim being to 'bring together in common action all friends of law and order for mutual defence and protection'.[33] Munster was suffering particularly from the system of boycotting, and those boycotted or without possession of a National League 'ticket' encountered difficulties in attempting to buy or sell goods and produce – organisational relief was provided in the form of postal supply of provisions, and the employment of labourers on landlord estates. H.L. Tivy, proprietor of the *Cork Constitution*, was a member of the CDU, and set up a subscription fund through his newspaper to elicit contributions from supporters in Ireland and Britain. Applications for relief also provided the loyalist press with testified evidence to reinforce propaganda against the National League. Accounts of boycotting received by the CDU were published in the press, along with evidence of the assaults on tenants who continued to pay rent. In the mid

30 *Irish Times*, 16 September 1881.   **31** *Cork Constitution*, 21 October 1881.   **32** *Dublin Daily Express*, 19 January 1886.   **33** *Boycotting in the county of Cork: what boycotting means* (Cork Defence Union), pamphlet, 1886, pp i–ii.

LEAFLET=No. 4]   [SIXTH SERIES.

THE MUTILATION

OF

DUMB ANIMALS.

Mr. John Dillon, speaking at Kildare (15th August, 1880), said :—
"In the County of Mayo, where the organization is pretty strong, we
have many a farm lying idle, from which no rent can be drawn, and there
they shall lie, and if the landlord shall put cattle on them, the cattle
won't prosper very much."—*Official Report*, Queen *v.* Parnell, &c.,
p. 289.

IN his charge to the Grand Jury of Co. Kerry at the
Spring Assizes, 1891, the Irish Lord Chief Justice
congratulated the Jury on the marked diminution of
boycotting. "In the year 1887," said the Judge,
"there were 273 persons boycotted in the County
Kerry. There are in this present year but five."
Thanks to the administration of the Crimes Act, this
subtle, cruel, and demoralising form of crime has
consequently almost ceased to exist in one of the worst
spots in Ireland. Turning from the question of
boycotting, the Judge referred to that most dastardly
species of crime, the mutilation of animals, and said :—

"Now it is melancholy to record this sickening detail, but what is
the remedy for it? I should be very sorry indeed—and I am sure
that you should be very sorry to think that it would be necessary to
have recourse to flogging in this country—as an Irishman, and you,
as Irishmen, should be very sorry that that species of degrading
punishment was thought necessary; but, after all, can any person be
more degraded than the man who commits this loathsome form of

3 'that most dastardly species of crime' – The Mutilation of Dumb Animals,
Irish Unionist Alliance pamphlet, 1893.

1880s the newly established Irish Unionist Alliance catalogued the grievances of
loyalist Ireland for publication. Hundreds of thousands of unionist leaflets were
distributed in Britain, and Irish unionist newspapers were posted to libraries, work-
ingmen's clubs and to individual campaigners, particularly in Liberal constituencies.

The Plan of Campaign published in *United Ireland* in 1886 was, according to the
loyalist press, a deliberate assertion of the efficacy of illegality. The *Irish Times* claimed

that the Plan was intended to emphasise the domination of a limited portion of the nationalist population in the control of politics, to demonstrate that the government was powerless, 'that in fact all authority, sway, cunning and keen sight belong to the League – all blunder, fumbling, impotency and failure to the law and its administration'.[34] Though the Plan was in effect on over 200 estates at one point, the loyalist press implied that the movement was only fuelled by severe coercion on the part of nationalist politicians against tenants. It was implemented with rigorous force on the estate of Arthur Smith-Barry in Tipperary, and in the case of an attack upon a landlord, the loyalist press had traditionally assumed the role of defending the personal character of the man involved. Smith-Barry was portrayed as a virtuous, 'generous and kind-hearted' citizen whose tenants had 'flourished'[35] and had been extremely contented prior to the enactment of the Plan of Campaign. The loyalist press also claimed that the Plan itself had little support from tenants, but that the threat of coercive boycotting, and sanction of local priests, had soon put paid to any reluctance to go along with the mob. The Tenants Defence Fund had raised large sums – a fact that might be accepted as evidence, according to the *Cork Constitution*, 'of how ready the people still are to submit to blackmail, in order to conciliate those whom they know would not hesitate to hurt them'.[36]

The effects of governmental inadequacy in dealing with Irish disorder represented to many in the press that the welfare of Irish loyalists was deliberately disregarded. It seemed that criminality was rewarded, and that such rewards were offered at the expense of Irish loyalists. Coercive legislation on the part of the new Conservative administration was welcomed in unionist quarters – this measure was not only seen as a necessary, if belated, response to crime in Ireland, but as a vindication of the grievances of the loyal. Cynicism at the 'noble' cause of tenant right became widespread in the press, and even those who had acknowledged that injustice existed in the landlord system in earlier years were now inclined to refer to nationalism, as opposed to landlordism, for the causes of Irish discontent. The *Irish Times* and several contemporaries had not survived the Land War with all original liberal policies intact. Reformative legislation, respectful of property rights at all costs, had been advised by this section of the press at the outset of Gladstonian policies. By the late 1880s the effects of Liberal legislation, along with concurrent crime and disorder, had been observed, and 'liberals' in the press began to adopt the hard-line attitude of conservatives – sympathy for the tenant seemed to dissipate. In 1889 the *Irish Times* recommended and printed a pamphlet entitled *The Irish Question*, the author of which asserted that Irish landlords were 'the most senselessly abused and the worst-treated set of men within the wide bounds of Her Majesty's vast dominions, while the Irish tenant is the most petted and the most highly privileged under the sun'.[37] Accusations surrounding communistic leanings within the Land League appeared less frequently in the liberal loyalist press, but the perception of a rush

34 *Irish Times*, 4 December 1886. **35** *Cork Constitution*, 10 October 1890. **36** Ibid., 20 May 1890. **37** Dr A. Hamilton Bryce, *The Irish Question*, *Irish Times* pamphlet, 5 April 1889.

towards economic suicide pushed these liberals into a position concordant with that of conservative contemporaries. The liberal press had previously treated landlords with relative objectivity, but the enactment of land agitation served to classify all loyal and propertied individuals as victims, and thus gave further impetus to the unionist movement. Land agitation had also alienated liberal loyalists from original Home Rule proposals. The political convergence of loyalists assisted in forging uniformity in the creation of the unionist identity, which required that allegiances to Liberalism be forsaken for the wider benefits of the oppositional unionist movement.

The press comment of nineteenth century southern unionist newspapers, and the propaganda of the official unionist organisation, provides a perspective on land agitation which has gone largely under-acknowledged in Irish historiography. In southern unionist discourse 'the land' was often framed as a prefixed right of the 'Ascendancy' classes. Land agitation and remedial legislation, along with the disestablishment of the Church of Ireland, appeared to sanction the erosion of ascendancy values and succeeded in consolidating a political base for organised unionism after 1885. It became imperative for southern loyalist editors, reporters and pamphleteers to claim propagandist 'ownership' of the land issue in the sense that they, as representatives of the 'peaceful' citizens of Ireland, should be afforded paramount position in terms of accurately characterising the true nature of Irish nationalism for the benefit of the British voter. 'The land' became an issue that enabled unionists to emphasise the perceived oppression of their creed at the hands of nationalist sectarianism and British Liberalism, and, in the nineteenth century at least, provided official unionism with an effective propaganda weapon to counter self-government for Ireland.

Through a different lens: the Irish landscape as seen by mining promoters, 1835–80

WILLIAM H. MULLIGAN, JR.

One of the less well known aspects of the nineteenth-century Irish economy was mining, principally of copper but lead, gold and other minerals as well. In the mid 1820s, there was a 'boom' in Irish mining with the establishment of four firms, in addition to the privately owned Berehaven mines, that played the important role of calling attention to the potential of Irish copper mines. Of the four – the Hibernian Mining Company, the Mining Company of Ireland, the Royal Hibernian Mining Company, and the Imperial Mining Company – only the Mining Company of Ireland lasted beyond 1842 as an active mining company. Its copper mines in County Waterford at Knockmahon were very successful, as were its other ventures.[1] While small, usually unsuccessful mining ventures were almost ubiquitous, there were four areas where mines, especially copper mines, enjoyed some success. The most varied area was Co. Tipperary where small copper, lead, iron, and coal mines operated intermittently over the course of the century. At Knockmahon in Co. Waterford, the Vale of Avoca in Co. Wicklow and on the Beara Peninsula in Co. Cork large copper mines operated successfully until late in the century.

Travellers' descriptions of the nineteenth-century Irish landscape generally focus on the physical beauty of the landscape and the desperate poverty of Irish peasants they found in that landscape.[2] One group who travelled about Ireland looking at its landscape, however, focused on geology and Ireland's potential for mining development. Many, if not most, travellers saw an idealized Ireland, shaped to a considerable extent by their preconceptions of Ireland. Frequently these preconceptions were romantic – an idealization or abstraction of the realities of Ireland. Interestingly, the group one would expect to be more objective and less prone to miss the reality of what they saw because of their economic motivation – mining promoters and developers – were not, in the end, much different from the casual traveller in their ability

1 Des Cowman, 'The mining boom of 1824–25: Part 1', *Journal of the Mining Heritage Trust of Ireland* 1 (2001), 49–54; 2 (2002), 29–33. 2 See John P. Harrington, *The English traveller in Ireland* (Dublin, 1991) for a discussion of this vast literature. In addition to the works cited below, examples include, Sir John Carr, *The stranger in Ireland* (Philadelphia, 1806); Emmet J. Larkin (ed.), *Alexis de Tocqueville's Journey in Ireland: July–August 1835* (Dublin, 1990); John Barrow, *A tour round Ireland* (London, 1836); J. Stirling Coyne, *The scenery and antiquities of Ireland* (London, 1842); W.M. Thackeray, *The Irish sketchbook 1842* (Gloucester, 1990, reprint); Asenath Nicholson, *Ireland's welcome to the stranger* (New York, 1847); and S. Reynold Hole and John Leech, *A little tour in Ireland* (London, 1806).

to move beyond preconception and idealization. Many in this group were Cornish miners; others were geologists, sometimes amateur. They published their descriptions in contemporary geological society journals, the press, and after 1835 when it began publication, *the Mining Journal*. Their perspective was very different from other travellers and has not been much studied. It did, however, reflect a significant level of activity for much of the nineteenth century. Before discussing these mine promoters' perceptions of the Irish landscape, it is useful to discuss several travellers or commentators on Ireland who described mine sites in Ireland as part of a more traditional traveller's account or description of Ireland.

TRAVELLERS' AND GENERAL OBSERVERS OF THE IRISH LANDSCAPE

One of the more prominent early nineteenth-century travellers who commented extensively on Ireland was Lady Chatterton [Henrietta Georgiana Marcia Lascelles]. In *Rambles in the South of Ireland* (1839), she describes her trip through the Beara Peninsula, including a visit to the Allihies mines, the largest and most successful copper mines in Ireland, in a manner typical of such accounts:

> From their station [Hungry Hill] the Kerry Mountains are seen to great advantage. The Hungry Hill adventurers descended to a projecting rock which they described to me as a very picturesque position, overhanging a hollow in the mountain in whose wild bosom lay a black and gloomy lake, said, nevertheless, with another near it, to abound with peculiarly bright trout.[3]

The next day she describes the ascent to Allihies, the site of the Puxley family's copper mines, the most productive in Ireland in the nineteenth century:

> The view as we ascended was very fine, including the bay and the headlands, and much of the mountain scenery was now familiar to the gentlemen from their visit yesterday to Hungry Hill.
>   After we passed the highest point of the ascent, we had a magnificent view over that part of the Atlantic of which the mountaineers were deprived yesterday by the fog. Dursey Island and Blackball Point, which has a tower upon it, form one side and Sheep's-head the other, of the entrance to Bantry Bay. The Skilligs ... made their appearance in the extreme distance. They are two remarkable rocks, which seem to be nearly similar in shape, and stand about ten or twelve miles out to sea. Before us were the Hogs, two rocky islands apparently lying just south of the Kenmare river; beyond was

3 Lady Chatterton, *Rambles in the South of Ireland*, 2 vols, 2nd edition (London: Saunders and Otley, 1839), i, 72.

1 'View of the mines at Allihies, County Cork', from
Lady Chatterton, *Rambles in the South of Ireland* (1839).

Darrynane Bay, with its lofty mountains. Then, nearer, Cooleagh Bay, which
is the summer harbour of the mines.[4]

As in most of the narratives, Chatterton comments on the dire poverty of the
Irish peasants she encounters and the filthiness of their homes and persons,
comparing them unfavourably to the English, in this case Cornish miners: 'On our
return, we visited some of the cottages, and with all my partiality for the Irish peasants, I could not but see the striking superiority in point of cleanliness of the cottages
belonging to the English [Cornish] miners.'[5] She also notes, 'the English [Cornish]
and the Irish, not withstanding a difference in religion, agree perfectly well together.
It is said that for ten years there has not been a quarrel among the workmen, owing
to a rule, which is strictly enforced, that whoever quarrels is immediately dismissed.'[6]

Lady Chatterton's observation of harmonious relations between the Cornish and
the Irish in Allihies may well have been what she saw. However, the small number of
Cornish who had come over when the mines were first opened lived in stone
cottages built for them by the Puxleys quite near the mines, quite apart from their
Irish co-workers. They worshipped in a stone Methodist chapel, also built for them
by the Puxleys. The Irish miners provided their own housing and walked some
considerable distance from their homes to the mines – and no Catholic chapel was
provided for them.[7] In Hancock, Michigan some years later Irish (largely from

4 Ibid., i, 74–5.   5 Ibid., i, 79.   6 Ibid., i, 76.   7 See, R.A. Williams, *The Berehaven Copper Mines*, Northern Mine Research Society, British Mining No. 42, 1991; C. O'Mahony, 'Copper mining at Allihies, Co. Cork,' *Journal of the Cork Historical and Archaeological Society*

2 'View of Castletown Berehaven' from Lady Chatterton,
Rambles in the South of Ireland (1839).

Allihies) and Cornish miners worked for the same company, but never together and regularly engaged in massive brawls on the main street. They can hardly be said to have gotten along.[8] In any event, Lady Chatterton sets forth the themes common to much of the travel writing about Irish mining districts – the physical beauty of the setting, the charm of the people, despite their dire poverty and squalid living conditions – and also displays the detachment from reality that is also common in such narratives.

In 1824, about fifteen years before Lady Chatterton's tour T. Crofton Croker published *Researches in the South of Ireland, etc.* Croker is not primarily concerned with scenery or mineralogy, offering instead very general and wide-ranging observations. However, in chapter seventeen he addresses 'Mines and Minerals' and begins with a disclaimer: 'Although it does not come within the design of this work to treat on the geology of the south of Ireland, yet I feel satisfied that a brief account of its mines and minerals will not be misplaced, and may tend to direct some attention to an important though neglected pursuit'.[9]

92 (1987), 71–84; Des Cowman, 'Life and labour in three Irish mining communities circa 1840', *Saothar*, 9 (1983), 10–19 for descriptions of the Allihies Mines and living conditions there. **8** William H. Mulligan, Jr., 'Irish immigrants in Michigan's copper country: assimilation on a northern frontier,' *New Hibernia Review*, 5:4 (2001), 109–22. **9** T. Crofton Croker, *Researches in the south of Ireland, etc.* (London, 1824), p. 310.

Croker is among the earliest writers to describe of the state of mining in Ireland, writing only twenty years after Colonel Hall reopened an ancient mine on Ross Island and essentially began the nineteenth-century Irish mining boom. His chapter includes nearly all of the sites that were to become important in Irish mining during the century. His description of the mines at Allihies is typical, interestingly, of later efforts to promote Irish mining, combining promotion with description:

> Besides paying the proprietors very handsomely, the blessing which this mine has been to the surrounding country can only be appreciated by those who have witnessed such a scene. The place where, but a few years since, the barren and rocky mountains could scarcely sustain the lives of a few half-starved sheep, is now the scene of busy and useful employment, dispensing compe-tence and comfort to hundreds. The principal works are carried on about a mile and a half from the water, and the ground rises to a considerable eleva-tion. The vein crosses the regular strata of the country, which is a hard rock of greywacke, at a small angle, taking a direction about two points to the south of east and the same to the north of west. The matrix of the vein is a white opaque quartz, in part of its course of the amazing width of sixty feet (which has been proved by cutting through it), but the ore has seldom exceeded three feet in breadth.[10]

While discussing the iron mines at Silver Mines in Co. Tipperary, Croker attributes the mine's problems to mismanagement and waxes enthusiastic about the potential economic benefits for Ireland. Both these ideas, the tremendous economic benefit Ireland could gain from its mineral resources and the need for proper (generally meaning Cornish or English) management remain important themes in the discus-sion and promotion of Irish mining for the rest of the century, as does Croker's positive view of English activities in Ireland:

> but mismanagement seems to be the order of the day in Ireland ... Many places may be mentioned where mineral treasures expose themselves to the view of the passing traveller; but a repetition of circumstances that admit little or no variation occasion a tiresome monotony, and enough has probably been said to show what an extensive field of speculation and research the south of Ireland presents: indeed, as useful employment is acknowledged to be the grand desideratum in that unhappy country, and as England has proved herself so nobly solicitous in every effort to raise the indolent and misguided Irish peasantry from their present state of wretchedness and discontent, what better opportunity could be wished for them than this subject presents? – Companies of wealthy individuals might be formed at this side of the water; and if qualified persons were engaged to superintend the works, such associ-

10 Ibid., p. 314.

ations would not only be attended with every probability of profit to those concerned, but they would at once administer extensive employment, and no doubt, greatly tend to tranquilize the peasantry.[11]

In 1883, nearly sixty years after Croker, Samuel Hall, the son of one of the first Irish mining promoters Colonel Robert Hall, described the state of Irish mining as the industry wound down with mines closing across the country:

> The failure of schemes for working mines in Ireland to repay their projectors has generally been traceable to one of two causes – bad management or insufficient capital, and sometimes the two combined ... but in copper, lead, sulphur, and marble, various districts are rich, and greater rewards than have already been obtained probably await those who shall in the future bring capital, skill and energy to the working of these deposits.[12]

Mining, particularly of copper, came to be a major focus for efforts to develop alternatives, or supplements, to agriculture as the principal foundation of the Irish economy through the 1860s. Hall's various efforts had had mixed success. In several instances, especially the Berehaven mines at Allihies in Co. Cork, the Knockmahon mines in Co. Waterford, and the Avoca (sometimes spelled Ovaca) mines in Co. Wicklow, success was substantial enough to suggest to proponents of mining development that with sufficient capital and 'proper,' that is, English, management many more successful Irish mining ventures were possible. The successful mining operations in these three areas became models for what proponents of Irish copper mining, especially the trade paper *The Mining Journal* saw as possible with sufficient capital and efficient management. The reality of the repeated failure of mining ventures in Ireland was invariably attributed to poor management, not the changing world market or overly optimistic projections.[13]

MINING AND INDUSTRIAL JOURNALISTS

Between Croker and the younger Hall there was a great deal written describing the mineral resources of Ireland with the intention of promoting mining generally as well as individual mining ventures. These efforts range from the very general and relatively objective discussion of Ireland's mining districts in Robert Kane's *The Industrial Resources of Ireland* to newspaper articles on various mining ventures and proposed

11 Ibid., pp 317–18. **12** S.C. Hall, *Retrospect of a long life from 1815 to 1883*, 2 vols (London, 1883), ii, 344. Hall had written a more traditional travel account with his wife some years earlier: Mr and Mrs S.C. Hall, *Ireland: its scenery, character, &,* 3 vols (Hall, 1841). **13** D. Cowman and T.A. Reilly, *The abandoned mines of west Carbery: promoters, adventurers and miners* (Dublin, 1988). There is a great deal about the failure of the Audley Mines, which led to prolonged litigation, in the *Mining Journal*.

3 Gold mining, County Wexford from Lady Chatterton,
Rambles in the South of Ireland (1839).

ventures and several industrial journals. These include two short-lived publications,
the *Irish Railway Gazette* and the *Irish Industrial Magazine,* and the more successful
Mining Journal, Railway and Commercial Gazette (hereafter, simply the *Mining Journal*),
which is still published today.

Sir Robert Kane's *The Industrial Resources of Ireland,* first published in Dublin in
1844 with a second edition appearing in 1845, is in many ways the key work for nineteenth-century Irish economic development efforts. Kane extensively and
exhaustively catalogued and discussed various mining and manufacturing operations
in Ireland. He also called attention to a wide range of underdeveloped economic
resources in Ireland, such as waterpower sites and mineral deposits that were suitable
for development.[14] Kane's work was regularly cited in newspaper and magazine articles and other essays on Irish economic potential during the second half of the
nineteenth century. It attracted a great deal of favourable notice among those interested in Irish economic development, but the level of investment activity and
economic diversification Kane and other advocates of mining in Ireland hoped for
never developed. The trade papers present a combination of reporting and opinion
that are not always clearly distinguished. The *Mining Journal* had regular correspon-

14 Robert Kane, M.D., *The industrial resources of Ireland* (1845 second edition.)

dents who provided a great deal of information, some of which conflicted with the editor's position on some ventures. Many pieces were not signed, or were signed with a penname.[15] There are also advertisements which explicitly promote various ventures and letters to the editor, which seem to be the best source for identifying problems within the industry.[16]

Another aspect of nineteenth-century journalism that must be taken into account is the practice of reprinting articles from publications obtained on exchange. Finding several articles on a particular mine at a particular time, or on the opportunities being promoted in a particular district is almost always due to reprinting, not reporting by different people that might offer different perspectives. Still, after all the caveats are noted and taken into account, the *Mining Journal*, the publication I will focus on here, does appear to be a useful window into the world of Irish mining in the nineteenth century. Focusing on the *Mining Journal*, a specialized industrial publication has many advantages over relying on general London, Dublin, Cork, Waterford or regional Irish newspapers in terms of yield, to borrow a mining term. Before looking at the *Mining Journal* it is useful to look at two, short-lived Irish magazines that also promoted and commented on Irish economic development.

The *Irish Industrial Magazine* which was published in Dublin was an attempt to produce an Irish publication focused on the economic development of the country. Established in 1866, the *Irish Industrial Magazine* avoided reprinting items and published some very trenchant and insightful original articles. In its first issue E.H. Wadge, a Fellow of the Geological Society, published the first of several articles entitled 'On Mining and Quarrying in Ireland'. The first had the subtitle, 'as source of industrial and profitable employment'.[17] Wadge touches on some familiar themes as well as presenting some new perspectives:

> The vast improvement in the localities amongst which mining industries are pursued far more than counterbalance the trifling loss of the surface land destroyed by their operations; ... It should be remembered, also, that mines are generally found in wild, barren, mountainous districts, the reclamation of which would of itself be a positive national advantage. How full is Ireland of such situations and of such premises![18]

He then proceeds to the great nineteenth-century cliché on Irish mining, that the development of mines would solve the problem of poverty in Ireland and once the problem of poverty was solved political agitation would stop and English rule would be accepted:

15 It has not been possible to determine how anonymous, within the industry, such contributions would be. The little evidence that does exist strongly suggests not very. 16 The *Mining Journal* published many such prospectuses as display ads throughout the century. The letters to the editor were generally on pages two or four and in smaller type. The letters are often in the form of a pointed question. 17 *Irish Industrial Magazine*, January 1866, pp 24–9. 18 Ibid., p. 25.

'What to do for Ireland?' has long been the question of questions to successive governments, and a difficulty to the most sagacious of statesmen. What
we should advise would be – cultivate and foster her mining industries; for
she does indeed possess vast mineral riches, as witness her mines of sulphur,
copper, and lead, in Wicklow and in Monaghan; her splendid mines at
Berehaven; her mines comprising the property of the Mining Company of
Ireland, and many other companies.[19]

Wadge does point out that Irish copper ores, on average, brought twice the price of
British ores at the Swansea sales, the major market for copper ore. He fails to point
out, or perhaps notice, that Irish ores brought far less than Australian and Chilean ores
in the same market.[20] He describes mines, slate and marble quarries, and coal mines
in some detail. He even offers the standard critique of apathy toward the development of Irish mineral resources by investment in mines. Wadge then offers a very
spirited, and unusual, defence of the Irish labourer and his suitability for mine work
and compares his position with that of the Cornish miner:

> The aptitude of the Irish labourers for pursuits such as quarrying and mining
> is well known and admitted, both *at* home and *from* home. [emphasis orig-
> inal] When properly instructed, they make workmen in all respects equal, in
> many superior, to the average of the men among whom they are employed,
> especially for the harder and more dangerous portions ... The most cursory
> ramble through a mining district or village will convince the most sceptical
> of the manifold advantages which the employment offers.[21]

The longest-term promoter of Irish mining was the *Mining Journal,* a weekly
trade paper based in London. On 29 August 1835 Henry English launched the *Mining
Journal and Commercial Gazette* to serve the British mining industry. Its scope was
broad, incorporating coverage of railroad and canal development and all types of
mining and quarrying in the British Isles. It also covered mining where British capital
was invested and other mining areas, such as the Lake Superior region of the United
States, where British investment was minimal. Between 1835 and 1880, when Irish
copper mining was most extensive and most active, the *Mining Journal* focused more
on copper mining than on any of the other economic activities it covered. Within a
few months the *Mining Journal* had its attention drawn to Irish mining:

> We have to thank 'Adventurer' for his communication. The mines of Ireland
> are deserving the attention of the capitalist. The mineral resources of that
> country are as yet unproved, and the application of capital would, we doubt

19 Ibid.   **20** The results of the bi-weekly Swansea ticketings appeared in various British
and Irish newspapers and after 1835 regularly in the *Mining Journal* and after 1848 in a series
of reports by Robert Hunt.   **21** *Irish Industrial Magazine,* January 1866, p. 28.

not, be as productive of advantage to the adventurer, as we are assured it would to those employed in developing its riches. Why do not Irish landlords and Irish patriots put themselves forward? They would get support, but while they are supine, how can it be expected that the English capitalist should be moving?[22]

In 1845 the West Carbery and County of Cork Mining Company published a prospectus, hoping to attract £200,000 by selling 10,000 shares at £20 each. It listed the advantages the site offered: proximity to the sea, water power, and cheap labour. These characteristics appear in other prospectuses in different combinations over the next few decades. [23]

A few months later an article by 'A Practical Miner' was reprinted from the *Cork Southern Reporter* on 'Mining in the County of Cork'. The points in the prospectus are made and expanded upon:

> the natural advantages and facilities for working mines in the west of the county are superior to any in the world. Here we have safe and commodious harbours, at convenient distances, all around the coast; and from the position of the mineral districts, the important item of land carriage is saved – here we have numbers of streams and rivers, that might be applied to mechanical purposes, to an unlimited extent – and here we have the valuable lodes staring us in the face in broad day-light, as if in mockery of the apathetic capitalist.[24]

In the end the venture was a failure – an almost complete failure, as were nearly all ventures in this area of Ireland developed after the 1830s. Despite the 'promising' geology, none of these ventures lasted very long – although a number were revived from time to time with glowing prospectuses in the *Mining Journal* – or made any significant return on the investment made.[25]

Sea access and potential for development of water power appear frequently in the prospectuses for new mining ventures and in the articles discussing them in the *Mining Journal*. Another theme is similarity in geological formation or location to one of the more successful mining ventures, especially the Berehaven Mines at Allihies. Frequently, these similarities become the principal justification for investment. After a romantic description of the geology of the Kenmare area, one promoter makes the case for investment based on proximity to the Berehaven Mines:

> The Kenmare Bay, from its entrance from the Atlantic to the town of Kenmare, is about 30 miles long; at the south side are the Berehaven Mines, and on the north side, near West Cove, the Hartopp Mines. The formation at

22 *Mining Journal*, 12 December 1835, p. 132.   **23** Ibid., 11 October 1845, p. 529.   **24** Ibid., 8 November 1845, p. 628.   **25** Cowman and Reilly, *The abandoned mines of West Carbery*, passim.

either side of the entrance to the bay is of a similar character – viz. compact clay-slate, and large quartz veins running obliquely to the strata. And if the same *cause* produces the same *effect*, judging from surface indications, there is no assignable reason why good mines may not be found in the West Cove Mountains as in those at the opposite side of the bay.[26]

Sometimes what starts out as flowery description turns technical, as with this opening paragraph for an article titled 'Ireland – Its Geology and Mining':

Assuredly a brighter era has dawned upon Ireland. The genial sun of a manifestly providential visitation is now fairly above her horizon; its revivifying rays have already called into life and activity the latent forces of civilization, which have for untold ages lain dormant within her prolific womb; they are rapidly dispersing the hitherto stagnant mists, and removing those foul blotches – moral, social, political – which during the protracted period of a chastening ordeal, affixed themselves like vampires upon her, to the great exhaustion of the life blood of her national existence, and to the sad disfigurement of those physical features, which nature herself, has rendered so eminently attractive.

We find a considerable development of the lower Silurian rocks in Waterford, bordered on the north and west by the old red sandstone, and to the south by the trap-rocks already referred to; in this district many valuable copper and some lead mines have been discovered.

The lower Devonian, or old red sandstone formation, constitutes an extensive and very picturesque tract in this part of the whole of the county of Cork ... In fact [copper mines] stud this part of the country even down to the extremity of that old red sandstone peninsula which stretches farthest out into the vast Atlantic; for here, on the shores of Crookhaven Harbour, a place greatly resorted to by shipping, are situated the famous purple copper ore and silver lead mines of that name.[27]

Examples of this approach to the landscape and mineral resources of Ireland can be multiplied. The West of Ireland Mining Company (Limited) which sought to develop 'one of the richest and most varied mineral deposits in the British Islands' mentioned in its 1857 prospectus that:

the whole is intersected with rivers and streams, so that the water power is inexhaustible, while the sea frontage affords every opportunity for shipment, either by the formation of quays to suit circumstance, or by means of existing and well-known ports of Killeries [*sic*] and Westport.[28]

---

26 *Mining Journal*, 29 January 1853, p. 68. **27** Ibid., 17 September 1863, p. 580. **28** Ibid., 16 May 1857, p. 350.

Descriptions of the Irish landscape presented by those promoting mining ventures have some things in common with travellers' accounts, primarily a focus on the poverty of the people. Mining promoters or observers, almost always hold up mining as the solution to this poverty. There are a number of things that are specific to mining promoters – Ireland's coasts are seen as advantageous for providing low cost transportation for mines located nearby. Picturesque rivers ands streams are sources of water power. Colourful rock formations and strata in cliffs are not merely scenic, but evidence of mineral wealth waiting development:

> The mines of Ireland have of late assumed so important a position in the tick-eting papers, of the sale of ores, at Swansea that it is with pleasure we advert to the circumstances, as it must be gratifying to all, whether embarked in mining adventures or otherwise, to learn that the mineral products of the sister isle are daily developing their riches affording employment to thousands, who otherwise must, in all notability, be in a state of starvation, and giving to trade in the vicinity of the mines that impetus which Ireland much requires. It is pleasing to find English enterprise and Irish industry this combined, yielding as they do, in most cases where prudent management in pursued, returns amply remunerative to the capitalist, and of an advantage to the peasant.[29]

The 'problem' of Ireland for the *Mining Journal* it becomes clear was the country's endemic extreme poverty and political restlessness and agitation against English rule. Industry and especially mining was seen as solutions that would provide employment for the peasants and develop a cash economy. Ireland, and the Irish, would quickly become more like the English and harmony would soon prevail.

So committed was the *Mining Journal* to its optimistic vision of an Ireland led to industry and modernity by mining that it was especially reticent about discussing negative aspects of the Irish mining industry throughout the 1860s and on numerous occasions accepted and believed overly optimistic assessments of the future of individual mines. When mining ventures that had drawn extravagant editorial praise when first proposed and offered to investors ended up in the wonderfully named 'Winding Up Court' or the principals were indicted for fraud, there was seldom editorial comment or notice taken in a formal article. One usually has to read the very fine print on page two for letters from subscribers who were shareholders in the failed ventures or the occasional column of the paper's always unnamed 'Dublin Correspondent' to find any hard questions being posed or negative information reported about failed ventures or proposals to reopen abandoned workings. The *Mining Journal*, however, remained optimistic in the face of mounting evidence that copper mining in Ireland was not going to be a profitable industry on an extensive scale. In fact, the paper seems not to have been able to see the negative prognosis for

29 Ibid., 2 April 1836, p. 112

British Isles copper mining generally. Copper mining would not be the solution to the 'problem' of Ireland; rather it became just another factor that produced emigrants – not only from Ireland, but from Cornwall as well.[30]

Changes in the world market that began in the 1830s and accelerated dramatically during the 1840s changed the situation for Irish mining ventures. The much larger and better established Cornish copper mines also suffered. Miners from both Cornwall and Ireland were beginning to emigrate in significant numbers by the 1840s because of the contraction of the industry and declining incomes for Irish and Cornish mines.[31] In Ireland this situation was made worse by the large number of relatively new ventures that brought people into mining, or, as appears more to be the case, led them to relocate to the newest venture that promised work. While reporting all of these developments, the *Mining Journal* consistently underestimated their significance. Initial reports on the tremendous copper finds in the Keweenaw Peninsula in Michigan, for example, were initially dismissed as so spectacular as to be impossible. When the reports were confirmed by experienced Cornish mining captains, the Michigan mines were still dismissed as serious competition because any resource that rich could not last long.

While Cornish miners soon became ubiquitous and visible in hard rock mining districts around the world, Irish miners were less visible and more likely to go to the United States or Australia. After 1845 production in the Lake Superior district increased making the prospects for Irish (and Cornish) copper mining ventures even less promising.

It is clear that the *Mining Journal's* view of the condition, and potential, of mining in Ireland was seriously flawed. While this is especially obvious during the Famine when the population was debilitated by hunger and disease, it was also true during the following decades. Its desire to promote industrial development, especially mining, in Ireland led its editor to underestimate the problems facing any effort to develop mining ventures, particularly during the Famine, and to continue to promote mining as a solution to the problems of poverty and political unrest in Ireland after the Famine.

The paper heralded what would become its standard call on 12 September 1846 under the heading 'Distress in the County Cork Mining Districts':

> Our chief object in our present notice of the condition of the poor in the districts referred to is to urge the propriety of different companies working mines and quarries therein to as extensive an employment of the poor in the respective vicinities, as the nature of their operations may allow. By their so

30 William H. Mulligan, Jr., 'From the Beara to the Keweenaw', *Journal of the Mining Heritage Trust of Ireland*, I (2001), 19–24.   31 Ronald Rees, *King Copper: South Wales and the copper trade, 1584–1895* (Cardiff, 2000) offers a sound, brief discussion of the changing world production of copper ore. For the United States see Charles K. Hyde, *Copper for America: the United States Copper industry from colonial times to the 1990s* (Tucson, 1998) and Mulligan, 'From the Beara to the Keweenaw' and 'Irish Immigrants in Michigan's Copper Country'.

doing, it may be very fairly assumed, that so far from suffering a loss, or even a reduction of their profits, in all remunerative mines they will increase those profits – because it is a well-ascertained fact, that there is nothing like a sufficient application of labour and capital to the development of the wealth of even the most productive mines in the mineral districts of the county of Cork.[32]

Such appeals for investment in Irish mines were a regular feature during the course of the Famine; occasionally with the variation that government aid money would be better spent expanding mining in Ireland to provide employment, and would thus be a long-term solution to both the current crisis and the long-term economic problems of Ireland. A correspondent from West Carbery, a mining district in Co. Cork, where many copper mining ventures had failed, who signed himself 'A Miner', highlighted one major problem with the approach suggested. While calling for assisted emigration to the mines in Australia, 'A Miner' described:

> our starving fellow-creatures, hundreds and thousands of whom are dying daily in this country from *starvation*? – men, who a few days ago were in full vigour, health and strength, are now reduced to mere skeletons; and such is the misery and extreme destitution to which they are reduced, that when employment on the public work is afforded them, they are unable to perform it – and numbers who stagger out in the morning to the roads and other works now being carried on, drop dead from exhaustion.[33]

The debilitated condition of the Irish working class was a serious impediment to solving Ireland's problems, at least in the short run, with industrial occupations like mining that required physical energy and some skill. The public works jobs provided by the Russell government were beyond the physical capacity of the population.

What is remarkable is that these images of the economic potential of Ireland's mineral resources, and the optimism attached to them, did not change during the entire period Irish mining was an active industry despite the failure of large numbers of mining ventures. The same things were being said as the industry was declining as were being said when it might have had a future. Actually, nearly everything quoted comes from the period of marked decline in production. Optimism reigned supreme. Perhaps it was a denial of the harsh realities that would destroy the great hope – that mining would provide a solution to the poverty of Ireland. Experience does not seem to have had any impact on how promoters saw the potential for mining. Take for example the Allihies mines in Co. Cork and the Knockmahon mines in Co. Waterford. Both are located on, or very near, the coast. Neither, however, gained much economic advantage from that. There is no good anchorage at the Knockmahon mines and lightering ore to ships was both expensive and dangerous. Allihies ores initially were processed near the beach at Ballydongan but access for ships was so dangerous there that the mine owner was forced to buy his own ships – and even he soon accepted the necessity of bearing the cost of shipping the ore six miles overland to Castletown Berehaven for shipment to Swansea. Neither area ever received rail service during their mining days, or afterwards. Experience proved the value of coastal location given the specifics of each site a myth, but it appears time and again in descriptions of Irish mining ventures as an advantage. It is even more puzzling that there were no efforts to develop railroads to move ore economically to better harbours. Plans for Irish mining development seem to have operated in an idealized world, not the real world.

The landscapes mining promoters saw, whether honestly or dishonestly, were much more landscapes of hope than landscapes of reality. This is not uncommon when people are confronted with an unfamiliar landscape. John Logan Allen has written extensively about how the American explorers Lewis and Clark took many months as they moved west into increasingly unknown areas to begin to see what was actually in front of them and not what they had expected to find.[34] The optimistic promotion of Irish copper mines continued nearly until the time the industry died. The peak years for production for Irish copper mines were from roughly 1835 to 1847. The lowest level during that period was in 1841 when 14,321 tons of copper was produced. From 1847 until 1882 when the Swansea ticketing sales ended that level was exceeded once and approached twice. Irish copper production did not exceed 8800 tons after 1870. It was an industry in decline because it could not compete with Chilean and Australian copper or compensate for the complete loss to the British copper industry of the American market after the development of the Lake Superior copper mines after 1845.

In my research on Irish copper mining and, peripherally, on nineteenth-century Irish mining and economic development generally, the most striking thing is the wishful thinking; that mining could be a solution to the problems of Ireland by providing employment to the native population, therefore it must be possible. In the real economic world after 1845 when large copper fields in the United States, Chile, and Australia began to be developed there was no future for the copper mines in Ireland or the more established and better funded mines in Cornwall. Those who saw mineral wealth in Ireland's landscape never saw the realities of that landscape in the larger perspective of the copper market of the nineteenth century. They never abadoned their landscapes of hope for the landscapes of reality.

---

34 John Logan Allen, *Passage through the garden: Lewis and Clark and the image of the American Northwest* (Urbana, 1975), passim. The sub-field of historical geography known as geosophy deals with these dissonances between expectation and reality.

'Old lords of the soil': *The O'Donoghue* (1845) by Charles Lever

JAMES H. MURPHY

Charles Lever, 'Dr Quicksilver', was once a star of the Victorian novel, compared with Scott and a rival to Dickens, his near contemporary. A doctor in the Irish country-side, a literary editor in Dublin, a diplomat in Italy: life provided him with a wide range of material to be transformed into fiction.[1] Yet he managed to alienate audiences on both sides of the Irish Sea by means of an early commercialism, on the one hand, which appealed to English audiences but not Irish critics, especially Carleton, and the mid-life blossoming of a social concern and an artistic aspiration, on the other, which reduced his standing in Britain as he became more critical of the polit-ical predicament of Ireland. As a result his novels are today not in print and register only occasionally on the academic radar. A recent biographer, indeed, dubbed him 'the lost Victorian'.

The O'Donoghue (1845) marks the transition in Lever's fiction.[2] James McGlashan,

1 Tony Bareham, 'The famous Irish Lever,' in Tony Bareham (ed.), *Charles Lever: new evaluations* (Gerrards Cross, 1991), pp 1–17; Edmund Downey, *Charles Lever: his life and letters*, 2 vols (Edinburgh, 1906); W.J. Fitzpatrick, *Life of Charles Lever* (London: Ward, Lock, 1884); Lionel Stevenson, *Dr Quicksilver: the life of Charles Lever* (London, 1939); Stephen Haddelsey, *Charles Lever: the lost Victorian* (Gerrards Cross, 2000); James H. Murphy, *Ireland: a social, cultural and literary history, 1791–1891* (Dublin, 2003), pp 83–5. 2 The story: the mid 1790s.
The O'Donoghue, an aged, self-absorbed, bankrupt Irish chieftain, lives in the ruinous castle of Carrignacurra in the valley of Glenflesk, between Macroom and Bantry Bay, bordering counties Cork and Kerry. With him are his Scottish brother-in-law, Sir Archibald McNab, his discontented elder son, Mark, his academically-inclined younger son, Herbert, and his French-convent-educated niece, Kate, who has given her £10,000 fortune to her uncle and whom Mark secretly loves. Mrs Branaghan is his cook and Kerry O'Leary his servant. Most of the valley is now owned by Sir Marmaduke Travers, an English banker intent on improving the conditions of his tenants. Having previously relied on his agent, the evil Capt Hemsworth, and his assistant, Sam Wylie, Sir Marmaduke takes up residence in his local home, the Lodge, with his daughter, Sybella, and son, Frederick, a captain in the guards. The Lodge is attacked by a group of French smugglers though it is saved from burning down by Terry the Woods, a local eccentric. The two families are brought together socially when Herbert saves Sybella from a flood, though it nearly costs him his life. Mark and Frederick, however, dislike each other. Mark allows himself to be persuaded by Lanty Lawler, a horse dealer, and Mary McKelly, whose inn conceals a secret store of arms and explosives, to aid the secret preparations of the United Irishmen for a French invasion. The Traverses spend the winter season in Dublin, together with Kate. Kate and Sybella become the central attractions of fashionable society. Herbert studies at Trinity College and becomes a

who represented Lever's publishers William Curry, was so disturbed by the adverse reaction to the book of Tories, who had accused it of supporting repeal of the Act of Union, the great nationalist cause of the 1840s, that Lever had to find a new publisher for his future books in Chapman and Hall.[3]

In terms of genre it is in part an old-fashioned national tale[4] – with a possible national marriage in the offing between Kate O'Donoghue and Frederick Travers – but also a satire of the travel literature of the early nineteenth century. In part it also looks forward to the realistic analysis of Ireland's social and political situation of Lever's later novels, while occasionally lapsing into the comic stereotyping of his early work. It is also an historical novel, set against the backdrop of the United Irishmen though tellingly it culminates in the failed French landing in Bantry Bay in 1796, rather than in the bloody internecine conflict of the rebellion of 1798.[5] Above all though the novel is an ostensible attempt to open up a new line of communication between Britain and Ireland, to find a common language for a renewal of under-standing and sympathy between the two countries. In attempting this highly pressurized enterprise, however, Lever forces history into unaccustomed grooves and seems to embark on a policy of degrading possibilities for knowledge and communication between characters within the novel, and undermining the traditional reliability of the narrator for the reader.

One of the most manifest issues in the novel, especially of the early part, is the satire not only of travel writing as a genre but of liberal and utilitarian English attempts to understand and improve Ireland. It is a necessary part of the novel. For Lever to assert that new ways are needed by which England might understand Ireland he must first disabuse the English of their belief in their hitherto accustomed ways.

Protestant. Mark, too, visits the capital in the company of a man whom he believes is a revolutionary called Harry Talbot, though others allege that he is a common criminal called John Barrington. Mark learns from him of his father's dishonest dealings with Hemsworth over money. Hemsworth both seeks to endear himself to Kate and to pressurise Lawler for information about the rebellion which he hopes to use to his advantage with the government. Two months later Mark is in hiding in the valley of Glenflesk as a suspected rebel. Kate has also returned to the area, having refused Frederick's marriage proposal, and is now being seriously wooed by Hemsworth, though the latter ruins his chances by threatening not to help Mark if she does not marry him. Mark unsuccessfully tries to raise the local peasantry to rebellion when the French fleet arrives in Bantry Bay, though when the French are unable to land he decides to leave with them and join the French service. Hemsworth is killed in an explosion, when he maliciously burns down Mary McKelly's inn, not knowing it houses gunpowder. The O'Donoghue dies, Herbert becomes a Member of Parliament and Kate returns to schooling in France. Nearly twenty years later, in 1815, Mark and Kate, now married to each other, return to visit the valley.   **3** Haddelsey, *Charles Lever*, p.73; Stevenson, *Dr Quicksilver*, pp 142–3.   **4** It has been said to be based on Edgeworth's *Ennui* (Haddelsey, *Charles Lever*, p. 21) and Morgan's *Wild Irish Girl* (Stevenson, *Dr Quicksilver*, p. 134). In addition, the character of The O'Donoghue himself bears a resemblance to the irresponsible landlords in Edgeworth's *Castle Rackrent*.   **5** Stevenson, *Dr Quicksilver*, p. 149. Lever had actually originally thought of continuing the story until 1798 but McGlashan had opposed it.

Of key importance is the land and the relationships it sets up between landlord and tenant. Lever centres the issue on Sir Marmaduke Travers, a London banker of landed background, who arrives in Glenflesk determined to be an improving landlord and to educate his tenants in enlightened ways.

The narrative links Sir Marmaduke's role as someone in the traveller-analyser tradition with his ambitions as an improving landlord. The problem is that though the traveller appears to be observing the realities of Irish life he is doing so through the lens of obdurate *a priori* assumptions:

> The state of Ireland had latterly become a topic of the press in both countries [...] The strange phenomenon of a land teeming with abundance, yet overrun by a starving population, had just then begun to attract notice; and theories were rife in accounting for that singular and anomalous social condition [...] Sir Marmaduke was well versed in these popular writings [...] and so firmly was he persuaded that his knowledge of the subject was perfect, that he became actually impatient until he had reached the country, and commenced the great scheme of regeneration and civilization [...] Like most theorists, no speculative difficulty was great enough to deter; no practical obstacle was so small as not to affright him.[6]

Sir Marmaduke believes the Irish to be ignorant, superstitious, and lazy. In order to bring about his 'Irish reformation'[7] – a phrase tellingly used about his efforts – he reduces rents and increases wages, and provides schools, medical help and better houses. The narrative warns the reader in a more general analysis, however, that comparisons between the husbandry of landlords and the recalcitrance of Irish tenants conceal a more exploitative reality:

> If, then, the eye ranged over a district poverty-struck and starving peasantry [...] let the glance but turn to the [well-cultivated] farm around the Lodge [...] and the astounding lesson seemed to say: 'Here is an object for imitation. Look at yonder wheat; see that clover, and the meadow beyond it. They could all do likewise [...] but yet ignorance and obstinacy are incurable. They will not be taught'. [...] Yet what was the real cause? [...] Duty-labour calls the poor man from the humble care of his own farm to come, with his whole house, and toil upon the rich man's fields [...] Duty-labour is the type of slavery that hardens the heart [... until] the wretched man grows reckless of his life, while his vengeance yearns for that of his taskmaster.[8]

When it comes to describing Sir Marmaduke's particular interactions with his own tenants, however, the novel lapses into the use of stereotypes. One morning Sir Marmaduke reviews his lack of progress and 'unhesitatingly ascribed to the prejudices

---

6 Charles Lever, *The O'Donoghue: a tale of fifty years ago*, 2 vols (Boston, 1899), i, 16–17.
7 Ibid., i, 138.   **8** Ibid., i, 140.

of the peasantry what with more justice might have been charged against his own unskilfulness'.[9] The better tenants had refused to become involved in what the narrative describes as his worthless schemes for improvement while the worse ones 'became converts to any doctrine or class of opinion which promised an easy life and a rich man's favour'.[10] One woman wants the new slates on her roof replaced with a thatch; a man returns the key to the shop he has been given as everyone wants credit; and another man, with a swollen face, reports that he has had to destroy the bees Sir Marmaduke gave him, though it emerges that he had placed the beehive within his house.

None of this though is intended as an argument for the return of an older order, quite the contrary. Though one character praises the former rule of the O'Donoghues it is because there was always a keg of spirits in the servants' hall and the ham was boiled in sherry wine: '"Them was the raal improvements."'[11] And Sir Marmaduke's earnest interaction with the peasantry can be compared with that of the careless O'Donoghue who is seen laughing at a window when beggars arrive at his castle for the morning distribution of alms.

Two ironies appear to attend the novel's critique of English observation and improvement. The first is that the novel's own authority for the critique is that Lever himself has been 'wandering through the south of Ireland' and concocting his own theories about Irish character.[12]

There is another minor curiosity here. Lever's 1872 preface to the novel recalls his 1844 summer tour of southern Ireland when he had visited Glengariff and Glenflesk.[13] He recalls meeting a poor old man and being told later that his son, Tim O'Donoghue, was now a prosperous attorney in Tralee – an odd mixture of the Wordsworthian and the mercantile. This decides him on using the location and name O'Donoghue in the novel that was taking shape in his mind.[14] However, this smacks of disingenuousness because Lever uses the name for a character who was that rarest of survivals, an old Irish chieftain, and one from that very area. Few of them had survived the Elizabethan, Cromwellian and Williamite eras. One of those who had done so, however, was The O'Donoghue of the Glens, Lord of Glenflesk, a cadet branch of the extinct O'Donoghue Mór.[15]

The second apparent irony concerning Lever's satiric view of English improvements is that of course Sir Marmaduke's schemes for his land are in themselves perfectly good ones, though perhaps inexpertly introduced, and are not necessarily

---

9 Ibid., i, 158. **10** Ibid., i, 159. **11** Ibid., i, 10. **12** Ibid., i, vii. **13** Stevenson, *Dr Quicksilver*, pp 129–30. **14** Lever, *The O'Donoghue*, i, pp vii; x. **15** In spite of being on the losing side the family had managed to retain its lands throughout most of the conflicts of the sixteenth and seventeenth centuries and, indeed, the chieftaincy is still extant today. Ironically, the then holder of the title would become prominent in politics shortly after Lever had written his novel. Daniel, The O'Donoghue of the Glens (1833–89) was a Member of Parliament between 1857 and 1885 and for a time in the early 1860s, when he was known by the soubriquet, The Young Chieftain, it seemed likely that he might even accede to the leadership of the constitutional nationalist movement.

the 'absurd efforts' of the novel's appraisal.[16] More generally, there is a persistent problem of knowledge, communication and judgement within the novel, a work whose ambition is to find new channels for the communication of knowledge. Sir Marmaduke finds the peasants 'uncommunicative and shy [...] Their very idiom required translating, and he could not advance without an interpreter'.[17] In turn they consider him 'a mere simpleton' in his ideas for improvements and therefore they do not engage with him.[18]

The attack on Sir Marmaduke's home, the Lodge, to take another example, is a locus for great hermeneutic dispute. After the attack is repelled almost all aspects of it, including the number and disposition of the attackers involved, become disputed. The more the facts are questioned the more individuals become certain of their own particular accounts, 'circumstances dubious a moment before, were then suddenly remembered and sworn to'.[19] The O'Donoghue's Scottish brother-in-law, Sir Archy is the only one who seems alert to the complexities of meaning. When the O'Donoghue's niece Kate shows him the evil land agent Hemsworth's letter to her offering help for the O'Donoghue's elder son Mark, Sir Archy notes that '[s]tatements seemingly clear and open, were in reality confused and vague'.[20]

The problem with knowledge and communication in the novel affects more than the relationships between the characters. It also impinges on the relationship between narrator and reader and the latter's trust for the former's pronouncements. Time and again the narrator's analysis of what is happening and his moralising upon it, are in stark contrast to what appear to be the facts of the case. When Mark, in spite of his better interests, promises to remain by his father's side, the narrator's comments seem to presume that he has done the opposite: 'Mark mistook his selfishness for a feeling of independence; he thought indifference to others meant confidence in himself – and he was not the first who made the mistake'.[21]

When Kate returns to the castle from her continental education she is shocked by the poverty in which her family are living. The narrator considers that the worst aspect of poverty is that '[i]t is in the plastic facility with which the poor man shifts to meet the coming evil that the high principle of rectitude is sacrificed'.[22] This means that the worst aspect of poverty is the way in which it makes the individual sacrifice honour and principle. Yet, this is precisely the reverse of the case as far as The O'Donoghue and Mark are concerned. Their problem is that they refuse to adjust their views of themselves and their family honour to take account of their diminished circumstances. Even the O'Donoghue's death occasions an unsustainable response from the narrator. A short time before he had behaved so badly that the ever loyal Kate, 'stung by the old man's selfishness, spoke almost angrily'.[23] And yet when he does die the narrator goes into unqualified eulogy mode: 'The courage that withstood every assault of evil fortune – every calamity which poverty and

16 Lever, The O'Donoghue, i, 164.   17 Ibid., i, 42.   18 Ibid., i, 43.   19 Ibid., i, 111.
20 Ibid., ii, 36.   21 Ibid., i, 130.   22 Ibid., i, 181.   23 Ibid., i, 159.

distress can bring down – failed at last. The strong heart was broken, – the O'Donoghue was dead'.[24]

All of this is part of a general critique of traditional forms of perception and judgment of Ireland. The practice of pronouncements upon Ireland, even by the narrator of Lever's own novel, is no longer to be trusted. But what better form of communication can be found for the relationship between England and Ireland? *The O'Donoghue* experiments with two options, both of them related to the land. The first is the notion of nature, though more than in a simply Wordsworthian sense. The second is the idea of chivalry.

Nature is an important theme in the earlier part of the novel. In some ways it is determinant of human experience. The valley of Glenflesk seems both 'wild and picturesque'[25] and noticeably bereft of human beings:

> In vain the eye ranges to catch sight of one human being, save that dark speck be such which crowns the cliff, and stands out from the clear sky behind. Yes, it is a child watching the goats that are browsing along the mountain, and as you look, the swooping mist has hidden him from your view.

Because of his isolation, his thoughts must be 'sad and melancholy,' his dreams 'mournful' and his superstitions 'fearful,' shaping the clouds so that they seem 'things of life and substance'.[26] Sybella Travers, daughter of Sir Marmaduke, is the closest character in the novel to a Wordsworthian:

> the tall and peaked mountains lost in the white clouds, the waving forest with its many a tangled path [. . .] realized many a poetic dream of her childhood, and, she felt that visionary happiness which serenity of mind, united to the warm imagination of early life, alone can bestow.[27]

As for the peasants she thinks they seem grateful and affectionate: 'All appealed to her mind with a very different force from what they addressed themselves with to her father's'. She liked their 'figurative eloquence,' their 'fervour of fancy she had believed an attribute of highly wrought temperaments only she found here amid poverty and privation'.[28] And yet though she fantasizes about the good nature of the peasantry she is changed neither by them nor by nature. Indeed, she assumes that nature exists for her own personal consumption: 'It was a fairy existence to live thus secluded in that lonely valley, where the flowers seemed to blossom for them alone'.[29]

Later the Lodge is transformed to fully utilize its position in a location of natural beauty and thus to enhance its function of providing domestic pleasure:

> The ample windows, thrown open to the ground, displayed a suite of apartments furnished with all that taste and luxury could suggest, – the walls

24 Ibid., i, 161.   **25** Ibid., i, 1.   **26** Ibid., i, 2.   **27** Ibid., i, 42.   **28** Ibid., i, 43.   **29** Ibid., i, 42.

ornamented by pictures, and the panels of both doors and window-shutters formed of plate glass, reflecting the mountain scenery in every variety of light and shadow. The rarest flowers, the most costly shrubs, brought from long distances at great risk and price, were here assembled to add their beauties to a scene where nature had already been so lavish.[30]

The locals, who see the land in terms of food production, are generally perplexed by the Traverses' admiration for the least fertile parts of the valley:

'whenever we passed a little potato garden, or a lock of oats, it was always, "God be good to us! But they're mighty poor hereabouts"; but when we got into the raal wild part of the glen, with divil a house nor a human being near us, sorrow word out of their mouths but "fine! beautiful! elegant!"'[31]

Nonetheless, their relationship with nature is also the way in which the locals situate themselves and their experience, particularly through their contemplation of art. When Herbert, The O'Donoghue's younger son, reads passages from Homer to a nine-year-old boy the child likens the sound of one to 'the cry of the big stag-hound at Carrignacurra' and of another to 'the way the thunder comes down the glen'[32] and when a local man is ushered into Sir Marmaduke he notices a painting on the wall of a local scene and insists on identifying himself with a figure in it, 'ay, there's a fellow going up – musha that's me'.[33]

Nature plays a role in a whole variety of ways in the lives of the principal characters. For Mark nature is the occasion of an epiphany in his progress from reckless youth to mature adult:

In tranquil spendour the planets shone on, as though to say, the higher destiny is rather to display an eternal brightness than the brilliancy of momentary splendor, however glittering its wide career [...] The stars looked down, like eyes, into his very soul, and he felt as if he could unburden his whole heart of its weary load, and make a confidence with heaven [...] '*They* point ever downwards,' said he to himself, as he watched the bright streak of the falling stars, and moralized on their likeness to man's destiny.[34]

Immediately afterwards he sees supporters of rebellion marching silently through the countryside. The transcendent moment has an immediate political corollary.

Kate uses nature for didactic purposes. Lecturing the Traverses about her nationalist beliefs she dramatically illustrates her point that life is full of surprises by drawing their attention to the evening landscape: '"That mountain peak was dark but a moment back; and now, see the blazing fire that has burst forth upon it."'[35] Finally,

30 Ibid., ii, 29.   **31** Ibid., i, 13.   **32** Ibid., i, 54.   **33** Ibid., i, 115.   **34** Ibid., i, 131.   **35** Ibid., i, 245.

Mark's climb to the top of a mountain and ecstasy when he sees the arriving French fleet is accompanied by the pathetic fallacy of a storm which mirrors his climatic emotions. He and his brother Herbert struggle up the mountain, in spite of dangerous precipices and gullies.

> If at such times as this the eye ranges not over the leagues of coast and sea, long winding valleys and wide plains, the prophetic spirit fostered by such agencies looks out in life, and images of the future flit past in cloudy shapes and changing forms. There, see the back mass that slowly moves along, and seems to beckon us with giant arms. You'd not reject an augury so plain.[36]

Mark finally reaches the summit. "'As if he had left his load of care with the nether world, his light and bounding movement, and his joyous voice, spoke of a heart which, throwing off its weight of sorrow, revelled once more in youthful ecstasy,'"[37] and he speaks of "'a secret whispering at my heart'"[38] that his time of disaster is over and the turning point of his life has come.

It is though with the language of chivalry, a code of behaviour reliant on a hierarchical structure of social relations that derives ultimately from possession of land, that the novel attempts to communicate a sympathetic understanding to an English audience of an Irish rebel such as Mark O'Donoghue, with whom that audience might normally have been disinclined to identify. The novel is a Bildungsroman of Mark's development from ill disciplined youth to disciplined maturity:[39]

> His course was rather to throw passion and impulse into the same scale with circumstances, and take his chance in the result. He had little power of anticipation, nor was his a mind that could calmly array facts before it, and draw the inference from them.[40]

And yet by the end he has learned those very skills. Indeed, Lever attempts to make the novel a new mode of communication between Irish experience and an English audience in terms of the presentation of Mark, heir to The O'Donoghue name, within a tradition of chivalry with which an English Victorian audience might identify.

Of course the utilitarian Sir Marmaduke cannot understand 'the alliance between pride and poverty – between the reverence for ancestry and an utter indifference to the present' which he detects in The O'Donoghue and his position as a chieftain.[41] The latter feels that Sir Marmaduke has no sympathy for relationships based on a connection with the land and intends "'to banish the old lords of the soil'".[42] The O'Donoghue's demeanour is truly aristocratic, in an uncompromising but rather

---

36 Ibid., ii, 99.   **37** Ibid., ii, 100.   **38** Ibid., ii, 101.   **39** Haddelsey, *Charles Lever*, p. 60.
40 Lever, *The O'Donoghue*, ii, 36.   **41** Ibid., i, 119.   **42** Ibid., i, 128.

useless sense, inasmuch as when he receives Kate's inheritance his instinct is not to pay off his debts but to spend more as '[t]he very act of succumbing [by paying debtors] smacked of defeat'.[43] The serious issues concerning the family, its position and future, devolve therefore on his son Mark.

Lever attempts to show how Mark O'Donoghue struggles through personal diffi-culties towards a sense of chivalrous honour which, no matter how its political ends differ from those of an English audience, can nonetheless be admired by that audi-ence. Lever shows this as a complex issue, touching matters of personal character, class and politics.

Mark's notion of self-identity is rooted in his family's connection with their ancestral lands. During his first appearance in the novel he remarks of his family's position that '"[c]onfiscation cannot take away a right"'.[44] Ironically, however, the O'Donoghues have not had their lands confiscated in the manner of so many Irish chieftains: they have lost them due to importunity. This though is not a point that Mark, seeing himself as a representative of an aristocracy based on a connection with the land, can afford to recall.

At times his resentment can be haughtily aristocratic. When Frederick Travers, Sir Marmaduke's son, who has made the unforgivable error of mistaking Mark for a game keeper, compliments Herbert's courage in saving Sybella from a flood, Mark retorts '"It is not out custom here to listen to compliments on our courage. We are O'Donoghues"'.[45] His jealously over Frederick's attentions to Kate also leads to an aristocratic incandescence:

> 'That fellow's gay jacket and plumed hat are dearer to her woman's heart than the rude devotion of such as I am. Curses be on them! they carry persecu-tion through everything – house, home, country, rank, wealth, station – ay, the very affection of our kindred they grudge us. Was slavery ever like this?'[46]

Though his resentments grow from his sundered relationship with the land, Mark's commitment to rebellion and revolution as a matter of honour and chivalry is, ironically, learned from Frederick Travers, a British officer and his rival in love and enemy in politics. His chivalry is thus subtly presented as an English quality which he has acquired. When Frederick warns him that the government knows of his correspondence with the leaders of the United Irishmen, he accuses Frederick of wishing 'to humble me by an obligation'.[47] Frederick's reaction is to apologise to Mark for his behaviour to him when they first met. Mark '"could better have looked on Travers wounded and bleeding than have seen him thus elevated above himself by temper and manly candour"'.[48] Frederick goes on to recognise Mark's bravery but also to suggest that he redirect it, '"the courage that would seem madness in a hope-less cause will win you fame and honour where the prospects are fairer"'.[49] Mark

43 Ibid., i, 242. **44** Ibid., i, 5. **45** Ibid., i, 200. **46** Ibid., i, 206. **47** Ibid., ii, 9. **48** Ibid., ii, 10. **49** Ibid., ii, 10.

should go to India where war has all the features of chivalry, where personal daring and heroism are surer roads to distinction than influence and patronage.[50] Mark responds with a grudging recognition of all that Frederick has done for him but says he cannot go to India as it would involve wearing the same epaulette Travers does and this would be a disgrace to him. However, his final parting from Frederick, when the latter, in a move surely at odds with his own loyalties, lets him escape from his custody, is more fulsome, "'Few, either friends or foes, have done me the services that you have'".[51]

The novel ends with a vignette set in 1815 on the conclusion of the Revolutionary and Napoleonic wars. A couple, identified as foreign, visit the valley of Glenflesk. They meet a local woman who recognizes them as Mark and Kate, who had left Ireland after the failed French landing at Bantry Bay. She refuses their money, because "'it isn't by a purse full of gold you'll ever make up for desarting the cause of ould Ireland'".[52] The political situation of Ireland thus remains properly contentious. But then the novel has never sought directly to elicit its readers' sympathies for the cause of rebellion; far from it. What it has done is to evoke respect for Mark as an honourable and chivalrous individual, albeit one in some way representative or typical of Ireland. Lever has sought to establish what he would undoubtedly have considered a new and metapolitical form of communication of understanding and respect between England and Ireland. What the novel has argued for is that, allowing for a different political context and setting aside all the superficial marks of French foreignness about him, Mark O'Donoghue, schooled by Frederick Tavers, has become something akin to an English gentleman. Irish land, for all the antagonism it creates, can thus sustain an acceptably English mode of being, according to Lever.

---

50 Ibid., ii, 11.   51 Ibid., ii, 149.   52 Ibid., ii, 165.

Mounds of rubbish and the shades of extinct churches: perceptions of archaeological field monuments in nineteenth-century Ireland[1]

MÁIRÍN NÍ CHEALLAIGH

In nineteenth-century Ireland as elsewhere, the study of the remains of the past underwent a metamorphosis that saw antiquarians abandoning flights of speculative imagination in favour of the more empirical and phenomenologically-based approaches of the natural sciences. While Irish remains were shaped by the local specifics of climate and topography as well as by the island's history, the increasingly 'scientific' vision of the Irish past was part of broader European political and educational trends that culminated in the establishment of archaeology as a discipline. Those who engaged in literate discourses regarding the nature of the Irish past focused more and more closely on the stones, wood and earthen banks that marked the sites of past human activity within the landscape. This discourse was further predicated on specialized historical knowledge of 'lost' or decayed sites, and privileged this form of literate and empirical knowledge over the co-existing and sometimes competing visions of the past held by many other members of nineteenth-century Irish society.

Alternative perceptions of monuments varied according to the social, cultural and economic situation of the individual visitor, and according to often interacting sets of literate and orally transmitted beliefs. While antiquarians may have privileged archaeological remains as evidence of past human societies, monuments were also locked into dense networks of narratives that included popular histories, local and tourist experiences of particular places, supernatural lore, visitor expectations and wider economies. The role of such narratives in defining identities and the nature of communities and social groups meant that archaeological monuments were perceived in a variety of ways that often differed significantly from antiquarian approaches. These different ways of seeing and understanding archaeological monuments were implicated in the attribution of 'value' and meaning to sites within their

1 This paper and the research upon which it is based were facilitated by an IRCHSS Government of Ireland Postgraduate Research Scholarship. The work was further rendered possible by the research facilities made available to me in my capacity as Postgraduate Research Scholar at the Humanities Institute of Ireland, UCD.

wider landscape settings. In this paper, I examine some of the lenses of perception through which archaeological monuments were viewed, including antiquarian modes of vision, which, since the nineteenth century, have come to dominate modern popular understandings of the past.

SEEING ANTIQUARIAN SITES – WILLIAM WAKEMAN IN FERMANAGH

In the early 1880s, William Wakeman, antiquarian and artist, published a paper in the *Journal of the Royal Society of Antiquaries* on the subject of 'several rock scribings and rock markings, found in the north-west of Ireland, with suggestions for their classification'.[2] Rather than launching immediately into an account of these features, and of the classificatory system that might be used in their description, he instead began his paper with a portrait of the beauties of Co. Fermanagh, that might even today cause a glow of pleasure in the breasts of the Northern Irish Tourist Board. He asserted that the county had not 'hitherto received that attention from artists, antiquaries, geologists or botanists, which its varied treasures of the past, or of the present, [could] legitimately claim'[3] and argued that perhaps nowhere else in Ireland and the United Kingdom was there 'a richer quarry of geological, prehistoric, and even of medieval monument'. The list of sites that followed these statements included round towers, the sixth-century church of St Molaise, abbey churches including one dated by a 'Lombardic' inscription, the ecclesiastical sites of Inishmacsaint, Inishkeen, and Cleenish, stone circles and 'kindred monuments', various caves which were thought to have been ancient dwellings, and 'cromleacs' or prehistoric tombs. Only after completing this list and commenting on various prominent antiquarian debates associated with some of the monument-types listed did he finally turn to consider the topic of his paper, namely a consideration of the nature of ogham writing.

Although it might appear at first glance that Wakeman's encomium on the beauties of Fermanagh was simply a tangential start to a consideration of a highly specialized antiquarian topic, it is arguable that it also demonstrates the context in which such studies were undertaken in nineteenth-century Ireland. Not only did his account allow Wakeman to demonstrate his knowledge of contemporary archaeological debates to his fellow antiquarians, it also illustrated the close ties between tourist experiences of the Irish landscape, and the presence of antiquities within that landscape. His positioning of Fermanagh and its surviving archaeological sites within a wider British context also demonstrated the international nature of antiquarian and scholarly experiences.[4] His expressions of pride in these can, moreover, be linked to

2 William F. Wakeman, 'On several sepulchral scribings and rock markings, found in the north-west of Ireland, with suggestions for classification', *Journal of the Royal Society of Antiquaries of Ireland*, 15 (1879–82), 538–60. 3 Ibid., p. 538. 4 See for example Mairéad Ashe Fitzgerald, *Thomas Johnson Westropp (1869–1922): an Irish antiquary*, Seandálaíocht, Monograph 1 (Dublin, 2000), pp 57–65; Eve Patten, *Samuel Ferguson and the culture of nineteenth-century Ireland* (Dublin, 2004), p. 161.

the coincident rise in nationalist and patriotic sentiments, and the application of romantic landscape aesthetics to the wider Irish landscape.

More importantly, Wakeman's account also demonstrated a particular attitude towards the landscape that manifested itself in his recommendation of particular sites as deserving of the attention of visitors. These sites were united by their association with the remains of past human actions through which they were held to embody particular points on linear historical trajectories. As a group, they created a network of places, which (according to Wakeman) made Co. Fermanagh a place worth visiting. It should also be noted that Wakeman was presenting an image of Fermanagh that was not necessarily aimed at local people, who were likely to have already been familiar with the sites and the landscape in which they were set. His list and his assertion that Fermanagh was not sufficiently known to a wider world, indicate that his account was aimed at people travelling to or through the county from outside its borders. Such visitors would, he expected, replicate his vision of the county by seeking out and viewing with their own eyes the sequence of sites listed. Moreover, his confident listing of sites indicated a belief in his own ability to predict and identify what would interest other antiquarians. Writing in his capacity as both an antiquarian and an artist, he articulated a particular vision of Co. Fermanagh that privileged the remains of the past over other possible attractions. In a nineteenth-century context, this vision was given precedence over understandings that promoted particular areas of rich and well-husbanded land, notable houses of local aristocrats, mineral springs, areas of picturesque beauty and a variety of other natural and manmade features.

SEEING THE PAST IN THE RUINS OF THE PRESENT: RECOGNIZING SHADES OF EXTINCT CHURCHES

In his list of archaeological attractions, however, Wakeman didn't include a detailed inventory of what *exactly* visitors to those places might be expected to see when and if they got there. He included no enumeration of structures, descriptions of banks, or references to architectural details in his list, perhaps because such details were redundant. He was, after all, writing for a readership comprised of his antiquarian peers, and on a topic ostensibly only slightly related to the beauties of Fermanagh. Other antiquarians, it might be assumed, would presumably have had at least a general idea of the type of remains that would be likely to survive at such sites. His attitude implied that they would also be capable of recognizing those remains even where they had been eroded and blurred by the passage of centuries and the workings of what the Reverend Lukis some twenty years earlier had termed 'the ravages of time, and the destructive hands of man'.[5]

5 W. C. Lukis, 'Observations in reference to Mr. M. [*sic*] Du Noyer's Paper "On Cromleacs near Tramore"' in *Journal of the Royal Society of Antiquaries of Ireland*, 8 (1864–66), 494.

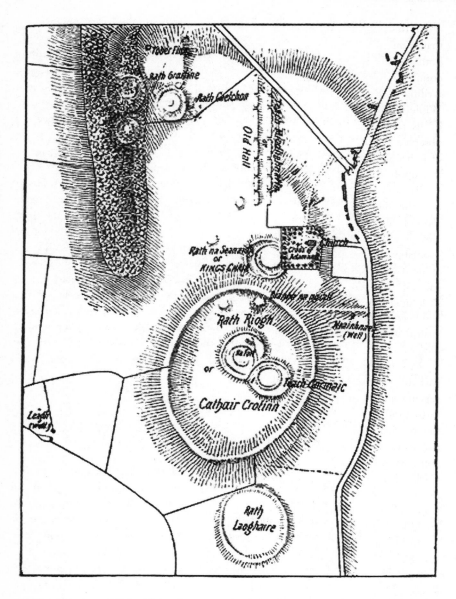

1 'General plan of the earthen remains on the Hill of Tara'. From W.G. Wood-Martin,
Pagan Ireland: an archaeological sketch. A handbook of pre-Christian antiquities
(Longmans, Green, and Co., 1895), fig. 35, facing p. 202.

In this respect, perceptions of antiquarian visitors to Fermanagh, and to the sites that in antiquarian terms rendered Fermanagh visible, were likely to have differed – both literally and metaphorically – from those of other visitors and many of the county's inhabitants. This distinction had already been articulated by William Wilde, writing in 1850 of tourist visits to the famous royal site of Tara in Co. Meath (fig. 1). While visitors were, presumably, drawn to the site by its historical significance, and by its prominent position in evocations of a glorious national past,[6] Wilde had observed that 'casual visitors', as opposed to those with a more specialized awareness of archaeological remains, often 'spen[t] an hour at Tara', and some read the commentary upon it, and [then] acknowledge[d] that they [were] none the wiser'.[7]

Part of the reason for their confusion was that they were disconcerted by the fact that the site was comprised of a physically unimpressive 'collection of earthen mounds and grassy undulations, a few-time worn stones, and an old churchyard crowning the top of rather an unpicturesque hill'.[8] While historical accounts of Tara – notably George Petrie's magisterial study, which was published in the *Transactions of the Royal Irish Academy* in 1839[9] – contained references to banqueting halls and palaces, the casual visitor to the site could not relate the physical remains of these structures to the banks and hollows before them. In practice, without having eyes that had been trained, in the words of Wilde, to perceive 'the forms of ancient remains,'[10] visitors were in many cases unlikely to be able to directly relate historical or archaeological narratives to surviving landscape features.

In some instances this was hardly surprising, as the process of identification of particular features was frequently based on their comparison with descriptions of varying quality in early medieval historical sources.[11] This process was fraught with further difficulties, not least because the descriptions did not necessarily reflect either the 'original' functions or the nature of the surviving features that were visible at archaeological sites. In this context, many of the identifications were based on a combination of guesswork and a somewhat beleaguered faith in the accuracy of Gaelic manuscript sources and their applicability to both Irish history and to the remains of the ancient Irish past.[12] In light of the fact that links drawn between narratives and features were sometimes erroneous, seeing sites through antiquarian eyes could lead to the perception of things that were literally not there.

In the case of Tara, for many of those visitors who left the site none-the-wiser, it was likely that the gap between popular narratives regarding the site and what

6 See, for example, Mairéad Carew, *Tara and the Ark of the Covenant: a search for the Ark of the Covenant by British-Israelites on the Hill of Tara (1899–1902)*, (Dublin, 2003). **7** William R. Wilde, *The beauties of the Boyne, and its tributary, the Blackwater*, second edition, enlarged (Dublin, 1850), p. 121. **8** Ibid. **9** George Petrie, 'On the history and antiquities of Tara Hill' in *Transactions of the Royal Irish Academy*, 18 (1839), 25–232. **10** Wilde, *The beauties of the Boyne*, n. 7, p. 121. **11** Conor Newman, 'Tara Project' in *Discovery Programme Reports: 1. Project Results 1992* (Dublin, 1993), p. 70. **12** Michael Herity (ed.), *Ordnance Survey letters Meath: letters containing information relative to the antiquities of the County of Meath collected during the progress of the Ordnance Survey in 1836* (Dublin, 2001), p. 79.

remained in the field was too great to allow unified visions of the past to animate physical features. Wilde was probably correct in arguing that the relative unfamiliarity of the historical narratives, the strange names, the alien practices and structures of Tara meant that many visitors were unsure of what they were supposed to see in the first place. This confusion was probably not confined to the perception of unfamiliar prehistoric or early medieval sites, but was also likely to have been experienced by the average literate visitor when faced with sites that were, in theory, more accessible. For example, liturgical and social changes over the centuries had de-familiarized the spatial organization and various features of ecclesiastical sites such as those listed by Wakeman. They were as a result difficult to relate to contemporary understandings of what Christian sites looked like, and how they worked.

This meant that visitors to such sites would not necessarily be capable of 'recon-struct[ing] from authentic data the dilapidated [medieval] pile, and call[ing] up before the minds eye the manners and everyday occupations of its quondam inmates'.[13] Nor is it likely that they would have been able to identify the barely visible traces that were often all that survived of prehistoric sites, or the shadowy remains of what the Revd William Reeves termed the 'shades' of 'extinct' churches.[14] It is instead more likely that when they looked at sites such as these, they saw, as at Tara, only banks, mounds and ditches, shorn of any framework that would allow them to become the foundations from which mental reconstructions of long-demolished structures could be projected (fig. 2).

ALTERNATIVE VISIONS AND INDIFFERENCE TOWARDS HISTORICAL NARRATIVES

Archaeological sites that were not filtered through antiquarian visions were likely to have been experienced and perceived as elements of landscapes that were constructed and represented through the conventions of contemporary landscape aesthetics. Through such perceptions, monuments were less likely to have stood out in imag-ined topographies as singular, spatially discrete and sharply defined places in which specified past human activities had taken place. Many archaeological remains, partic-ularly those that were comprised of earthen mounds and banks, or that survived only in very fragmentary forms, may have been subsumed into wider landscapes comprised of a range of natural and manmade features of varying dates. They would have been qualitatively undistinguished from walls, rock outcrops, plough-headlands, eskers, field-drains or tree-clumps, and subject to the same forms of treatment. Indeed, where the remains of antiquities were 'difficult to distinguish' they, like other landscape features, could be removed.[15]

13 James Graves, 'Ancient street architecture in Kilkenny', in *Journal of the Royal Society of Antiquaries of Ireland*, 1 (1849–51), 41. **14** William Reeves, *Memoir of the church of St Duilech, in the diocese of Dublin; commonly called 'Saint Doulagh's': containing a paper read before the Royal Irish Academy, on Monday, April 11, 1859* (Dublin, 1859), p. 5. **15** Sara Champion and Gabriel

2 'Cemetery on the Hill of Usnagh (Ord. Map of Westmeath, Sheet 24)'. From Samuel Ferguson, 'On the Ancient Cemeteries at Rathcroghan and elsewhere in Ireland (as affecting the Question of the Site of the Cemetery at Taltin)' in *Proceedings of the Royal Irish Academy* vol. 15 (vol. I, Ser. II, Polite Literature and Antiquities), [1879?], p. 119.

This was particularly the case where the landscape aesthetics involved in the perception of sites were those of the improving landowner or holder. In such cases, the value of well-cultivated and profitable lands superseded either antiquarian visions or pictorially derived perceptions of picturesque scenery. For those familiar with the structures of rural landscapes and indifferent to the claims of historical or aesthetic narratives, archaeological remains were just another series of more or less decrepit traces of past human activities in contemporary worked landscapes. According to such understandings, Wakeman's list of sites worth visiting was more-or-less meaningless, except as a way of identifying unsympathetically viewed 'old' places characterized in a way that was at odds with the forces of progress and change.

The privileging of an awareness of the wider settings (fig. 3), rather than the archaeological remains of sites did not, however, lead visitors to automatically discount the potential truth of narratives told of those sites. Nor did it preclude the use of sites, no matter how invisible or unimpressive to the untrained eye, as guarantors of the truth of those narratives, whether historical or popular. For example, the

Cooney, 'Naming the places, naming the stones' in Amy Gazin-Schwartz and Cornelius Holtorf (eds), *Archaeology and folklore* (London and New York, 1999), p. 206.

3 'Site of Clonenagh, Queen's County. Engraved by Mrs. Hillard. Drawn by Henry O'Neill'. Frontispiece of John O'Hanlon's *Lives of the Irish Saints, with Special Festivals, and the Commemorations of Holy Persons, compiled from Calendars, Martyrologies and Various Sources, relating to The Ancient Church History of Ireland,* vol. II (James Duffy & Sons; Burns, Oates, and Co.; The Catholic Publishing Society, n.d.).

author of a 'Romance of Irish History' published in 1846,[16] was still prepared to accept that Glendalough in Co. Wicklow had originally been the location of 'splendid churches, [and] many religious edifices'. This was despite the fact that, at the time of writing, the author considered their remains to have been 'an undistinguished heap of ruins' rather than a potential source of information that could lead to a better understanding of the site or of past religious practice.

The use of sites in order to confirm the accuracy and 'truth' of narratives that were in many cases unrelated to the way in which those sites had been used in the past was not confined to literate imaginings. Orally transmitted and traditional tales also featured accounts of archaeological monuments as a way of emphasizing the 'truthfulness' of narratives. By relating stories to physical remains as they survived in the present, the stories were reinforced while the sites gained additional importance as arenas of human or supernatural actions.[17] This, while not reflecting the empirical

16 Anon., 'Romance of Irish history – No. 1: The Tanist's Daughter (by the author of Tales of Irish Life)' in the *Irish National Magazine and Weekly Journal of Literature, Science and Art,* 1 (1846), 6.   17 Philip Moore, 'Giants' graves. No. I' in *Journal of the Royal Society of Antiquaries of Ireland,* 1 (1849–51), 13; Patrick Cody, 'Folklore. No. II' in *Journal of the Royal Society of*

emphasis of archaeological visions, used sites to similar effect. In some instances, there was also a similar emphasis on a more spatially defined awareness of sites. The description of specific elements of archaeological sites in traditional stories, while not predicated on the need for their scientific classification, may nonetheless have created a heightened awareness of those elements.[18] Where these different ways of seeing sites overlapped, monuments were likely to be accorded a considerable degree of protection, and visitors were likely to be drawn from the ranks of those conversant with both sets of understandings. On the other hand, where the elements considered significant by archaeologists or tradition-bearers differed, the resulting mutual incomprehension might (like the application of wider landscape aesthetics to sites) result in the destruction of all, or of parts of monuments.[19]

THE VALUE OF VEGETATION – THE 'WILD WOOD' AND MOUNDS OF RUBBISH

Given that perceptions of the significance and importance of monuments changed to reflect the beliefs of those who visited and viewed them, it is worth returning to a consideration of the nature of surviving remains in more detail. As indicated above, these varied considerably from the smoothly grassed sward of Tara's banks and ditches, to the surviving masonry walls of medieval buildings. Other sites were identifiable as crooked and displaced megaliths or as tangled and disturbed piles of masonry interspersed with nettles and vegetation (fig. 4). Many sites had been damaged or subjected to vigorous plant growth due to neglect and the fact that such structures were no longer actively curated by local people and communities, and no longer featured as important places in local narratives. In many instances, the heavily overgrown nature of many archaeological sites was the probable result of traditional beliefs that proposed them as points of contact with a supernatural otherworld. These beliefs generally precluded the removal of vegetation, or even the trimming of overgrown bushes associated with sites for fear of supernatural reprisals. Such beliefs were a common element of stories associated with early medieval ringforts and other earthen monuments. Prohibitions on vegetation removal and on interference of any sort with the remains of monuments meant that such sites often survived even where economic or agricultural considerations would otherwise have led to their removal.

Antiquaries, 2 (1852–53), 101.   **18** Moore, 'Giants' graves. No. I', n. 16; see also Patrick Cody, 'Primæval remains in the Mullinavat district' in *Journal of the Royal Society of Antiquaries*, 1 (1849–51), 385–8.   **19** Such divergent ways of seeing monuments may have led, for example, to the dismantling of surviving medieval church buildings by local populations in order to re-use carved stone fragments as headstones. This re-use, while based on a popular perception of the value of worked stone was anathema for many antiquarians, whose vision of archaeological remains required the retention of all structural remains in situ. For example, see Otway, Caesar, 'Paper on the ruined abbeys in the province of Connaught' in *Proceedings of the Royal Irish Academy*, 1 (1836–40), 210–11.

This, in concert with inevitable antiquarian exaggerations and romanticized perceptions of an artificially ancient land, may explain the fact that some foreign tourists in the nineteenth century remarked that Ireland was a land abnormally well-endowed with ruins.[20] Such observations may have reflected the strength of popular beliefs as well as the high visibility of many archaeological remains due to their heavily and paradoxically obscuring blankets of vegetation. In this context, it is interesting to consider that in the relatively deafforested Irish rural landscape of the nineteenth century, many overgrown sites appear to have functioned in a fashion analogous to the 'wild wood' of German and other European folktales.[21] They were places whose rampant vegetation signalled their role as places where 'protagonists g[o]t lost, me[t] unusual creatures, under[went] spells and transformations, and confront[ed] their destinies'.[22] Where overgrown early medieval ringforts, medieval buildings or prehistoric sites were located in the middle of fields, or on the edges of villages or towns, their uncut hedges and vegetation may have acted as counterpoints to tilled agricultural landscapes or to small-scale urban activity.[23] Indeed, a part of the value of heavily overgrown sites may have been that their very wildness enabled the crisper outlines and more regulated features of farmed and worked landscapes to be more clearly perceived.

However, the visual contrast between archaeological monuments – particularly more overgrown or fragmentary examples – and farmed, domesticated landscapes was not always perceived in a positive light. Accounts of the destruction of archaeological monuments were frequently recorded in learned journals and antiquarian publications throughout the nineteenth century. It is significant that in many instances interference with sites was often related to what might be seen as agricultural 'progress' and profit, involving the reclamation of land for tillage, the recovery of stones as building materials, and the removal of organic layers and archaeological deposits for spreading as manure.[24] It would appear that in many instances, individual farmers and landlords were unprepared to accept the implicit claims embedded within many traditional narratives that archaeological monuments were communal psychological and physical resources. They thus rejected the validity of the partial conversion of sites into monetary resources by communities acting according to traditional understandings. These included beliefs such as 'gold-dreaming', where

20 For example, Marietta Lloyd, *A trip to Ireland, giving an account of the voyage scenes and incidents on landing; also a graphic description of travel and sightseeing in Ireland, interspersed with historical legends and stories of her remarkable antiquities; including a romantic tour on the lakes of Killarney* (Chicago, 1893), p. 46.   21 Robert P. Harrison, *Forests: the shadow of civilization* (Chicago and London, 1992), p. 169.   22 Ibid.   23 Charles Smith, *The antient and present state of the county and city of Waterford, containing a natural, civil, ecclesiastical, historical and topographical account thereof,* second edition, with additions (Dublin, 1774), p. 352.   24 Gillian Smith, 'Spoilation of the past: the destruction of monuments and treasure-hunting in nineteenth-century Ireland' in *Peritia: Journal of the Medieval Academy of Ireland,* 13 (1999), 134–72.

protagonists dreamt three times of the location of treasure, and were thus given a limited form of supernatural permission to interfere with sites that were otherwise inviolable.[25]

Those who claimed individual or legal ownership over sites as landscape features also tacitly or explicitly denied the communal value of many archaeological sites as places in which social issues, such as marital infidelity or the acquisition of wealth, could be negotiated or examined without rupturing the social fabric.[26] Such individuals also denied the assertions of antiquarians such as Wakeman, who claimed archaeological sites as part of a 'national' heritage that was morally owned by an idealized Irish people whose claims were held to supersede those of individual members of society. Hence, farmers who viewed archaeological sites as integral elements of personally owned landscapes often felt no qualms about altering sites in pursuit of their own beliefs and understandings. This often involved the superimposition of visions of improved social status or productivity onto particular lands, which were then altered to correspond to those visions.

It was obviously easier to remove the physical traces of past human activity, and to ignore the existence of sites except as integral parts of contemporary landscapes, where archaeological remains (such as the ghostly traces of the medieval church at Balgriffin)[27] were barely visible. In such cases, farmers and local communities were being asked to take assertions of their existence and value on trust. As illustrated by the traditional mockery of antiquarian pursuits in popular culture,[28] however, this trust was not always available, nor freely offered. The failure of casual visitors to perceive the structures and features identified by Petrie and his Ordnance Survey colleagues at Tara, for example, may have led those visitors not only to question the truth of historical narratives, but also the accuracy of archaeological 'visions'. This may have had a knock-on effect on belief in the legitimacy of associated antiquarian demands that such sites be set aside from the processes and uses of contemporary agriculture and industry. In turn, this reduced the claims of the primacy of archaeological visions over competing claims and perceptions. Thus in those instances where the fundamental value of antiquarian visions was in question, the very confidence of assertions made by Wakeman and fellow antiquarians may have resulted in accelerated rates of monument destruction and the conversion of archaeological monuments to agricultural or infrastructural purposes.

This did not mean that a general belief in the truth and accuracy of antiquarian visions of particular sites automatically protected those sites from destruction or

25 William R. Wilde, *Irish popular superstitions* (Dublin & London, 1852), p. 98.   **26** Angela Bourke, *The burning of Bridget Cleary: a true story* (London, 1999), pp 37; 86.   **27** These traces were identified under grass-sward by the Revd William Reeves, *Memoir of the church of St Duilech,* p. 5.   **28** For example, Anon., 'The Antiquary', in *Dublin Penny Journal,* 3:3 (1834–35), 51; also Michael O'Flanagan (ed.), *Letters containing information relative to the antiquities of the county of Mayo collected during the progress of the Ordnance Survey in 1838,* vol. II (RIA typescript: Bray, 1927), p. 69.

dismantling. Incidences of destruction were particularly likely to occur where those engaged in destructive processes were ideologically opposed to the beliefs and understandings projected onto monuments by antiquarians or other 'protectionists'. The visible remains of sites could be removed by those acting upon sectarian differences,[29] or upon a 'modernist' hostility towards the 'superstitions' that led many local people to curate or preserve particular places in the landscape.[30] In other instances, the association between particular sites, painful historical episodes, and lost ancestral gentility could lead to their destruction. The logic behind this type of destruction was that as monuments embodied memories,[31] those memories could be obliterated by the destruction of the monuments in which they were contained. The resulting empty and memory-free space could then be filled by other structures more expressive of contemporary prosperity, such as the genteel terraces of prestigious housing developments.[32]

The formulation of what constituted visual evidence of an 'acceptable' prosperity often diverged considerably from the values that underpinned antiquarian visions of archaeological sites. Prosperity was frequently understood in terms of the moral and aesthetic values that had been articulated with respect to land improvement and agricultural and industrial development since the later eighteenth century onwards.[33] As a result, the overgrown and unworked remains of archaeological sites would appear to have been a source of discomfort to those who took pleasure in the straight boundaries, reclaimed fields[34] and intensified agricultural practices associated with and indicative of land improvement.

Such views manifested themselves even within the antiquarian community, and they may have been what led Thomas O'Conor of the Ordnance Survey to charac-

---

29 Michael O'Flanagan (ed.), *Letters containing information relative to the antiquities of the county of Down, collected during the progress of the Ordnance Survey in 1834* (RIA typescript: Bray, 1928), pp 3–4; also Robert M. Young, 'The Priory of St Columba, Newtownards, County Down' in *Journal of the Royal Society of Antiquaries of Ireland*, 15 (1879–82), 145.   **30** Wilde, *The beauties of the Boyne*, n. 25, p. 11.   **31** See Adrian Forty, 'Introduction', in Adrian Forty and Susanne Küchler (eds), *The art of forgetting* (Oxford and New York, 2001), p. 2.   **32** For example, James Hardiman on urban towerhouses in Galway city in his book on *The history of the town and county of Galway, from the earliest period to the present time, Embellished with several engravings, to which is added, a copious appendix, containing the principal charters and other original documents*, facsimile of 1820 edition (Galway, 1975), pp 312–13.   **33** For example, Charles Coote, *Statistical survey of the county of Armagh, with observations on the means of improvement; drawn up in the years 1802, and 1803, for the consideration, and under the direction of the Dublin Society* (Dublin, 1804); J. B. Ruane, 'Introduction' in A. W. Hutton (ed.), *Arthur Young, A tour in Ireland 1776–1779*, vol. I (reprint, Shannon, 1970), pp v–ix; Arthur Young, *A tour in Ireland; with general observations on the present state of that kingdom: made in the years 1776, 1777, and 1779, and brought down to the end of 1779* (Printed for T. Cadell; J. Dodsley, 1780).   **34** Charles Kickham, *For the old land: a tale of twenty years ago* (Dublin, 1886), p. 56; Charles E. Orser, 'Of dishes and drains: an archaeological perspective on Irish rural life in the famine era' in *New Hibernia Review*, 1:1 (1997), 120–35.

terise the piled remains of Friarstown priory in Killerig, Co. Carlow, as 'a mound of rubbish, covered over with grass'.[35] In his terse account of the site, he also included the information that it lay 'in Mr Douce's land, about fifty perches to northeast of Russelstown Road'. His positioning of the site within the local farming topography rather than within historical narratives can be seen as an indication of the relatively low symbolic significance that he accorded the priory's remains. As a result, it was effectively transformed from sacred site into prosaic parcel of land integrated into a contemporary farming landscape and bordered by a modern road that led elsewhere.

Somewhat ironically, this unofficial 'deconsecration' was also likely to have stemmed from O'Conor's antiquarian tendency to create an interdependent network of associations between identifiable architectural elements, the nature of ecclesiastical sites and the value attributable to those sites. The interdependence of these factors meant that a failure to identify architectural fragments or features could lead to the conclusion that the site in question was so 'damaged' as to be effectively valueless. O'Conor's identification of Friarstown Priory as 'rubbish' thus constitutes an acceptance and recognition of the site's physical state in the nineteenth-century present. By refusing to people the site with ghostly actors living out an imagined medieval existence, and by failing to perceive the priory's remains as clues to its 'original' state, he asserted the reality and irreversibility of Friarstown's decay. In this example, antiquarian perceptions, in a manner analogous to those of more casual visitors had failed to reconstruct the 'original' state of an almost obliterated site and had failed to repopulate it with its past occupants.

O'Conor's perception of Friarstown also resembled the understandings of those who saw analogous sites as an affront to a sensibility that equated beauty with utility.[36] According to this sensibility, the retention of ruined structures or inconvenient banks and ditches simply because they were places where things had happened in the past was unsympathetically viewed. According to such understandings, the 'cannibalizing' of antiquities for their materials and their consequent obliteration might be interpreted not as acts of random destruction stemming from ignorance, but as the rehabilitation of offensively 'dead' or decayed buildings into the realm of the 'living' local farming economy. If O'Conor had been asked to compile a list of Carlow sites that – like Wakeman's inventory of Fermanagh locations – were worth visiting for their antiquarian value, it is likely Friarstown Priory would not have been among the places listed.

35 Michael O'Flanagan (ed.), *Letters containing information relative to the antiquities of the county of Carlow collected during the progress of the Ordnance Survey in 1839* (RIA typescript: Bray, 1934), p. 8. **36** John Barrell, *The idea of landscape and the sense of place, 1730–1840* (Cambridge, 1972), p. 73.

CONCLUSION: DIVERGENT VISIONS AND FORTUITOUS
OVERLAPS IN THE PERCEPTION OF ARCHAEOLOGICAL
SITES IN NINETEENTH-CENTURY IRELAND

The vision of a landscape in which contemporary prosperity could be expressed
through the removal of traces of decay can be set against William Wakeman's evocation of Co. Fermanagh as a place defined through and by identifiable remains of past
human activities. In antiquarian perceptions, those features in the landscape which
spoke of contemporary activities, or of lives lived in the present were not necessarily
visible or were not actively regarded by eyes which had been trained to prioritize the
ghostly presence of extinct monuments. This is of course something of an exagger-
ation, as antiquarians, as much as any improving farmer or bearer of oral traditions,
were the products of the society in which they dwelt. Indeed, O'Conor's perception
of the Friarstown Priory as a pile of building rubble rather than the site of ecclesiastical activities indicates the degree to which the contemporary condition of
monuments might negatively impinge upon even the antiquarian consciousness.

Antiquarian perceptions, however, had a disproportionately large impact on the
treatment and understanding of surviving archaeological remains. This is clearly indicated by the fact that despite their inability to 'see' the past through those remains, a
wide range of people were nonetheless prepared to follow the itineraries set out by
Wakeman and others. They also remained willing to visit visually unintelligible sites
like Tara. In this way, the proposition that Fermanagh or other places in the Irish
landscape were primarily visible through the remains of the past became self-
fulfilling. People sought out those remains as observation points from which the past
could be observed, even if they couldn't themselves perceive it. It should be borne
in mind, however, that the burgeoning influence of archaeological understandings
and their official codification in later nineteenth-century protectionist legislation
probably had as much to do with cultural and political nationalism, as with a blanket
acceptance of the truth of archaeological visions. It is also likely that the wider social
prestige of antiquarianism[37] as well as fear of public condemnation united to dilute
the attractiveness of monument destruction as an articulation of the aesthetics of land
improvement. It is certainly the case that traditional prohibitions on the destruction
of archaeological monuments greatly facilitated the wider establishment of antiquarian modes of perception, as it was easier to train the eye to see the 'shades' of
churches and other lost structures where multiple and comparable examples survived
in the contemporary landscape. Antiquarian understandings, on the other hand,
tended to lead to the deconstruction of popular narratives, as they often required a
clear view of remains that could only be achieved by stripping sites of their protec-
tive vegetation.[38]

---

37 Philippa Levine, *The amateur and the professional: antiquarians, historians and archaeologists in Victorian England, 1836–1886* (Cambridge, 1986), pp 8–11; Bruce G. Trigger, *A history of archae-ological thought* (Cambridge, 1994), pp 14–15.   **38** For example, Public Works, Ireland, *Sixty-*

There may have been overlaps between various ways of understanding and seeing archaeological field monuments in nineteenth-century Ireland. At their extremes, however, divergences in vision led to radical differences in the ways in which those monuments were treated. The survival or otherwise of archaeological sites as places within the human landscape often depended on the translation of those ways of seeing into actions. This in turn could lead to the physical reconstruction of monuments in ways that reflected a belief in the primacy of their 'original' states, hence, for example, the re-erection of the fallen arch of one of the churches of Clonmacnois.[39] It could also lead to the translation of the very fabric of archaeological sites into the 'realities' of the contemporary present, as they were quarried and hauled away in response to the dictates of modernity or the aesthetics of prosperity.

ninth report of the Commissioners of Public Works in Ireland: with Appendices (Dublin, 1900–1), pp 15; 46.   **39** James Graves, 'Report of the receipts and expenditure of the works of repair and conservation at Clonmacnois and brief statement of what had been done', in *Journal of the Royal Society of Antiquaries of Ireland*, 8 (1864–66), pp 368–70.

Inside and outside the frame: landscape pictures and real debates in *The Untilled Field* (1903) and *The Lake* (1905)

MARY S. PIERSE

The titles of two books by George Moore, *The Untilled Field*[1] and *The Lake*,[2] convey visual images of countryside and suggest the material for landscape pictures. Moore even said of *The Lake*, 'it is my landscape book'.[3] For those familiar with the titles Moore had bestowed on his earlier books, ones like *Esther Waters, Evelyn Innes, Sister Teresa, Celibates,* and *A Drama in Muslin*, the choice of landscape connections must seem particularly noteworthy as it represents such a total departure from previous practice. The move appears all the more remarkable because the author, as the main promoter and interpreter of Impressionist painting in Britain, would have been perceived as favouring the uncertainties of Impressionism, with its evocative and ephemeral qualities, over the detailed and often didactic narrative nature of mid to late-Victorian landscape depictions. Moreover, it can be argued that linking the short story with landscape was not an obvious choice for the writer of fiction at the time, and definitely not one driven by popular demand. The combination of these factors – not to mention Moore's own political nature and leanings – raises the possibility, then, that the author has turned to landscape with a very definite purpose. This essay seeks to explore some of the varied vistas that are to be found in these two examples of George Moore's 'Irish' fiction. It will suggest that Moore aims to reclaim landscape from those who, either visually or verbally, annexed that genre to portray rural idylls, utopian dreams and dubious national constructs, and that he utilises landscape in a most imaginative way as an influential and flexible medium for presenting ideas.

Expectations and individual perceptions are central to the reactions to landscape, whether portrayed in visual or verbal media. Kenneth Clark is of the opinion that most Englishmen, if asked to depict beauty, would launch into a description of a scene that included a lake, mountain, white-washed cottages, gardens, a little harbour with red sails. Without explicitly deploring such preferences on the part of 'the average man', Clark records 'a complete divorce between popular and informed taste'.[4] Such predilections are not confined to Englishmen though, but are shared by thousands in several countries, as the geographically wide-ranging Melamid/Komar

---

1 George Moore, *The Untilled Field* (1902–3), (Gloucester, 1970). 2 George Moore, *The Lake* (1905), (Gerrards Cross, Bucks., 1980). 3 George Moore, *Letters 1895–1933 to Lady Cunard,* ed. Rupert Hart-Davis (London, 1957), p. 45. 4 Kenneth Clark, *Landscape into art* (London, 1976) p. 230.

investigations of the 1990s show.[5] However, while Clark leans towards the existence of common, innate and instinctive attraction to an identifiable pastoral perfection in landscape, Simon Schama is emphatic that culture and convention, rather than congenital partiality, dictate the choice of image and the framing of the design: 'Landscapes are culture before they are nature, constructs of the imagination projected onto wood and water and rock.'[6] Whether the reader is culturally aware or innocently instinctive, both of these beliefs are relevant for interpretations of what is framed by George Moore in his landscape picture gallery since they are equally reflective of the perennial popularity and attraction of landscape. Also germane to analysis of the Moore approach is the aesthetic idea that non-verbal images augment verbal ones, thus doubling the aesthetic force and ensuring delivery of the intended conceptual impact.[7] In an examination of the texts, it will be seen that Moore's painterly touch is much in evidence: the verbal accounts provide the outlines of recognisable scenes; any ideas that are not totally comprehended at first will be copperfastened in memory by the visual after-images that linger and penetrate the consciousness. For example, in looking at the mountains, cottages, lakes, woods and bogs in the two volumes, it becomes clear that the landscapes therein are not spaces intended for idle contemplation of the Romantic sublime or for luxuriating in nature;[8] neither does their presence aim to provide reassurance concerning controlled governance in the realm by showing a fixed and immutable hierarchical order appropriate to an Enlightenment age. It will be observed that the Moore landscape scenes – notwithstanding their beauty, balance and ornamental qualities in *The Lake*, and despite brevity and apparent simplicity in *The Untilled Field* – are structured and organised in order to stimulate thought and provoke vigorous discussion on the state of the world.

At a first glance, the landscapes in *The Untilled Field* seem hard to discern. Under that umbrella landscape title, the names of the individual short stories do not have any landscape or geographical links (see table 1). The nearest to such nomenclature is 'A Play-house in the Waste', first published as 'San nDiotramh Dubh' in *An tÚr-Ghort*, the shorter Irish-language version of the volume whose publication preceded *The Untilled Field*. The story called 'In the Clay' does not refer to agricultural land, nor even to graveyards, but to the modelling clay for a statue.

In addition, these stories – whether the 8 in *An tÚr-Ghort* or the 13 in *The Untilled Field* – are short. The tales move on through brief conversations, scraps of thought and a minimum of linking narrative; they are relatively shorn of description and such description as can be found is frequently of barrenness. For instance, in 'The

5 Malcolm Andrews, *Landscape and Western art* (Oxford, 1999), pp 20-1. In 1994, Alex Melamid and Vitaly Komar constructed paintings based on worldwide survey of popular preferences: the majority opted for landscape, with water, mountain and trees. The resulting composite images were published on the internet. 6 Simon Schama, *Landscape and memory* (New York, 1995), p. 61. 7 Benedetto Croce, *The aesthetic as the science of expression and of the linguistic in general*, trans. Colin Lyas (Cambridge, 1992), pp 105-8. 8 Kenneth Olwig, *Nature's ideological landscape* (London, 1984), pp 1–10, in particular.

Table 1: The story titles of *An tÚr-Ghort,* and the corresponding and additional titles in *The Untilled Field*

An tÚr-Ghort (1902)	*The Untilled Field* (1903)
	'In the Clay'
'Naomh Áitiúil'	'Some Parishioners
'An Deoraí'	'The Exile'
'Galar Dúiche'	'Home sickness'
	'A Letter to Rome'
	'Julia Cahill's Curse'
'San nDiotramh Dubh'	'A Play-house in the Waste'
'An Gúna-Pósta'	'The Wedding Gown'
'Tóir Mhic Uí Dhíomasuigh'	'The Clerk's Quest'
'An Déirc'	'Alms-giving'
	'So on he fares'
'Tír Grádh'	'The Wild Goose'
	'The Way Back'

Exile', the elements of landscape description are few: the first one (in a story that runs to a mere 21 pages) relates to the priest's house: 'There were trees about the priest's house, and there were two rooms, on the right and left of the front door'.[9] In terms of traditional landscape painting, that would not even equate to a preliminary sketch. Some pages further on, there is a recreation of what were, and are, recognisable tourism poster-pictures of Connemara: 'The mare trotted gleefully; soft clouds curled over the low horizon far away, and the sky was blue overhead; and the poor country was very beautiful in the still autumn weather, only it was empty'. Those last four words mark the economic and social reality, the failure of the political system. The next few lines elaborate only briefly, but quite strikingly: 'The fences were gone, cattle strayed through the woods, the drains were choked with weeds, the stagnant water was spreading out into the fields'.[10] The contrast is set out between propaganda for tourists and the conditions on the ground, but it is only momentarily before the readers' eyes and then the text moves on. A point has been registered but not over-worked; two disparate pictures have been shown. There is a tinge of irony in the fact that, as an art expert would know, both the scene of neglect and decay, and that of the fluffy clouds, share some faint affinity with classical landscape paintings in that they are empty of humans. Their juxtaposition here removes any grounds for possible idyllic or Arcadian associations. The clear signal is that the deliberations arising from the landscapes of this story cannot be confined to the picturesque; they will inex-orably involve political agendas and social problems, whether for landlord or tenant, ruler or colonized.

9 Moore, 'The Exile', p. 4.   **10** Ibid., p.14.

The next description in that same story, 'The Exile', is of arrival in town. This vista too provides a quick glance, but a suggestive one:

> Very soon the town began, in broken pavements and dirty cottages; going up the hill there were some slated roofs, but there was no building of importance except the Church. At the end of the main street, where the trees began again, the convent stood in the middle of a large garden.[11]

Afterwards, in a story where people hardly ever talk, there is nothing that would normally evoke the word or the image of landscape; neither is there anything dramatic or sudden in the half-unfolding of tragic elements in the lives of the central characters. Yet, as Moore intended, the bare narrative and the small glimpses of terrain create an atmosphere and etch the memories; they carve out a space where social issues – though merely skimmed over in the text – are unavoidable, and the encouragement is towards reflection, cogitation and more complex reasoning. Moreover, the paltry few pictorial landscapes contained within the tale tell many other stories: there is the physical structure of the Irish town with the poor down at the edge in cottages, the church dominating the area, and the more solid and slated houses of the shopkeepers between them; the double-fronted house of the priest is not a usual structure but the existence of those 'two rooms, on the right and left of the front door' is a reminder that they were often used to accommodate the priest's unmarried sisters and relatives, and sometimes a housekeeper, whom he supported financially and who cared for him materially. The apparent comparative prosperity of the priest could often be accompanied by the relative poverty of others, whether financially or in their choices. The trees at his house, and at the convent, are indicative of the higher echelon of society from which their occupants come, and of a degree of prosperity. The fact that 'the nuns were doing well with their dairy and their laundry' marks the result of organized collective work, partly funded by the property of those who joined the congregation. The socio-economic reality is that the running of the convent farm, dairy and laundry depends on the practical knowledge of those from small farms and tenant holdings, rather than on the capacity of sisters from the slated houses. As Pat Phelan says about the nuns: 'I'm sure there isn't one of them could boil pig's food like Catherine herself', an opinion corroborated by the Reverend Mother who says to Catherine as she plans to leave the convent, 'we have got no one to take your place'.[12] Catherine then writes out farming instructions for another nun, although it is far from certain if a written guide will guarantee the same success.

Several social issues are discernable in those particular landscape frames from 'The Exile', and, in their entirety, the stories of *The Untilled Field* contain a veritable catalogue of rural Ireland's predicaments and afflictions at the end of the nineteenth century: the poor prices for cattle and pigs, and the sale of American bacon in a land that had its own; the state of the roads; depopulation and its consequences for

11 Ibid., pp 14–15.   **12** Ibid., pp 15; 17; 18.

marriage partners and care of the elderly; the generous, self-sacrificing gestures made, at enormous personal cost, to help others prosper; the hurtful badges and gradations of class and degree; the phenomenon of faraway hills that make the exile a perpetual wanderer, drawn by material necessity to America and by emotional bonds to return to Ireland, but never to settle in either place. In that last context, it is rather poignant that the titles for two of the stories in *The Untilled Field* are interchangeable: 'The Exile' could as easily be called 'Home Sickness'.[13] In the entire collection of stories, other potentially sad subject matter occurring outside the landscape frame includes, for instance, the made match, marriage for love or convenience, the fate of unmarried pregnant women, the murder of 'bastard' babies, the quirks of religious belief, fundraising for large churches in impoverished communities, excessive drinking, governmental insistence on follies as relief work, women considered as property. The stories lack traditional landscape mounting – the total number in the collection amounts to a mere handful – but the paucity of such pictures makes the few the more remarkable, outweighed as they are by the evidence of social malaise.

In the absence of numerous or detailed framed landscapes, it must be asked why 'The Exile' or any of the other tales should appear in a book bearing a landscape title. At least four possible reasons might be suggested: firstly, that the simple titles are alluring for a readership that believes itself secure in its understanding of such landscape concepts; secondly, that George Moore seeks to stimulate questioning and expansion of those popular viewpoints, his belief being that landscape should be more about the reality of living than about the picturesque because it is the people who should count. It must be the social ills rather than the identifiably Irish heather and the mountains in those barely-delineated landscapes that should remain more memorable for the reader. Thirdly, with the strong impetus in the volume towards forcing acknowledgment of compound human motivations and complex psychological features, the concept of landscape is to be expanded; it must include mindscapes or inscapes and mirror their different scenes. Fourthly, it seems that there is an invitation to readers to paint in landscapes, and to augment and decorate them themselves with their own ideas, knowledge and experiences. Whether in the local scene or in the mindscape, predetermined responses are to be queried and space provided for spontaneous, individual reactions. This is a new aesthetic wherein the author, by minimal reference, generates a myriad of reader responses. The result is that, in the ultimate liberalisation and democratisation of art, literature and thought by Moore, the untilled field of the overall title is to be worked by the reader. In literary terms, this is groundbreaking in more senses than one.

Cutting-edge originality is evident also in *The Lake*, a book that is recognised as the first English stream-of-consciousness novel.[14] The tale was originally intended as

13 This same possibility occurs with the first and last stories in James Joyce's *Dubliners* some years later: 'The Sisters' and 'The Dead' could also exchange titles. It is recognized that Joyce took Moore's *The Untilled Field* as his structural model for *Dubliners*. 14 Adrian Frazier, *George Moore, 1852–1933* (New Haven & London, 2000), p. 347.

the last story in *The Untilled Field* but it contrasts markedly in style from the stories of that volume. It is not just that the characters' thoughts and speech are provided at greater length than in the brief sentences of the short stories, but rather that this book is crowded with landscape pictures, a striking aspect of which is their sensory quality. In this text, the abundance of visual, tactile and aural elements achieves an intensity that is comparable in force, if not in tone, to that generated by the stark and spare scenes of *The Untilled Field*. Moore's rendering of the storm in *The Lake* provides a multi-dimensional experience of colour, darkness, flashes, fauna and flora, pattering and thundering, and is reflective of the disparate elements in Father Gogarty's mood.[15] The aural constituents include the sounds that resonate for the reader from the page, whether of curlews, wind or lake water; they also arise in the arrangement of words on the page to create literary music. That latter quality is the extension of Moore's writing into another art form – verbal music in prose rather than in poetry, what is often referred to as the melodic line. This is landscape painting enhanced, a remarkable expansion of the artist's repertoire into *son et lumière* and beyond that into '*grain et parfum*', or touch and odour. These aspects of evocative landscapes in *The Lake* contribute significantly to enrichment of the text, as do the faint contemporary references that are delicately woven into both *The Untilled Field* and *The Lake*.

The Lake is the story of a priest's gradual realisation of how he had made the wrong choice in joining the clergy and of how he must escape from this position. The tale of this slow coming to terms with himself unfolds in stream of consciousness, internal monologue and in letters, interwoven with a succession of depictions of natural landscapes in all their variety and seasons. The early idea of landscape as locus amoenus (or pleasant place) can surely be applied to some of these drawings – so, too, would the later romantic notion of the sublime and wild landscape. The pictures of nature can act as mirror, or as counterpoint, to the states of mind and actions of Father Oliver Gogarty, the central character. There is implied contrast between Gogarty's cultivation of exotic garden flowers and the proliferation of natural species that flourished around the lake and on the hermit's island but, in an unspoken expansion of the concept in *Candide* of 'cultiver son jardin', the picture is complicated for the reader by the absence of any single, exact horticultural or moral prescription.[16] Symbolism abounds and the comparison is facilitated, but not forced, between on the one hand, the predictable course of the seasonal cycles, the close-up views of flora and fauna, and on the other hand Gogarty's jolting, shuddering journey of mind and soul down blind alleys of self-delusion to an ultimate greater awareness. Evident also, but again not obtrusive in its presentation, is the contrast between the solidity of rich visual images and the shakiness and volatility of the priest's psychological and rational processes: the episode of his hallucinations concerning Nora provides a good example of Moore's method in this regard.[17] When Gogarty finally decides to leave and to fake his own death by drowning, his gravitation is towards what he sees as natural, and his justification is expressed in the language of nature and

15 Moore, *The Lake*, pp 91–2.   **16** Ibid., pp 95; 161–2.   **17** Ibid., pp 115–16; 138.

landscape pictures: the images are of the curlew, the 'old decrepit house' from which the shutters fell to look at 'splendid sun shining on hills and fields, wooded prospects with rivers winding through the great green expanses'; he will not resign himself 'to a frog-like acquiescence in the stagnant pool'.[18]

The lake of the story is not that 'stagnant pool'. It is the central, beautiful, natural feature of the countryside, first introduced as being 'like a mirror that somebody had breathed upon'. On each appearance, it adds to the wealth of imagery and, on occasion, its presentation has a musicality and sonority that is mesmerising: 'The ducks were talking in the reeds, the reeds themselves were talking, and the water lapping softly about the smooth limestone shingle'. The lake reflects the mood of the beholder as well as its physical surroundings: it was 'refined and wistful, with reflections of islands and reeds, mysteriously still. Rose-coloured clouds descended'. Despite several depictions of its loveliness and the predominance of those pictures, it becomes apparent that, for Oliver Gogarty, it is still an inland waterway and he was 'certain that if he had such a boat he would not be sailing her on a lake, but on the bright sea, out of sight of land'. Some islands on the lake have ruined castles, another was the site of a hermit's cell, and one will be his staging post when he 'ungirds' for his swim across the lake to a new life. As time progresses, Gogarty wonders if the lake reminds him of a shroud or a ghost, but then decides that 'Every man has a lake in his heart'; that phrase is repeated and somewhat elucidated finally as 'he listens to its monotonous whisper year by year, more and more attentive till at last he ungirds'.[19]

Landscape painting continued to interest the wider public at the beginning of the twentieth century, and indeed well beyond that date although, in part influenced by nineteenth-century developments in photography, the genre had diminished in importance and prestige in the eyes of artists and critics. That popular taste could well be part of the reason for Moore appearing to proffer landscape to his readers in these book titles, while ultimately delivering images and messages that the reading, looking public had not bargained for. Thus, the author could combine literary experiment with general reader appeal and reach a wider audience. In the landscape scenes of *The Lake*, in particular, the text displays some of the detail typical of the style of Victorian landscape artists; in *The Untilled Field*, the panoramas are suggested rather than executed. For the contemporary reader, there is also the comfort of recognising the familiar in items that are of their time and place in Ireland, with some confirming the modernity and others emphasising ancient heritage or links with Celtic myth and legend, subjects that were topical in the Celtic Revival period. In 'Home Sickness', Bryden looks 'at the old castles, remembering the prehistoric raiders,'[20] in 'The Wild Goose', Ned mentions 'Finn McColl', and he and Ellen plan to see Tara, Clonmacnoise, Cashel and Glendalough. 'The Aran Islands tempted them, for there was Gaelic Ireland'[21] – the topicality and contested nature of that last assertion was picked up by James Joyce in 'The Dead'. Similarly, Father Moran's assertion that 'the

18 Ibid., pp 144; 145; 176.   **19** Ibid., pp 1; 25; 5; 35; 179.   **20** Moore, *The Untilled Field*, p. 28.

questioning of any dogma would mean some slight subsidence from the idea of nationality'[22] is an echo of contemporary debate and dispute. In *The Lake*, Father Oliver's thoughts 'lingered in the seventh and eighth centuries, when the arts were fostered in monasteries – the arts of gold-work and illuminated missals – "Ireland's halcyon days"'.[23] On the modern side, it emerges in both books that train services reach remote Connacht; it is 'as easy to go from London to Ireland as it is to go to Margate'; it seems simple also to travel to Antwerp, Munich, Rapallo and Cairo or Turkestan.[24] Market prices would be of concern to many and odd snippets are painted in on the varying prices of livestock, the yearly salary of a school teacher (£50), and the relatively high church fees demanded for conducting a marriage for a labourer – minimal information that enlivens the pictures.[25] The ubiquitous village gossip is drawn with an accuracy that makes the figure totally plausible for any age or place.[26]

There are other allusions with local and contemporary interest. Some relate to ecclesiastical quarrels and they surface in the comparisons made between Roman and Celtic Christianity in *The Lake*: 'Religion in Ireland in the seventh and eighth centuries was clearly a homely thing full of tender joy and hope, and the inspiration not only of poems, but of many churches and much ornament'. Here one finds hints of postulated ingredients for a national identity, and echoes of the support given by Moore's father to Archbishop McHale in his disagreements with Cardinal Cullen and John Henry Newman and the ultramontanes of the time;[27] there are also shades of interdenominational prejudice and bigotry, in particular over the baptism of a child when the adherents of the two main religions seek to claim it.[28] On the secular side, there is even a subtle nod in the direction of a controversial murder insinuated into *The Lake*; the death was that of Bridget Cleary, an alleged witch, in 1895. While the entire episode faded from view in the succeeding years, Bridget's name would have been very well-known a century ago. Moore's references to Bridget and his treatment of the tragedy seem to have gone entirely unnoticed then and since, even though the case of Bridget Cleary has once again become familiar in recent years.[29] Moore's attitude to the primitive happenings near Clonmel in Co. Tipperary can be deduced from the manner in which he links coopers with the past, a 'Bridget Clery' cottage with Father Gogarty's unenlightened state, and then Gogarty's move away from it is made to coincide with the dawning of greater self-understanding, his 'liberation from prejudices and conventions'.[30] The cottage that is so much part of idealised and traditional landscape pictures is symbollic here of a dark past and suggestive of its lingering presence. Depicting the depopulation of the west and the collapse of abandoned cottages forms a part of George Moore's continuing riposte

21 Ibid., pp 150; 168.   **22** Moore, *The Lake*, p. 47.   **23** Ibid., p. 43.   **24** Ibid., pp 76; 83–4; 97; 99; 133.   **25** 'The Exile', p.2; *The Lake*, pp 60–1; 168; 'Patchwork', p. 47.   **26** Moore, *The Lake*, pp 20-2.   **27** Ibid., pp 96–7.   **28** Ibid., pp 69; 89; 98; 153–66; 168.   **29** See, for example, Angela Bourke, *The burning of Bridget Cleary: a true story* (Dublin, 1999); Tom Mac Intyre, *What happened Bridgie Cleary* (Dublin, 1985); *Hidden History*, RTE 1 television, 1 November, 2005.   **30** Moore, *The Lake*, pp 2; 14; 44–5; 53; 145; 172.

to travel writers of the nineteenth century, and such scenes appear also in *The Lake*; they are approached, however, with much more subtlety than Moore had achieved in 1887 in his polemical book, *Parnell and his Island*. While these and many other elements are in the texts, they are not in the foreground nor do they constitute any kind of dramatic backdrop for the numerous landscapes of *The Lake*; yet, neither can they be detached from the pictures. They are often not visually presented but they are factors and questions that are hinted at, triggered by images, and they will not go away.

George Moore's focus on Irish contexts does not preclude attention to the mode of expression, a matter that is vital for him as art critic, literary man and connoisseur of French artistic trends in word and paint. His artistic decisions in these books are simultaneously concerned with literary genres and with preferences and movements in visual art, both of which were contested spheres in the period. His engagement with those spheres is signalled in *The Lake* by, amongst many other devices, mention of 'Landor's *Hellenics*', a Rubens painting in Antwerp, Father Gogarty's musings on an unnamed woman who is instantly recognisable as George Eliot ('a learned woman, a learned philosophical writer and translator of exegetical works from the German') and a landscape scene (with wood gatherers) that is obviously reminiscent of a painting by Millet.[31] Indirect allusion to Millet recalls Moore's opinion that while the Frenchman was not 'a painter in any true sense of the word', he provided lessons for all on 'how to suggest rather than to point out, and how by a series of ellipses to lead the spectator to imagine what is not there'. Edgar Degas is praised in even more laudatory terms: 'in Degas the science of the drawing is hidden from us'.[32] Those are exactly the approaches taken by Moore, particularly in *The Lake*. In 1892, commenting on Corot's painting style, Moore had judged that 'it changed gradually, as nature changes, waxing like the moon from a thin, pure crescent to a full circle of light'.[33] It is no coincidence that such a description that could equally be applied to Father Gogarty's development in the novel and appropriately, on the night of his escape, there are two moon references in the text: 'A yellow disc appeared', and 'that great moon pouring silver down the lake'.[34] The recurrent intermingling of visual and sensory images in verbal portrayals of landscape and inscape will be an abiding concern for Moore, seen by him as a pattern originating with Cervantes and followed by Rousseau.[35]

In the case of *The Untilled Field,* the idea of a themed and unified collection of short stories was a literary innovation, as was the introduction of stream of consciousness and internal monologue into the English novel in *The Lake*. It is noteworthy that in each of these texts, Moore should decide on landscape as an instrument, and as an intrinsic part of his ongoing artistic developments and expansion of genre. On occa-

---

31 Ibid., pp 16; 77; 99; 105.   **32** George Moore, *Modern painting* (New York, 1913), pp 71; 278.   **33** Ibid., p. 75. The article on Corot had first appeared in August 1892 in *The Speaker* where Moore was art critic.   **34** Moore, *The Lake*, pp 177–9.   **35** George Moore, *Avowals* (London, 1919), p. 13.

sion, the landscape scenes of these texts evince a profusion of ingredients that would be in keeping with the crowded style of Victorian artists, and elsewhere readers are confronted by unembellished narrative; in both cases, a less than idyllic reality is evoked, the certainties of Victorian visual and verbal narratives are absent, and the elusiveness of agreed national identity is perceptible. The use and frequency of verbal paintings might differ in each book but, overall, the landscapes act as catalyst to the generation of imagined pictures by the readers, thus multiplying the images available. It could be said that, in two senses, Moore actually overlooks the mountains and the lakes of these stories: he takes a panoramic and bird's eye view of the Irish world, identifying the significant landmarks, physical features and fault lines, and sketches them in with minimalist pen strokes; downplaying the picturesque, he zooms in close to foreground the human situations. In each instance, his tactics highlight what he sees as crucial matters for debate, and the sensitivity of the topics for various different constituencies ensured that the subjects were not ignored by contemporaries: his landscapes and mindscapes inevitably become debating grounds for those issues. Had it been anyone other than Henry James who wrote that 'analogy between the art of the painter and the art of the novelist is, so far as I am able to see, complete', Moore might have concurred. However, in his view, the Jamesian verbal paintings lacked the political force that he sought to inject into *The Untilled Field*.[36] George Moore never mentions Horace either, but the Horatian dictum 'ut pictura poesis'[37] is also one that he could have fairly and proudly affixed to both 'landscape' texts. Moore took his own route with verbal landscape painting and developed a sophisticated technique that combined artistry with commitment, the medium with the message. Reflecting on landscape painting, Irish artist William Crozier, declares that, 'Landscape is not the subject; it is the vehicle through which I can express intangible things. Things which have no narrative. Loss, memory – all can be done through the language of landscape'.[38] Almost a century separates the Crozier interview from the first publication dates of *The Untilled Field* and *The Lake,* but his articulation of a landscape artist's attitude and practice would seem to coincide perfectly with Moore's innovatory literary methods of a hundred years ago.

36 Henry James, 'The art of fiction', in *Partial Portraits* 1888 (New York: Haskell House, 1968), p. 378.   **37** Horace, *Ars Poetica,* 361. Tr. 'as in painting, so also in prose'.   **38** Brian McAvera, interview with Bill Crozier, 'Construction in colour and light' in *Irish Arts Review,* 20:1 (Spring 2003), 66.

Landscape and the Irish asylum

OONAGH WALSH

The landscape of the West of Ireland has long been associated with a romantic prim-itivism, and a unique connection with both a spiritual heritage, and a direct link to a more elemental way of life. Folk belief persisted there for longer than any other part of the country,[1] and throughout the nineteenth century the province of Connaught became a happy hunting ground for proto-anthropologists, writers, and scientists who each sought their own particular evidence for the survival of a 'pure' Irish culture.[2] Severely affected by the famine, and never part of the limited wave of industrialisation that changed other parts of Ireland, the West remained a relatively unspoiled landscape, with a topographical profile in the nineteenth century little different from the seventeenth. There was one significant addition to this landscape from the start of the century, however, that both changed the appearance of the envi-ronment, and altered fundamental patterns of family and community life: the creation of the District Asylum system.[3] Grand in scale and aspiration, the asylums were a visible reminder of Ireland's relationship to Britain, coming as they did as part of a metropolitan desire to deal with an apparently growing problem, and also a self-conscious testament in stone to science and modernity. In this essay I will approach the relationship between the institution and the landscape from the perspective of the use of local landscape as a therapeutic tool, and the interior landscape of the asylum itself as a force for recovery.

BUILDING MORAL THERAPY

The Connaught District Lunatic Asylum was opened in 1833, and was one of the first, and largest, of the new wave of District Asylums built in Ireland in the early to mid nineteenth century. It is now St. Brigid's Hospital, Ballinasloe, and the original buildings are still in daily use (fig. 1).[4] The earliest structures retain a certain beauty,

1 This was also the case in other parts of the country. For an example of how folk belief survived in Co. Tipperary for a period alongside a more modern medical approach, see Angela Bourke, *The burning of Bridget Cleary: a true story* (London, 2001). Cleary fell ill, and her husband sought assistance from the local doctor, and the folk healer, simultaneously. 2 *Visions and beliefs in the West of Ireland* by Augusta Gregory (London, 1920), was the defining text, but J.M. Synge's plays, and Douglas Hyde's early work on old Irish literatures, confirmed the sense that the West remained the repository of an ancient way of life. 3 This was a nationwide expansion, which saw the construction of twenty-two asylums by the 1870s. 4 At the time of writing, the hospital is closing (having officially been scheduled

1 Main entrance with clock tower, from original buildings of 1833.

despite some drastic remodelling over the years, and stand as important, but sadly neglected, elements in Irish architectural history (Fig. 2). The important thing to note about the early construction of the CDLA is that it took place during a period when 'moral therapy' held sway in the treatment of the mentally ill. Pioneered in France, moral therapy came to prominence in Britain in the late eighteenth century, when the Tuke family incorporated key elements in the treatment of patients at the York Retreat.[5] In brief, moral treatment, also known as moral management or moral therapy, sought to eliminate force and coercion in all their forms. The treatment of the insane prior to this development had largely depended upon force as a means of control: patients were to be intimidated into good behaviour through a system of punishments and threats, backed by the widespread use of mechanical restraint in the form of chains, fetters, padded wrist and ankle muffs, and so-called 'straight waist-coats'. Institutions routinely used purging and bleeding as a means of weakening patients physically, and thereby making them more amenable to the instructions of their keepers. More drastic methods of control included the 'rotary machines', that whirled patients violently, and made them sick and disorientated – this description by its inventor, Joseph Mason Cox, indicates how effective it could be:

for closure in September 2006), and mental health services are to be provided on a community and out-patient basis. **5** For the best account of the workings of the York Retreat, see Anne Digby, *Madness, morality and medicine: a study of the York Retreat, 1796–1914* (Cambridge, 1985).

2 Admissions block, St Brigid's Hospital.

[It could produce] ... the most violent convulsions ... of every part of the animal frame. It could be employed in the dark, where from unusual noises, smells, or other powerful agents, acting forcibly on the senses, its efficacy might be amazingly increased. By reversing the velocity of the swing, the motion being suddenly reversed every six or eight minutes, pausing occasionally, and stopping its circulation suddenly ... [it secures] ... an instant discharge of the contents of the stomach, bowels, and bladder, in quick succession.[6]

This was, of course, nothing more than torture and exhaustion, a treatment, for want of a better word, which would result in cowed and debilitated patients who might be easier to deal with in the asylum. The rotary machines were most popular on the continent, although they were used in Britain and Ireland (at Cork in particular, where Dr William Saunders Hallaran refined the machine in order to protect the patient's neck, while ensuring the complete evacuation of stomach and bowels[7]) in the early years of the century. Much more common here though were purging, bleeding, and restraint, with various forms of hydrotherapy (especially immersion in cold water, that temporarily numbed the individuals) employed in many institutions.

6 Andrew Scull, *The most solitary of afflictions: madness and society in Britain, 1700–1900* (New Haven, 1993), p. 77. 7 Halloran was in fact a firm believer in moral therapy, but retained a belief that the 'circulating swing' produced favourable results. See Joseph Robins, *Fools and mad: a history of the insane in Ireland* (Dublin, 1986), pp 57–60.

However, none of these strategies were in any sense curative, and while they may have produced a more easily managed patient body, they did not result in a large number of permanent, or even semi-permanent, cures. But moral therapy, once popularised, did appear to hold out hope that patients could be rehabilitated and returned to the community as productive members of society. Moral therapy absolutely condemned all of the coercive forms of treatment mentioned above. Its underlying principle was that if patients were treated humanely and gently, they would eventually be restored to mental health. This meant that no form of violence was ever to be offered to patients, they were not to be punished or threatened in any way, restraint was only to be employed for their own safety, or the safety of other patients, and solitary confinement, a common punishment, was to be eliminated. Crucially, the patients were to live in an environment that would be conducive to their recovery. Thus, asylums were to be built on gracious lines, modelled on the great country seats of the aristocracy.[8] They were to be close to towns and cities, and not hidden away from view, and of course supervision. They were to have extensive landscaped grounds to be used for walking, painting, and light agricultural work for the labouring patients. Bars and screens should not be used, and as far as possible, the interior of the asylum should reflect a domestic environment, and not, as they had done to date, a prison. Patients should have unrestricted access to calming views of the countryside, and the grounds should include areas for games such as croquet, cricket, and later in the century, rugby and lawn tennis.

The rules and regulations of the institution also indicate how seriously moral therapy was taken at Ballinasloe,[9] and above all else, a rigid timetable was to be adhered to, in order to give patients the security of routine, and the calmness that physicians felt a structured existence would offer. The lives of staff and patients alike were to be governed by 'the large bell', which rang 'at the proper hours for the patients rising and retiring for the night, at the hours for breakfast, dinner and supper, and at the appointed times'. The smaller bells were used to indicate hours of exercise, to call work parties from the farm, and to indicate the start and end of indoor entertainments. Although perhaps suggestive to the modern reader of a repressive, penal structure, this was intended to provide patients with a living example of the benefits of a calm, regulated life. As Edward Shorter has noted in relation to similar regimes in France, '[this] timetable breathes the philosophy that orderly life is restorative'.[10] In many ways, it was a structure highly suitable for Ireland, echoing as it did the highly regulated existence of convents and monasteries, where one's life was also delineated by rigid structures, and the imperative of the bell.

If this sort of approach sounds a utopian ideal for a group that had routinely been abused and ridiculed, it is surprising how many asylums in Britain and Ireland actu-

---

8 For a discussion of the emergence of asylum architecture, see Christine Stevenson, *Medicine and magnificence: British hospital and asylum architecture, 1660–1815* (New Haven, 2000) **9** Bye-Rules and Regulations for the Government of the Connaught District Lunatic Asylum, 1853. **10** Edward Shorter, *A history of psychiatry: from the era of the asylum to the age of prozac* (New York, 1997), p. 19.

ally attempted to enshrine moral therapy in their buildings, and their treatments. Most of the District Asylums in Ireland followed moral treatment principles, especially in terms of the location of the institutions (usually close to town, often on heights) and in their handsome facades. The Connaught Asylum is for example less than ten minutes walk from the centre of Ballinasloe, and was described by Thackeray as being 'as handsome and stately as a palace'.[11] Indeed, the institution appeared in its planning to conform to the idealistic model outlined by no less an individual than W.A.F. Browne, a champion in Scotland and England of the enlightened treatment of the insane. In the 1830s, Browne had delivered a series of public lectures on the necessity to reform asylums, published as a single volume in 1837. The CDLA would appear to conform to his ideal notion of a modern institution:

> The next requisite is an establishment properly placed and constructed ... It certainly is indispensable that the situation chosen should be healthy, that it should possess the advantage of a dry cultivated soil and an ample supply of water, that it should be so far in the country as to have an unpolluted atmosphere, a retired and peaceful neighbourhood, and yet be so near to a town as to enjoy all the comforts and privileges and intercourse which can only be attained in large communities.[12]

The Ballinasloe asylum did just that. The River Suck winds to the rear and side of the institution (of which more later), following a basic moral therapy injunction to include river views where possible, and also provided the establishment with water. Although the land upon which the asylum was built was not in fact dry or cultivated (it proved unsuitable for farming), it was regarded as valuable for town expansion, and was relatively expensive to purchase. When the Dublin to Galway railway line opened in 1850, adding to the transport network provided by the Grand Canal (1828), the town and its asylum were indeed at the heart of both a vibrant community, and a reconfigured and sophisticated landscape, that possessed the most modern of infrastructures.

The very buildings at Ballinasloe also enshrined moral therapy principles. Rooms were light and airy, with views of the surrounding landscape. However, there were many difficulties inherent in implementing moral therapy at Ballinasloe, not least because as soon as the asylum opened, it was literally swamped by the admission of institutionalized, long-stay lunatic inmates from the workhouses and gaols of Mayo, Galway, Roscommon, Sligo, and Leitrim. These patients represented a cohort least likely to respond to moral therapy, since by the time of their arrival they were already deemed incurable. They were moreover often without relatives to either offer any

11 William Makepeace Thackeray, *The Irish sketch book* (London, 1883), p. 459.   12 W.A.F. Browne, *What asylums were, are, and ought to be* (Edinburgh, 1837), edited with an introduction by Andrew Scull, *The asylum as Utopia: W.A.F. Browne and the mid-nineteenth-century consolidation of psychiatry* (London, 1991), p. 181.

information as to their previous state of health, family medical history, or, crucially, to take care of them if they recovered and were released. The asylum authorities rapidly found that the buildings were ill-fitted to accommodate such patients, and were forced to make rapid alterations. The manager, for example, laid a report of deficiencies before the Board, which included the fact that many of the incontinent patients admitted from the workhouses had irreversibly damaged the wooden flooring, which could not be cleaned, and had made several abortive attempts to escape through the unbarred windows, which had conveniently low sills for the better enjoyment of the views. Within months, the Board was forced to approve of alterations that eliminated the moral therapeutic purpose of the original construction. The wooden floors were ripped up, and replaced with stone flags for easier cleaning. Bars were placed on the accessible windows, blocking the views of the landscape. The open fires in the day rooms, regarded as necessary to not merely heat the rooms, but provide a cosy, domestic atmosphere, were bricked up, leading to a constant debate regarding the difficulty of providing heat for the patients, without also providing a means of harm. Moreover, the rapidity with which patients were presented for admission, and the consequent overcrowding, made it a matter of urgency to find more accommodation. Highly unsuitable buildings were pressed into service, and in fact remained in use for almost fifty years. The manager reported that the 'defects [of overcrowded accommodation] have been partially remedied by converting a Store room and two workrooms into Dormitories containing 31 beds with Keepers apartments'.[13] The storeroom had no windows, and the workrooms high windows that let in light, but did not allow the patients to look out. In almost an instant, then, the therapeutic benefits of landscape views were lost to the patients, and in the case of bedridden inmates, all visual contact with the environment was severed. The Board were hampered by governmental insistence upon saving money where possible – the adaptation of these rooms cost not more than £20, according to the manager.

LOCAL POLITICS, PUBLIC HEALTH

The architecture of asylums has attracted academic attention in recent years, and reveals a good deal regarding the manner in which the state, and individual cities and towns, regarded the mentally ill. Contrary to the earlier impulse to disguise the buildings, or place them in remote areas, and by extension hide their inmates from view, nineteenth century asylums were bold additions to expanding towns. Indeed, competition to secure the new asylums was intense, and the subject of vigorous political lobbying. Such an institution was a tremendous boost to the local economy, bringing extensive employment, and adding considerable sums to the annual turnover, through wages and contracts. In 1846, for example, despite the collapse of the economy because of the famine, the Ballinasloe asylum expended almost six

13 Board of Governor's Minutes, 7 June 1837.

thousand pounds locally. Successive boards of governors jealously sought to protect their institutions, even to the point of opposing the construction of others elsewhere. When the new asylum was proposed for Sligo in the early 1850s, and another at Castlebar a decade later, there was strenuous opposition from Ballinasloe, despite a history of many years complaint to the lord lieutenant regarding the overcrowded nature of the institution, and the necessity for expansion. It would appear that there was a reluctance to allow any another asylum to be constructed in Connaught, in case it would undermine Ballinasloe's importance: there was no suggestion that the existence of the asylum itself was under threat, and the new institutions were intended to cater only for patients from their respective catchment areas. Nevertheless, the Ballinasloe administrators and governors resisted not merely its establishment, but also the transfer of Co. Mayo, Leitrim and Sligo patients to the new asylums on their opening. District Asylums were prestigious bodies, conferring a considerable status upon the local area, despite the anxieties some felt regarding the congregation of mentally ill. As significant public institutions, asylums should also be regarded as civic statements, and expressions of a public pride in modernity itself, as well as modern medicine. Like the town halls and public libraries of nineteenth-century Northern England, Irish asylums were not merely a response to concerns regarding the treatment of the mentally ill, but a marker of progress.

But of course, as so often occurred with regard to lofty ambition, there was a significant gap between aspiration and reality. Although the Ballinasloe asylum occupied a prominent position in the town – on the main Dublin to Galway road, and unavoidable as travellers entered the town – its interior landscape failed to match the hopes of its planners. In the first instance, although the institution proved an imposing structure, it was far less impressive as a working asylum. Indeed, one might argue that in an attempt to ensure that the asylum stood as an emblem of modernity and progress, the architect achieved a triumph of form over function. The handsome facades hid a multitude of problems, some of which contributed materially to the ill-health of the patients and staff. A pressing problem was the sewerage system. The main sewer ran underneath the centre of the asylum, discharging foul smells, and worse. In 1845, the clerk of the asylum requested that he be given an increase in salary, to compensate for his increased duties, but also to allow him to rent apartments in the town, as he could no longer bear the smell from the main drain which permeated his rooms.[14] As these were three floors above the drain itself, it is an indication of how foul the air had become (the request was rejected by the lord lieutenant's office, and the clerk went on to rent accommodation at his own expense). However, there were patients housed in the basement rooms of the institution, which lay directly above the offending drain. As the inspector noted in successive years, this had a detrimental effect upon the inmates in these rooms, but it proved impossible to find alternative accommodation for them. Even when the drain was implicated in several outbreaks of dysentery, the lord lieutenant's office was reluctant to fund repairs, or

14 Board of Governor's Minutes, 24 December 1845.

consider alternative waste disposal. Indeed, it was not until extensive building works were undertaken in the 1880s, almost fifty years after the asylum opened, that the drains in the original building were temporarily modernised. Even then, the work was done both because, as the resident medical superintendent noted, 'the overflow sewerage drain [had] become offensive to the neighbouring householders', and also because the solution (to simply use the effluent as fertiliser on poor land) allowed one of the governors, the earl of Clancarty, to lease additional acerage to the asylum.[15]

One might ask why there appeared to be such reluctance to address a pressing problem. An obvious answer lies in the cost of renovation: correspondence between the asylum and the lord lieutenant's office amply demonstrates the difficulties the board of governors experienced in extracting anything more than the bare minimum of funding from government. And the asylum inspectors were also conscious of the necessity to keep the County contributions to the lowest level, in light of the impoverished population of the West of Ireland. In discussing a proposed building programme to accommodate the estimated 358 'excess' patients in residence in 1897, the inspector noted that 'it is of course most desirable that in the chronic section, the structural arrangements should be as simple and inexpensive as possible, and having regard to the poverty of the holders of so many wretched tenements in this district, it rests as a special duty on all concerned to try and keep down expenditure which has to be defrayed out of a tax – the county cess – which is levied on the poor as well as on the wealthier classes'.[16]

But one might also suggest that it reflects a complex response to the individuals who were admitted to the hospital, and one that signalled a somewhat ambiguous attitude towards the pauper insane in Ireland. On the one hand, they were legitimate objects of sympathy and concern, driven out of their minds through no fault of their own. As such, they ought to have fulfilled the demanding Victorian criteria of 'deserving poor' without difficulty, all the more because there was a general consensus that no one would enter an asylum unnecessarily. On the other, though, there was a sense that the standard of living offered in the asylum was in many cases so superior to that they had enjoyed at home, they should be grateful for the treatment and shelter offered, and endure any discomforts that would prove too costly to remedy (even if, as in the case of the defective plumbing, it was potentially fatal). For example, when a Catholic chapel was finally constructed in the asylum grounds, the inspector, Dr John Nugent, articulated a sense that pauper inmates might be expected to be a hardy lot. He instructed the resident medical superintendent 'to consider whether a costly heating apparatus for the Chapel is needed, it being unknown in ninety nine per cent of the ordinary Chapels throughout Ireland; in fact, under existing circumstances it appears to be uncalled for'.[17] Similarly in 1895 the inspector expressed only mild disapproval of the fact that 'the male wards on the ground floor

15 Report of the Resident Medical Superintendent, February 1882, p. 4. **16** Inspector's Report, 22 May, 1897, p. 9. **17** Letter from J. Nugent to R.V. Fletcher, October 25, 1881, included in the Ballinasloe District Asylum Annual Report for 1881, p. 7.

are infested with rats', and 'the male patients are so crowded in their dayrooms as to have barely room to sit down'[18]: His statements are made with quiet regret, rather than any real anger. Of course, the likelihood of such sums as were necessary to remedy all of the defects being released by the lord lieutenant were slim, and the Inspectors, as well as the asylum administrators, were careful to couch their criticisms as temperately as possible, to avoid the very real possibility of cuts in the government subsidy. But the sense that the patients were not to expect luxurious treatment was strong. In the same year, the Inspector reported on the case of a patient who died shortly after admission: 'In this case a woman, admitted on the 22nd December, had been driven a very long distance on an open car, in very severe weather, and was in a very exhausted state on admission, and never rallied. The Coroner's Jury considered that no blame was attachable to anyone. No doubt, both the police and the relatives considered it most advisable to remove the woman to the Asylum without delay, and in such remote parts it is impossible to get a covered vehicle'.[19]

WORKING THE LAND

In the first decade of its existence, the institution was continually under pressure to accept cases it regarded as incurable, and therefore not suitable inmates under its own rules (the Connaught Asylum, like the other district asylums, was intended for the treatment of curable cases only). However, even with this difficulty, the board of governors, and the asylum physician, continued to promote as far as possible a regime of moral treatment. In this context, the land and landscape surrounding the asylum came to play a key role. The majority of the patients were landless labourers and domestic or farm servants. Moral therapy called for the continuation as far as possible of the patient's ordinary mode of life while inside the asylum, and in the case of Ballinasloe this meant providing farm work for the men, and a variety of domestic labour for the women. But a problem immediately presented itself: the asylum had an original land holding of only eleven acres, most of it unfit for cultivation. The first years then were ones in which the majority of the male patients were unoccupied, and only a few of the women, principally in cleaning and in laundry work. However, the board steadily increased pressure upon the lord lieutenant to release funds for more land purchase, and the holdings increased substantially over the century. As the asylum grew, so too did the perceived importance of therapeutic labour on the farm, so much so that it became a prerequisite for release. As a patient's notes were updated, outdoor work featured increasingly as an indicator of mental health. One man, described as a difficult case, received a rather damming assessment from the admitting physician: 'He has one answer delivered after a long reaction period to all questions "I don't know" why he was sent here, what he did, where he is, or anything else asked. He is surly, obstinate, pig-headed, ignorant, impulsive and badly contorted

18 Inspector's Report, 1895, pp 8–9.   **19** Ibid.

but doubtfully insane in the strict sense but unsocial at all times and probably brutal when vexed'. A month later it is noted that he 'refuses food at times, [is] stubborn and obstinate emotional without cause; has to be dressed at times and resists; does no work; memory bad'. Within five months, however, he gradually consented to work on the farm, and his final note stated that he 'is now in ward 12 and much improved. Works well in the division answers rationally and coherently but does not know why he was sent here except that he was contrary'.[20] He was discharged recovered within two weeks of this note, the curative power of work on the farm having taken effect. Thus the landscape came to play an increasing role in the rehabilitation of patients, and was a key strand within moral treatment at Ballinasloe. Through agricultural labour, patients could not merely be restored to mental health, but the successful completion of tasks set by the physician and keepers was crucial if a patient wished to be discharged.

However, this was not necessarily the case with the female patients, who, although the majority shared a background of manual, agricultural labour with the men, were not as central to the running of the asylum farm. Thus the emphasis in the male records is placed upon a willingness and ability to work well, and follow instructions without delay, whereas for women the criteria was rather more traditional: they were to present 'a neat and cheerful appearance', and to occupy themselves principally with laundry work and sewing. The healing properties of land, so often cited for the men, was rarely mentioned in the women's records, beyond the necessity for the patients generally to take the air in the exercise yards. But what was an absolute imperative, if the asylum was to continue to secure the support of government, was to demonstrate convincingly its efforts to achieve self-sufficiency. Every annual report detailed to the penny the amount of money either saved through the manufacture of food and clothing, or the actual profit turned by the sale of Asylum produce. This is not surprising in itself: in an era before mass mechanisation, the patients themselves came from backgrounds where they produced much of what they consumed throughout their lives. What is noteworthy, though, is the manner in which the medical discourse of moral therapy became entwined with a hard-nosed Victorian economic sensibility, that insisted upon a payment of some description in exchange for food, shelter, and treatment. Thus a general, and endlessly recycled, statement is made each year by the Inspectors about the value of farm labour as a therapy, followed by a minute presentation of how much money the farm saved and produced in the preceding year. Occasionally the two objectives are sandwiched together, with the distinctions between the differing objectives blurred:

> The purchase of the additional land has now been completed, and the acquired ground added to the farm, which now consists of 150 acres ... It will, therefore, be possible at an early date to supply at least part of the milk from the Asylum farm. Considering that the contract price for milk is at

20 Male Case Book, no. 3377, 11 September 1883.

present nine pence per gallon, this, if properly managed, ought to result in a very great saving. The extension of the farm should, therefore, tend to greater economy in management, but above everything else, will serve to render the lives of the male patients happier and will improve their mental condition.[21]

In 1891 a similar attitude had prevailed: 'A new and commodious Laundry has recently been erected, in which only 16 patients are at present employed, whereas, with a little more energy on the part of the female staff, five times that number might be usefully occupied. The employment of the more noisy and turbulent patients would result in peace and quietude in the Wards, and would aid, above all things, in improving their mental condition and adding to their happiness, while at the same time lessening the cost of their maintenance'.[22]

The board were no less concerned with the question of productive work from patients, and discussed frequently the advantages of using patient labour wherever possible. They noted that 'the Governors are of opinion that the importance of keeping the patients employed is too much lost sight of in ordering machinery and plumbing work',[23] and urged frequently that long-stay patients in particular be trained up in a variety of occupations, including tailoring, shoemaking and repair, masonry, and painting.[24] These skills were to be expended exclusively in the service of the asylum: even when patients had worked for several years at a particular trade or occupation, they rarely seem to have transferred that experience to the outside world.[25]

WATER AND THERAPY

As mentioned earlier, the Ballinasloe Asylum is built close to the River Suck, which winds about it in a pleasing manner. The river played an important part in the life of the asylum, providing water for the institution, and at one stage a means of waste disposal, and was to become an essential element in the farming calendar, flooding the callow lands in due season.[26] Despite its adherence to the best moral treatment principles, though, in providing a calming spectacle, the river was to play a far more sinister part throughout the life of the asylum, by becoming one of the principal means of suicide, and attempted suicide, for escaped patients. Indeed, if one wanted to go west from the asylum, and to avoid the public road, the river would have to be

21 Inspector's Report, 1894, p. 6.   22 Inspectors Report, 10 March 1891, p. 11.   23 Board of Governors Minutes, 3 January 1856.   24 Board of Governors Minutes, 5 March 1888. 25 It is difficult to show what occupation a patient followed on discharge, unless, ironically, they were readmitted, when a note was taken of how they had spent their time. Perhaps as a result of prejudice against former inmates, or a desire to protect the few semi-skilled jobs that existed in the area, discharged patients rarely continued the trades they learned outside the asylum, but reverted to agricultural labour, or unemployment.   26 Callow Lands are those lying near a river, and which are subject to flooding in winter and spring.

crossed at some point or other. Thus what may have seemed a logical and progressive element at the planning stages, proved something of a liability, especially as the asylum grew enormously throughout the century. The issue of suicide in the asylum is a difficult one. Although the authorities were vigilant in attempting to establish suicidal tendencies in a patient (indeed, a claim of suicidal intent was one of the easiest means to secure the admission of a relative), and constantly monitored such patients, attempts were regularly made in and out of the asylum. However, unless the cause of death could be absolutely established beyond doubt, the authorities were reluctant to label it as such. This was partly to avoid any charges of negligence: patients were supposed to be in the care of specialists, after all, but it also appears to have been in response to a contemporary horror of the mortal sin of suicide. Patients themselves testified to the dread with which they regarded suicidal tendencies: indeed, they reported urgings to commit murder more readily, and openly, than suicide. When an unexpected death occurred in the asylum (one unrelated to any underlying physical disease) it was the subject of at least a coroner's inquest, and often an official investigation. All suicides were supposed to be the subject of investigation, and in the cases of the unfortunate patients who hanged themselves, or inflicted fatal injuries with implements, these took place. It was a relatively straightforward procedure, as the cause of death, and the intent, were clear to all. However, the deaths by drowning were treated differently. Because all that the authorities had to go on was the fact of death by drowning, these cases were frequently described as accidental, and as having taken place as a result of escape attempts, as opposed to deliberate suicide 'One patient (WH), who escaped, was drowned on the 11th of June, 1891, while trying to swim the River Suck';[27] 'MD got into difficulties when attempting to cross the river, and drowned';[28] 'We have had one accidental death by drowning, of a male patient who attempted to swim across the River Suck.'[29] This approach allowed the authorities to record a verdict of accidental death, as opposed to suicide, which made a tremendous difference to the relatives. Suicide was not merely illegal, but carried a dreadful stigma. Suicides could not be buried in consecrated ground, and were considered to have brought great shame on a family, regardless of the obviously distressed nature of the individual who undertook such action.

Despite the continual complaints regarding overcrowding, underfunding, and the reservations some expressed regarding levels of comfort, the CDLA did attempt to cling to moral therapeutic principles, even when it had largely fallen from favour. In 1894, the inspector pleaded for the continued importance of a humane and generous approach. In expressing regret that not all of the patients could eat together, he indicated how Ballinasloe still held moral treatment in high regard:

> It must be a matter for regret that it was not found possible to build a hall sufficiently large to accommodate both sexes, as has been done with advan-

27 Inspector's Report, 30 June, 1893, p. 7.   **28** Resident Medical Superintendent's Report, 28 August 1888, p. 3.   **29** Resident Medical Superintendent's Report, 27 July 1895, p. 4.

tage in many of our other Asylums. Nothing breaks the monotony of an Asylum day better than bringing the patients together at meals, and nothing tends more to quiet and decorum than the example which the tranquil and orderly patients show those who are excitable or refractory. It is to be hoped that by degrees the resident medical superintendent will be able to introduce table cloths, glass and delph vessels, and knives and forks. These articles are now almost universally used. Some persons do not understand why we recommend such things for pauper lunatics, or why we should seek to surround them with amenities and comforts, to which they have been unaccustomed in their own homes. As we have already said, reporting on other Asylums of the Province, it is not because birds and flowers, and bright rugs and easy chairs are pleasing to the eye of visitors and inspectors that they are recommended. It is because such things, like the farm, which provides means of physical exercise, enter into the curative treatment, and help largely to divert the morbid thoughts and suggestions of the insane. Indeed the modern treatment of insanity might be almost summed up in the two words – occupation and recreation. In the farm and in the workshops we try to find a healthy vent for the patients excitement, while indoors we seek to turn their morbid thoughts into new channels by amusement and interesting objects.[30]

I want finally to return to the interior landscape of the Ballinasloe Asylum, and raise one particular element that was literally central to the patient experience. The Ballinasloe asylum was originally laid out as an 'X', with two 'arms' of wards and offices radiating from a central spoke, in which the reception area was and is housed. When patients were admitted, they passed through the main reception area, and before they were taken to their dormitories, they passed through a further small central area in which this enormous mirror is housed (fig. 3). It dominates the space, going floor to ceiling, and is lavishly decorated with a shell, life-sized birds, and floral details. As yet, I have not found any reference to the mirror, or to its function, in the asylum minute books. Some staff in the hospital believe that it was a gift from one of the Board members – representatives from the local gentry including Lord Cloncarty, Lord Ashtown, and Lord Clonbrock all served (or failed to serve) as board members throughout the nineteenth century – and this fantastic piece may well have come from one of their great houses. Others have said that they were told that the asylum was literally constructed around this mirror, as it is too large to have been taken in through any of the original doors or windows. Whether this is true or not, the mirror would have been an extraordinary part of patients' lives in the nineteenth century. They would have passed it repeatedly during their stay, and it must have made some impression upon them. One might speculate that it had some sort of therapeutic function, albeit for many a sort of shock therapy. When one thinks of Synge's *Playboy,* and of Christy's reaction to seeing himself properly for the first time

30 Report of the Inspector of Lunatic Asylums, 1893, pp 7–8.

3 Mirror, main reception block, St Brigid's Hospital.

in an unbroken mirror, it is a reminder that even hand mirrors were a luxury out of the reach of most Irish cottiers and labourers in the early and mid nineteenth century.[31] Imagine then the possible reaction amongst patients literally confronted by a full-length reflection of themselves for the first time, as they were brought to the

31 J.M. Synge, *Playboy of the Western World*, Act II (Boston, 1911), p. 44.

asylum, possibly in distressed or violent states. Was it hoped that this image would jolt them back into sanity? Were they supposed to retain their first view of themselves, to hold against the presumably calm and possessed reflection they would present on their discharge? Why have such a large and obviously valuable mirror in a District Asylum that catered for pauper lunatics, unless it was intended to provoke some sort of reaction? Mirrors were routinely banned in many English asylums, because of the danger they posed if broken by violent patients. Yet here is this enormous piece of baroque furniture in an impoverished West of Ireland asylum, placed where patients could secure regular glimpses of themselves. Was it part of the general impulse towards moral therapy, that drove the asylum throughout the nineteenth century, by providing not merely a functional reflection of themselves, but one framed in an exceptionally lavish way? Perhaps for patients who had limited interaction with others, they could at least be in the company of themselves.

Wandering home: Charles Robert Maturin and the subliming of Ireland[1]

TONI WEIN

My title plays on the multiple ironies associated with Irish literature. One such irony arises when critics credit place and space in Irish literature with the power to create a national and a personal identity, a kind of situational irony in which one must lose oneself to find oneself – in which one ultimately wanders home.[2] Dramatic irony looms when this interpretive claim about place and space collapses the theoretical distinction between public and private spheres, because such a claim reproduces the trope of the Big House in many early nineteenth-century Irish novels.[3] Sunny prognostications have overshadowed a more dire phenomenon, though: in many novels where the land becomes so palpable a presence as to take on the attributes of a full character in its own right, the collapse of distinctions simultaneously evokes terror.[4] And nowhere does forecasting more quickly veer off into foreboding than in Charles Robert Maturin's *Melmoth the Wanderer*. Coming at the end of the first wave of Irish novels by Maria Edgeworth and Sidney Owensen, Maturin's uses of landscape and the trope of the Big House seem self-conscious and consciously designed to produce negation: Maturin refutes the sense of destiny attendant on Big House novels. At the same time his text wanders from the very notion of home, no stable identity emerges from the wreckage. Yet Maturin's novel merely inverts the brooding pressure of cosmic irony. Mangled remains trumpet the prophetic: home, an Irish home, place and space on Irish soil, can never furnish surcease from wandering, exiled and alienated as it is from itself. Ireland *is* a wandering home.

The idea of vagrancy is reinforced by its form: the novel traverses place and space in the process of constructing a nested series of interpolated tales.[5] Characters and

1 I'd like to express my gratitude to the conference organizers and participants for the contributions their questions and formulations made to my thinking. If I've failed to honor their encouragement, the fault is mine alone.   2 See, e.g., Claire Norris, 'The Big House: space, place, and identity in Irish fiction', *New Hibernia Review*, 8 (Spring 2004), 107–21. 3 For a different interpretation of the Big House novel, see Robert Tracy, 'The "unnatural ruin": Trollope and nineteenth-century Irish fiction', *Nineteenth-Century Fiction*, 37 (Dec. 1982), 358–82.   4 According to Margot Backus, novelists gothicize the 'Big House' to evoke the cultural displacement felt by members of the 'Anglo-Irish colonial order': *The gothic family romance: heterosexuality, child sacrifice, and the Anglo-Irish colonial order* (Durham and London, 1999).   5 Most critical responses to the novel have rested on the embedded tales. The text frequently unsettles critics, who either flee the repetitions of primal trauma by declaring the text 'unspeakable,' or grapple for mastery by enumerating recurrent patterns.

events shuttle between England, Ireland, Spain, and India; they alternate between the seventeenth and the nineteenth centuries. These oscillations compose a kind of travel narrative, in addition to the gothicized strain of the Big House novel. Perhaps unsurprisingly, given the catalogue of refutations above, the novel works to undo these forms as assiduously as it establishes their echoes.

But in its deviations from conventional form, a new form emerges, one that I have termed the Irish sublime.[6] This form appears in staged encounters that freeze the otherwise panoramic sweep of the novel. Not all of these scenes occur on Irish soil, but each of them concerns itself predominantly with things Irish. Moreover, the form of the staging dissolves traditional boundaries of aesthetic thought, in that the sublime occurs simultaneously as literary, natural, and political phenomena, thus merging the ideas of Longinus, Kant and Burke.[7] However, crucially absent is the recuperatory moment shared by all three. In what follows, I concentrate on those sublime 'moments' in Maturin's text. I want to demonstrate that their principal source of terror arises from a fearful enactment of dissolution, whether the boundaries breached be those between the novelistic and the actual, the past and the present, the human and the animal, or England and Ireland. Whatever symbolic resonance these scenes might have, they imagistically fuse the human and the landscape, creating thereby what Eagleton in a different context called an 'eerily atavistic'

See, for example, Chris Baldrick, introduction to Charles Maturin, *Melmoth the Wanderer*, ed. Douglas Grant (New York and Oxford, 1989), p. x. **6** Terry Eagleton preempted my coinage by more than a decade; see his 'The Irish Sublime', *Religion and Literature*, 28: 2–3 (Summer 1996), 25–32. Like Laura Doyle's essay 'The Racial Sublime', in Alan Richardson and Sonia Hofkosh (eds), *Romanticism, race, and imperial culture, 1780–1834* (Bloomington and Indianapolis: Indiana UP, 1996) pp 15–39, Eagleton subtly traces the turning of the sublime from radicalism to conservatism, from an anti-representational strategy designed to facilitate civil and political disobedience to the same strategy deployed in the service of Anglo authority and submission. Eagleton locates the apotheosis of the Irish sublime in the Famine, the literal and figurative death of the signifier, which 'beggar[ed] the representational imagination and transcend[ed] all feasible speech'. Like Eagleton, I identify the Irish sublime with moments of crisis that freeze the narrative of history as well as of fiction; unlike Eagleton, I see the Irish sublime, as Maturin handles it, working as a gestural figuration of intellectual and moral decay. **7** A frighteningly elastic term, the word 'sublime' enacts its own properties by gathering to itself a host of hyphenated identities in recent years. From the sciences we acquire a technological, biological, electrical, ecological, physiological, and material sublime; public life gives us a political and a revolutionary sublime; private life yields the intimate and gay sublimes; philosophy contributes Hegelian, Wittgensteinian, and postmodern as adjectives; and aesthetics donates such qualifiers as apocalyptic, monstrous, Shelleyan, and comic. From leisure studies, we also speed into the notion of an accelerated sublime, associated with tourism. For examples of these diverse applications, see the special issue on *The sublime and the beautiful: reconsiderations*, cited below (*New Literary History*, 16: 2 [Winter 1985]); and *The Georgia Review* (Summer 2004) for its symposium on 'The Poetic Sublime'. Although I feel some guilt at expanding the term yet further, I do so in the hope that the contours I describe will help discriminate the Irish sublime sufficiently from its companion forms as to make it a useful tool.

moment and firmly entrenching the effect I describe in the register of the sublime. I'll try to suggest in my conclusion ways in which the identification of a specifically 'Irish sublime' can help us evaluate whether or to what extent the sublime becomes 'the representational mode in which cultural hegemony reproduces itself'.[8]

Scholars of travel literature have made a case for the role of that genre as a kind of first-stage participant in the production of a cultural hegemony. Speaking of travelogues of post-Union Ireland, for instance, Glenn Hooper has demonstrated how a colonialist canon reveals a 'desire for narrative coherence and authority', as part of an 'ideologically driven' need 'to stabilize engagement' and make it more 'structurally . . . acceptable'.[9] Maturin's description of land in the Indian tale fits the pattern Hooper identifies, and it furnishes a useful context against which to consider his sublime landscapes. Measurement, location, topography, climate, the findings of history, archeology and anthropology: all the naval and scientific discourses converge in the description of India:

> There is an island in the Indian sea, not many leagues from the mouth of the Hoogly, which, from the peculiarity of its situation and internal circumstances, long remained unknown to Europeans, and unvisited by the natives of the contiguous islands, except on remarkable occasions. It is surrounded by shallows that render the approach of any vessel of weight impracticable, and fortified by rocks that threatened danger to the slight canoes of the natives, but it was rendered still more terrible by the terrors with which superstition had invested it.[10]

From the information offered by an omniscient narrator, we move to details foisted upon the notice of the innocent, Immalee, by the sophisticate, the Melmoth of the title who has sold his soul to the devil for knowledge. The knowledge he gives her instructs her in the ways of viewing and knowing a foreign territory: he introduces onto her primitive island a telescope and teaches her the correct management of perspective. Training the telescope on a succession of buildings on the mainland of India, Melmoth recounts to her and for us the barbaric religious practices of the Indian subcontinent. Conveniently, this site makes the three principal religious competitors neighbours:

8 Peter Cosgrove, 'Edmund Burke, Gilles Deleuze, and the subversive masochism of the image', *ELH*, 66, (Summer 1990), 405–37.   **9** Glenn Hooper, 'Stranger in Ireland: the problematics of the post-Union travelogue', *Mosaic: a Journal for the Interdisciplinary Study of Literature*, 28 (March 1995), 25–47.   **10** Charles Robert Maturin, *Melmoth the Wanderer*, ed. Douglas Grant (New York and Oxford, 1989), p. 272. The passage is accompanied by a footnote from Maturin that directs the reader to 'Maurice's Indian antiquities', a scholarly work of 1806. This footnote is but one of many by which Maturin dissolves the boundaries between the fictional and the actual.

'You see,' said he, 'the coast of India, the shore of the world near you. – There is the black pagoda of Juggernaut, that enormous building on which your eye is first fixed. Beside it stands a Turkish mosque – you may distinguish it by a figure like that of the half-moon ... At a small distance you may see a low building with a trident on its summit – that is the temple of Maha–deva, one of the ancient goddesses of the country.'[11]

Immalee protests that she values the 'living things', the natural scenery more than dead buildings. Melmoth insists that the buildings indicate the modes of thought of those who use them; that to know ideas, one must look at actions. His examples, as well as the actions then furnished by the omniscient narrator, underscore this axiom by tracing a kind of reverse reciprocity: men reveal their inherent cruelty by conceiving a harsh and vengeful god; they signal their desire to inflict pain by imposing penances of suffering upon themselves as the conditions of holiness. This axiom unfurls over four pages of xenophobic imagination. If the reader, like Immalee, had held no preconceptions about the lands, peoples, and religions described, the chapter would fuse this meaning retroactively onto the buildings, so that the half-moon, the blackness of the pagoda, and the trident, all become hieroglyphs of apprehended imagination, to paraphrase Shelley.

Maturin's treatment of India and of colonial beliefs make the exotic 'available and ordered', as Glenn Hooper suggests. Conversely, the familiar, in the sense of family, acquires its status precisely because it eschews the spectacular. Despairing of humanity, Immalee discovers a 'small, obscure building overshaded by palm trees, and surmounted by a cross; and struck by the unobtrusive simplicity of its appearance, and the scanty number and peacable demeanour of the few who were approaching it,'[12] she demands to know what it is. Melmoth informs her that a new religion, 'PROTES-TANT' Christianity – for Maturin had already compared the martyrdoms of Catholicism to the self-immolations of the 'idolatrous' Juggernaut[13] – renounces splendor and magnificence because it knows that 'external devotion' cannot supply the 'homage of the heart'; that no 'artificial and picturesque religion' can stand against 'single devotion to G–d, before whose throne, though the proudest temples erected to his honour crumble into dust, the heart burns on the altar still, an inextinguish-able and acceptable victim'.[14] In sum, to paraphrase Hooper, the evocation of India writes that country as 'an epistemologically available terrain awaiting the interpreting eye of the traveler', while the space of India that has been already colonized, symbol-ized by the presence of the Protestant church, needs no outward show; it is a space and place that resonates with an unspoken sincerity to the initiated.

The Irish material engages a different level of discourse. The Big House is a spec-tacle of ruin, whose causes are natural and human, as are its effects. When young Melmoth arrives at his uncle's estate:

---

11 Ibid., p. 291.   **12** Ibid., p. 296.   **13** Ibid., p. 292.   **14** Ibid., p. 297.

The lodge was in ruins, and a barefooted boy from an adjacent cabin ran to lift on its single hinge what had been a gate, but was now a few planks so villainously put together, that they clattered like a sign in a high wind. The stubborn post of the gate, yielding at last to the united strength of John and his barefooted assistant, grated heavily through the mud and gravel stones, in which it left a deep and sloughy furrow, and the entrance lay open.[15]

In contrast to the foreign temples, the Irish estate contains signs which signify nothing but decay. Agricultural and medical metaphors combine: the sloo, in American, or slou in British pronunciation, signifying a depression filled with deep mud or mire, takes on the adjectival form 'sloughy', appropriate to the medical sense of 'dead tissue separated from a living structure'. The compound metaphor that governs the opening of the gate, the 'deep and sloughy furrow' which its passage has plowed, whose 'entrance laying open' invites the showering of new seeds, stifles productivity.

In place of the progressive narrative represented by productivity, fertility has run amok, in that the signs of decay consistently cross categories:

As John slowly trod the miry road which had once been the approach, he could discover, by the dim light of an autumnal evening, signs of increasing desolation since he had last visited the spot, – signs that penury had been aggravated and sharpened into downright misery. There was not a fence or a hedge round the domain: an uncemented wall of loose stones, whose numerous gaps were filled with furze or thorns, supplied their place. There was not a tree or shrub on the lawn; the lawn itself was turned into pasture-ground, and a few sheep were picking their scanty food amid the pebblestones, thistles, and hard mould, through which a few blades of grass made their rare and squalid appearance.

The passage begins with the personification of penury but quickly spirals into the sublime. Hardship takes on a threatening quality: penury aggravated and sharpened reveals the process whereby a gnawing weakness also draws its victims to a dangerous point. The 'uncemented wall of loose stones' that replaces property markers signals a double undoing, a habitual scavenging of historic remains of castles and forts by necessitous farmers,[16] as well as the artificial insemination of barren rock with hardy, if worthless, scrub. The sense of impending combat lurks in this evident struggle between nature and culture. Lawns typify patches of land designated for conspicuous consumption in a triumph of aesthetic spectacle, where 'civilization' flourishes its disregard for nature or natural needs; here, however, although the lawn has been recouped and pressed into service, we are not permitted to read a positive image of exchange and productivity.[17] Lack of cultivation provides only bare subsistence, as

15 Ibid., p. 9. **16** Ibid., p. 291. **17** An insight made possible by hearing Máirín Ní

though the decay of the estate and the decay of its tenants always, and inevitably, go hand in hand.

As though in retaliation, Nature usurps her place. Instead of growing on the ground, where it might nourish the livestock, the grass grows over the house, colonizing the steps and boarded windows.[18] The house only maintains a kind of stubborn integrity in its outline, but even this is a side effect of deprivation, since it stands strongly defined by virtue of its lack of ornament: 'there were neither wings, or offices, or shrubbery, or tree, to shade or support it, and soften its strong outline'.[19] This simplicity stands in marked contrast to the purity of aesthetic form evinced by the Christian church, 'overshaded by palm trees, and surmounted by a cross'.

If nature cannot supply wants, humankind succeeds no better at providing nourishment. Young Melmoth attempts to tip the servant boy, only to find his pockets empty. But here, Maturin suggests that the Irish peasants experience no suffering: 'the lad, on his return, cleared the road at a hop step and jump, plunging through the mud with all the dabbling and amphibious delight of a duck, and scarce less proud of his agility than of his 'sarving a gentleman'.[20] The corruption of human dignity into the 'dabbling' bipedalism of fowl 'naturally' accompanies the corruption of speech. Two implications flow from this portrait: either the native Irish are too like the dumb creatures of nature to notice their deprivation, taking sufficient pleasure in animal strength, or the native Irish too 'like' their colonizers, that is, admiration converts proximity into reciprocity, yielding a misplaced and implicitly inhuman pride that sustains in place of more tangible rewards. Other scenes involving the Irish Catholic servants of the Melmoth household repeat this pattern, with a native cunning and rapacity replacing the boy's more innocent play. In either case, we infer, the natives can take care of themselves.

What is knowable here is that the land, like its people, is unknowable: it has transgressed conventional categories of measurement. Thus the passages mark the transition from the travelogue, with its ordered and orderly detail, to the sublime. At the same time, with their emphasis on the breakdown of boundaries, the passages illustrate the manner in which the Irish sublime transgresses conventional aesthetic categories.

Normally, the sublime substitutes the qualitatively abstract for the quantifiably concrete, as when, for instance, Kant famously teaches us to look for 'Bold, over-hanging, and as it were, threatening rocks, thunderclouds piled up the vault of heaven, borne along with flashes and peals, volcanoes in all their violence of destruction, hurricanes, leaving desolation in their track, the boundless ocean rising with rebellious force, the high waterfall of some mighty river, and the like ... A good, if belated,

Cheallaigh's paper published in this collection.   **18** Compare the way Fraser Easton has characterized Maria Edgeworth: 'In her fictions of Irish society and Irish-English national relations Edgeworth freely adapts the ideas of exchange and productivity from which Smith's cosmopolitical thought derives': 'Cosmopolitical economy: exchangeable value and national development in Adam Smith and Maria Edgeworth' in *Studies in Romanticism*, 42 (Spring 2003), 99–126 at 99.   **19** Maturin, *Melmoth the Wanderer*, p. 10.   **20** Ibid., p. 9.

Gothic son, Maturin parcels out such Kantian scenes throughout his novel. Storms rage continually, shipwrecks abound, volcanoes and earthquakes shatter villages. In these scenes, in keeping with the conventional sublime, spectator and spectacle remain discrete. Moreover, the fear engendered by the scene never outweighs the pleasure it provides to the spectator. Maturin underscores this balance when he makes Immalee witness almost all of the Kantian examples, catalogued in a single retrospective that underscores its Wordsworthian debt:

> her soul took its colour from the sombrous and magnificent imagery around her, and she believed herself precipitated to earth with the deluge – borne downward, like a leaf, by a cataract – engulphed in the depths of the ocean – rising again to light on the swell of the enormous billows, as if she were heaved on the back of a whale – deafened with the roar – giddy with the rush – till terror and delight embraced in that fearful exercise of imagination. So she lived like a flower amid sun and storm ... [a]nd both seemed to mingle their influences kindly for her.[21]

Typographically as well as tropologically, the passage signals an imaginative participation from which the spectator can withdraw at any moment. This potential for detachment has led Luke Gibbons to call Burke's theory of the sublime 'a fraught, highly mediated response to the turbulent colonial landscape of eighteenth-century Ireland', which enabled similarly 'detached, spectatorial [British] responses to [Irish, or Indian] tragedy'.[22]

Burke's theory may enable a 'detached, spectatorial response'; Maturin's spectral sublime permits of no such detachment. Instead, a different mediated response occurs in the nexus between history and the sublime, or indeed, in the subliming of history. In *Melmoth the Wanderer*, history becomes sublime because it acquires speech, the speech of the dead. And because the dead speak through no mortal organs, their sounds penetrate the vain barriers thrown up by mortal ears.

Whereas conventional descriptions of the sublime merely evoke a hint of dissolution in the threat which nature's might poses to the spectator, in the novel nature's eruptions terrify less through their displays of might than through their intimations of a supersensible substrate, one not identified with Kant's divinely ordained 'Reason', however, but propelled by a demonically driven reason. Monçada describes this fear when he is thrust beneath the earth into Adonijah's cave and indentured servitude: 'It was a night of storms in the world above us; and, far below the surface of the earth as we were, the murmur of the winds, sighing through the passages, came on my ear like the voices of the departed, – like the pleadings of the dead'.[23] With

---

21 Ibid., p. 281.   **22** Andrew Keanie, 'Edmund Burke and Ireland: aesthetics, politics, and the colonial sublime', *Wordsworth Circle*, 35 (Autumn 2004), 177–8. This article reviews Luke Gibbons, *Edmund Burke and Ireland: aesthetics, politics, and the colonial sublime* (Cambridge, 2003), citing pp 23; 104.   **23** Maturin, *Melmoth the Wanderer*, pp 271–2

the exception of the scene with Immalee discussed above, this sense that nature speaks with more than her own voice gets repeated each time a storm rages, no matter which character makes the observation, nor what the circumstances might be. For example, when the writer tells the tale of Guzman to Don Aliaga in the Spanish inn, the scene is again framed by storm:

> The rising voice of the stormy night seemed to make wild and dreary harmony with the tones of the listener's feelings. The storm came on, not with sudden violence, but with sullen and long-suspended wrath – ... And as the stranger proceeded in his narrative, every pause, which emotion of weariness might cause, was meetly filled by the deep rushing of the rain that fell in torrents, – the sighs of the wind, – and now and then a faint, distant, but long-continued peal of thunder. 'It sounds', said the stranger, raising his eyes from the manuscript, 'like the chidings of the spirits, that their secrets are disclosed!'[24]

Were we to read the storm's wrath as a projection of the speaker, the passage would serve as an early instance of the pathetic fallacy. Instead, a series of words establishes the idea of a sympathetic union between hidden and exposed, living and dead. The storm makes a 'dreary harmony' not with spoken, but with the unspoken 'tones of the listener's feelings'. The speaker experiences not physical but emotional exhaustion, a weariness which produces in its turn the rhythmic syncopation of silence and speech. Where human speech ends, the speech of nature, or of the dead, begins; their duet sounds meetly, an adjective deriving from Anglo-Saxon that points not only to the idea of common ground, but also to a precise suitability in terms of moral rightness or justness.

Further, these last two mentioned episodes, with their staging of literary production, forge a common ground of the sublime, one that knits storytelling, manuscripts, and an outraged nature, thus combining the natural and the political sublimes of Kant and Burke with that of Longinus, for whom the sublime was predominately literary.[25] The intradiegetic manuscripts thus produced detail crimes originating from Ascendancy stock and saturated with the blood of Irish history, for the tenure of the Melmoth family begins with 'an officer in Cromwell's army, who obtained a grant of lands, the confiscated property of an Irish family attached to the royal cause,'[26] And it is with the introduction of history that the Irish sublime takes its final, most ominous form.

The provenance alone of the Melmoth family forms one hint about the historical moment in question. A number of the episodes take place in the 1680s, as, for example, the interpolated history of Immalee. However, even more numerous allu-

---

24 Ibid., p. 398.   **25** In characterizing Burke's sublime as political, I mentally include his *Reflections on the Revolution in France*, as well as the interpretations of his *Philosophical Enquiry* referenced throughout.   **26** Maturin, *Melmoth the Wanderer*, p. 26

sions bring the threat up closer in time and space; the coast the Melmoths inhabit is 'iron-bound,'[27] suggestive of imprisonment. As a storm impends, 'the clouds went portentously off, like ships of war after reconnoitering a strong fort, to return with added strength and fury'; once the storm arrives, 'Racking clouds' scud across the sky like 'the scattered fugitives of a routed army'.[28] These military metaphors, in which storms are compared to battles 'fought at once by sea and land, between hope and despair,'[29] impress more recent events into the net of association. Battles by sea and land invoke 1798. Although the novel buries overt discussion either of politics or of history, it cannot lay either politics or history to rest. Instead, history becomes a sublime revenant.[30]

This haunting begins long before Young John meets the Wanderer. As he travels to his uncle's estate through Co. Wicklow, 'The beauty of the country through which he traveled ... could not prevent his mind from dwelling on many painful thoughts, some borrowed from the past, and more from the future'[31]. With these thoughts and words, the novel opens. Young John tries to shake them off, but he has no other thoughts to supply their place. Thus he is forced to 'invite them back for company. When the mind is thus active in calling over invaders', the narrator tells us, 'no wonder the conquest is soon completed'.[32] Though it records no specific thoughts nor traces any specific route on which the main coach carrying young John as its only passenger travels, the path from Dublin to Wicklow lies along the military road built by the British government after the 1798 rebellion. And the deteriorating estate poised at the edge of a rocky promontory conjures up Black's Castle, built on land awarded to a partaker in the twelfth-century Anglo-Norman conquest and a site contested by Irish clansmen (the O'Tooles and O'Byrnes) until the sixteenth century. Doubling the sense of ruin while displacing revolutionary politics, the novel goes beyond the metaphorical collapse of public and private spheres; it buries ideological content and history beneath a terrain whose sublime exoticism can barely contain it.

At novel's end, we gain neither a restorative narrative nor linguistic strategies for imperial epistemologies. Instead, the Irish sublime functions as a cautionary tale, for, as Maturin tells us, 'Terror is very fond of associations; we love to connect the agitation of the elements with the agitated life of man; and never did a blast roar, or a gleam of lightning flash, that was not connected in the imagination of some one, with a calamity that was to be dreaded, deprecated, or endured – with the fate of the living, or the destination of the dead'.[33]

---

27 Ibid., p. 61.   **28** Ibid., p. 64.   **29** Ibid., p. 65.   **30** Maturin thereby extends indefinitely in the literary realm the effect of 1798 Kevin Whelan identified in a political register: 'The 1798 rebellion was fought twice ... The struggle for control of the meaning of the 1790s was also a struggle for political legitimacy, [. . .] the rebellion never passed into history, because it never passed out of politics'. Kevin Whelan, ''98 after '98: the politics of memory', in *The tree of liberty: radicalism, Catholicism and the construction of Irish identity, 1760–1830* (Notre Dame, 1996), p. 133.   **31** Maturin, *Melmoth the Wanderer*, p. 8.   **32** Ibid., p. 9.   **33** Ibid., pp 61–2.

II

The figurative status of the associations Maturin constructs above teeters unsteadily. To connect the agitation of the elements with the agitated life of man is to draw an allegorical correspondence. Yet the idea that natural upheavals cause human upheavals makes the equation register in the metonymic, as does the use of violent images such as roaring blasts and lightning flashes, equally proleptic of the ammunition unleashed by angry mobs. Here we see repeated the novel's evocation of Ireland as a spectacle of ruin whose causes are natural and human, as are its effects. This tropological sublime draws attention to its own aesthetic work when our narrator gestures explicitly at the role played by the imagination. However, the affect produced by that imagination exceeds both its source and its legislated tenure. The possible outcomes seem similarly imbalanced, since dread, deprecation, and endurance are scarcely commensurate reactions; yet the commas imply their equivalence. And, as I have been arguing, the sense that the 'fate of the living' is intimately bound up with 'the destination of the dead' creates the nexus between history and the sublime, or the subliming of history that I have identified as a key feature of the Irish sublime.

Two questions, however, still loom large. First, to what extent does this so-called Irish sublime conform to other definitions of the term? I've already drawn a very brief sketch of its continuities and discontinuities with Burke, Kant and Longinus, but now I want to turn to an appreciation of the way current critics use the sublime. By seeing the ways in which their versions or applications of the sublime differ from what occurs in Irish novels, we can better appreciate an Irish sublime as a more precise tool for analyzing Irish novels of the nineteenth century.

In 1992, Frances Ferguson complained about the tendency of her colleagues to value the sublime more for what it was not than what it was, to align the sublime with the poststructuralist 'repudiation of closure, comprehension, and totalization', with its celebration of the '[u]ndefined and indeterminate'.[34] Ferguson's comments summarized a critical history of the sublime that covered the middle decades of the twentieth century, and they marked a turn wherein critics had begun to sift the sublime for its political valence, for its role in the regimen that produced the individual as a member of the state. Three examples of this critical turn will stand as representative. Ferguson connected the sublime to the search for an escape from history: 'Solitude comes to be cultivated as a space for consciousness in which the

---

34 Whether the impetus was psychological, as in Thomas Weiskel's *The romantic sublime* (Baltimore, 1976) or Neil Hertz's reading of Weiskel in *The end of the line: essays on psychoanalysis and the sublime* (New York, 1985); phenomenological, as in Sartre's *Being and Nothingness: an essay on phenomenological ontology*, trans. Hazel E. Barnes (New York, 1956); or deconstructionist, as in Paul De Man's 'Phenomenality and materiality in Kant', in *Hermeneutics: questions and prospects*, ed. Gary Shapiro and Ala Sica (Amherst, 1984). Frances Ferguson, *Solitude and the sublime: romanticism and the aesthetics of individuation* (New York and London, 1992), pp 116–17.

individual is not answerable to others, and the waste landscape becomes the site of value because one can make it a peopled solitude, anthropomorphizing rocks and stones and trees, without encountering the pressures of a competing consciousness'.[35] Conversely, Ronald Paulson implicated aesthetics rather than individualism, and accordingly he characterized the 'problem of the historical sublime' as implying that 'Art remains the practical political accommodation which attempts to render the sublime (the revolution per se) manageable'.[36] Lastly, Peter Cosgrove melded the two approaches: he situated Burke's sublime in the shift away from the image not only in the history of aesthetics, but also in the history of judicial regulation articulated by Foucault:

> The sublime, then, is evoked by a tension internal to the mind, a functional tension instigated by the imagination's inability to retain a complete image narrowly defined as a bounded object. In other words, the pain and horror of the sublime is a form of iconoclasm that depends on the breaking of the imaging faculty rather than the breaking of images themselves. The active search for and the willing surrender to this experience is the heart of the moment of sublime terror experienced by the subject.[37]

The encounter with the sublime object forms the 'exercise of discipline', in Foucault's scheme; the failure of the imagination subordinates and subdues the individual to submit to a power which, in Cosgrove's explication, can only be achieved by an internalizion of the hegemonic threat.

Each of these accounts correlates with the interpretation of Burke's theory as enabling a 'detached, spectatorial response' because each buffers the individual from an empathic share in the dissolution. No such distance is ultimately possible with the Irish sublime. And, whereas the deconstructive readings of the sublime make the condition universal, the Irish sublime yet distinguishes itself by forming a mournful record rather than a celebration: the spectacle of dissolution preserves the remnants of an object and subject to dissolve; in the end, it is the object which breaks, not the imaginative capacity. In fact, the spectacle of the Irish sublime reveals a process at work even as it momentarily freezes that process, in a manner reminiscent of Wordsworth's 'woods decaying, never to be decayed'.[38] However, Ferguson's and Paulson's characterization of the sublime as the search for an escape from history echoes ironically against the Irish sublime. In the reduction of the human to the animal or mineral, we might witness the attempt to achieve a sense of independent solitude by petrifying those other, clamorous consciousnesses so that they become one with the landscape. Additionally, some sublime Irish landscapes lodge the desire

---

35 Ibid., p. 114.   **36** Ronald Paulson, 'Versions of a human sublime', *New Literary History*, 16:2 (Winter 1985), Special issue on *The sublime and the beautiful: reconsiderations*, 427–37. **37** Cosgrove, 'Edmund Burke, Gilles Deleuze, and the subversive masochism of the image', 405–37.   **38** *The Prelude*, Book VI, line 557. The revelation of the sublime as process is the very achievement Ferguson claims for Kant.

to escape from history, as I discuss below. Yet those very scenes frequently record, albeit obliquely, the history beneath. Thus they register the vain impossibility of such desiring. It is an attempt doomed to fail because history is too firmly moulded onto the land. Nor do these sublime scenes render the revolutionary violence manageable, even as they might offer a 'practical political accommodation'. So I think the Irish sublime might help us qualify Ferguson's and Paulson's reading, admirable as these might be.[39]

Here we arrive at the second question: does this application of a different sublime hold true in other Irish novels, or is it just another instance of Maturin's eccentricity? And, if it does, to what extent can the Irish sublime intervene in and contribute to our understanding of Irish novels? Novels like Maria Edgeworth's *Ennui* and *The Absentee* and Sidney Owenson's *The Wild Irish Girl* seldom get catalogued alongside a work like Charles Robert Maturin's *Melmoth the Wanderer*, except insofar as these are novels by Irish authors. On the surface, at least, these two types of novels seem diametrically opposed. One conveys the sense of solution; the other conjures up the spectacle of dissolution. One portrays the land and its people as legible, the other as illegible. But when we sift the novels of Owenson and Edgeworth for their use of the sublime, we find gradations of legibility. Further, a multitude of sublimes compete. In Edgeworth the Irish sublime once more arises; in Owenson, although we don't find a demonized dissolution of boundaries characteristic of the Irish sublime, we do see glimmers of a sublime that enables a colonialist disengagement.

Owenson often naïvely misnames a passage 'sublime'. Take, for instance, Mortimer's first description of Glorvina and the Prince:

> Once they paused, as if to admire the beautiful effect of the retreating light, as it faded on the ocean's swelling bosom; and once the Princess raised her

---

39 In distinguishing between the sublime and what he calls the pre-Romantic grotesque, Paulson offers a useful opportunity to more broadly discriminate the Irish sublime from other competing tropes of the period identified by critics, such as the grotesque and the traumatic. Paulson defines the grotesque as a violent assertion of change and transition in which incommensurables become interchangeable, and deems it satire, although he points out that this violence may, in practice, have served the ruling powers as a safety valve. His definition borders what I have been calling the Irish sublime, except insofar as its effect and satirical intent. Morton Paley records the existence of an 'apocalyptic grotesque' in the Romantic period whose function was also satirical, occurring chiefly in broadsides and caricatures: in it, a 'low' or mundane political reality was satirized by its parodic inversion of 'high' sublime visual tropes. See his *The Apocalyptic Sublime* (New Haven and London: Yale UP, 1986), pp. 184–6. Of course, parody makes the political substrate apparent, while the Irish sublime attempts to obscure the political it cannot bury. Finally, trauma theory allows for the seizure of terror that accompanies the bursting out of repressed or 'passive' memory, but these vestigial horrors appear to the unwilling spectator as unfragmented, intact apparitions instead of as the partially dissolved reminders which we encounter in the Irish sublime. Cf. Chad T. May, '"The horrors of my tale": trauma, the historical imagination, and Sir Walter Scott', *Pacific Coast Philology*, 40 (2005), 98–116.

hand and pointed to the evening star, which rose brilliantly on the deep cerulean blue of a cloudless atmosphere, and shed its fairy beam on the mossy summit of a mouldering turret.

Such were the sublime objects which seemed to engage their attention, and added their *sensible* inspiration to the fervour of those more abstracted devotions in which they were so recently engaged. At last they reach the portals of the castle, and I lost sight of them.[40]

Missing is the translation of the aesthetic image into an abstract concept. The images remain, if anything, too firmly embodied and too self-consciously assembled, the hallmark of the picturesque. A supplemental logic operates: sensible and ideal, like the oppositional 'fairy' and 'mouldering', combine rather than fuse. Consistently, Owenson undermines the notion of tension between the sublime and beautiful, as she accommodates the moral and the natural world, in more explicitly extended discussions of aesthetic theory,[41] an aesthetic comprehension in harmony with her meliorative politics.

Sensitivity to competing sublimes can help reveal how 'unnatural' is the very naturalness with which Owenson characterizes her sublime discourse. The sociability of this nighttime aesthetic exercise jars with the fundamentally solitary nature of the sublime. Unlike Glorvina, who is surrounded by her father, Father John, and a retinue of servants, Mortimer makes the more conventionally lone figure on the landscape. His gaze converts their human figures into part of nature, without projecting the kind of dissolution inherent in a similar Maturin moment. But the sense of scopic scrutiny or voyeurism lingers: 'I was the first to leave the chapel, and followed them at a distance as they moved slowly along. Their fine figures sometimes concealed behind a pillar, and again emerging from the transient shade, flushed with the deep suffusion of the crimsoned firmament.'[42] Upon their departure, he remains 'spellbound' and 'transfixed'. Like Mortimer, the reader is left uneasy, occupying a split perspective: we look at Mortimer looking at the 'sublime' landscape; we are simultaneously sustained and bereft.

When Owenson presents the progress of her young lovers through what she calls a sublime retrospective, as their lives slowly twine into one, two histories vie for attention:

> In (I believe) equal emotion, we both arose at the same moment, and walked to the window. Beyond the mass of ruins which spread in desolate confusion below, the ocean, calm and unruffled, expanded its awful bosom almost to infinitude; while a body of dark, sullen clouds, tinged with the partial beam of a meridian sun, floated above the summits of those savage cliffs which skirt this bold and rocky coast; and the tall spectral figure of Father John, leaning on a broken pediment, appeared like the embodied spirit of philosophy

40 Owenson, *The Wild Irish Girl,* p. 49.   **41** Ibid., p. 148.   **42** Ibid., pp 48–9.

moralizing amidst the ruins of empires, on the instability of all human greatness. What a sublime assemblage of images![43]

More than a naïve misnaming occurs here. We find a collision of nativist and colonialist sensibilities that forces us to reappraise the valorization of Owenson for
eschewing the colonialist uses of an aesthetic distance. For example, to Kevin Whelan
Owenson 'stresses an ethic of proximity' as opposed to the colonialist's 'aesthetic of
distance created by the separating function of the gaze'.[44] In this 'sublime assemblage',
though, the scenery itself is registered with the 'separating function of the gaze', even
as the items themselves in the landscape maintain their discrete existence; at the same
time, the 'spectral figure' of Father John is viewed with both an ethics and an optics
of proximity. Father John's height towers over the broken monuments of history, such
that the organic and the inorganic exchange postures of dominance. Nonetheless, the
lament that Father John's time has passed as surely as have the remnants of Irish greatness faintly looming on the horizon, like the broken pediment, seems underscored
by the adjective 'spectral' as well as by the self-canceling reference to him as an
embodied spirit of an abstract occupation.[45]   Father John's presence mediates the
resignation or accommodation inherent in the colonialist sublime, but his spectral-
ization converts mourning to melancholia. More important, this later 'sublime'
moment demonstrates the harmony subsisting between Glorvina and Mortimer, a
harmony that we must imagine as *learned* – transmitted from Mortimer to his apt
pupil in drawing, Glorvina, since we never see Glorvina participating in this kind of
aesthetic distancing until she has allied her heart to his. In other word, we can recognize that the sublime forms for Owenson a scene of instruction analogous to the
kinds of instructions transmitted by Burke.[46]

---

43 *The Wild Irish Girl: a national tale*, ed. Claire Connolly and Stephen Copley (London,
2000).   **44** 'Writing Ireland, Reading England', Foreword to *The Wild Irish Girl*, p. xvi. It
seems fairly conventional to separate eighteenth-century from Romantic versions of the
sublime, as does David B. Morris; he argues that the Romantics import the Gothic to
gesture at mystery. Curiously, though, his description of Longinus delineates how (anachro-
nistically, then) Longinus characterized the sublime as a kind of possession, in Longinus's
case by a literary text or voice on a reader or auditor. See 'Gothic sublimity', *New Literary
History*, 16: 2 (Winter 1985), 299–319. We might use this idea of the voice as a haunting or
possession to once again interrogate the way in which Owenson portrays her aesthetics of
proximity, since it depends so strongly on the use of Glorvina as voice.   **45** In contrast, the
moments in Maturin's novel that I have defined as the Irish sublime rely precisely on a
notion of proximal terror. However, Whelan's description of the way Owenson saturates
space with time (xviii–xix) – as in the Gothicization of ruins as historical seepage – does
correspond to what I am trying to describe.   **46** Steven Knapp's *Personification and the
sublime* (Cambridge, MA, 1985) still offers a valuable overview of ideas about the sublime in
the eighteenth-and nineteenth centuries. Two points are distinctly germane: he distinguishes
between the self-preservative role of the sublime and the social role of ambition in Burke
(pp 69–71); and he underscores the emphasis Kant placed on the inevitable need to be
educated in the sublime (pp 78–9).

Burke is seldom absent as a measuring stick against which critics assess the work of Maria Edgeworth; as Fraser Easton has observed, Burke 'has stood as the pole star to considerations of Edgeworth's national ideas'.[47] A scene like that in *Ennui*, when Glenthorn arises from his first night in the paternal castle to take the view, certainly conforms to the model of a colonialist aesthetic: '[I] saw that the whole prospect bore an air of savage wildness. As I contemplated the scene, my imagination was seized with the idea of remoteness from civilized society: the melancholy feeling of solitary grandeur took possession of my soul'.[48] Here we see the idealizing love of solitude, mentioned by Ferguson. Here, too, we can read with Luke Gibbons and Peter Cosgrove, who argue persuasively that the recuperation implicit in Burke's model, which becomes explicit in that of Kant, introjects the threatening, patriarchal/colonial law of the father. Glenthorn's reaction to the scene as one of 'savage wildness' and his rapture at isolation magnifies his sense of self, such that he feels possessed by a 'solitary grandeur'.

Ironically, perhaps, the sublime discourse above credits solitude with a civility that civilizes. In contrast, Glenthorn's description of Ellinor's cottage contains the blurring of categories between the animate and the inanimate, the human, animal, and vegetative, characteristic of the Irish sublime.[49] Moreover, such chaos is said to be the 'natural' condition for the Irish; it results from their lack of an innate or instinctive love of order. In consequence, the newly-built cottage of English design but of Irish manufacture suffers the same process of indiscriminating decay.[50] No introjected hope, however melancholy, consoles for this fall into illegibility.

As we have seen with *The Wild Irish Girl* and *Ennui*, each invokes the term 'sublime' as misdirection for the picturesque at the same time that it employs what I would like to call the Irish sublime as an unstated proposition.[51] Marrying the abstract with the concrete, the Irish sublime reveals the aesthetic conditions of Irish land to be haunted, if not deformed, by its material past and present. Moreover, considered from the vantage point of the sublime, these novels instance a surprising sense of increasing despair. In other words, the Irish sublime takes on a darker tone and becomes more pervasive as we move further away in time, or closer to our own period – a surprising shift since, if the Irish sublime melds the land with its history, the voyage towards today leads away from more immediate, more bloody memories.[52]

47 Maturin, *Melmoth the Wanderer*, p. 296.   **48** Edgeworth, *Ennui*, in *Tales and Novels*. The Longford Edition, vol. IV (New York, 1967), pp 252–3.   **49** Ibid., p. 260.   **50** Ibid., p. 274. **51** *The Absentee* complicates the issue even further when it mocks the sublime by domesticating it, reducing it to the status of a fashionable accessory in the demonized household of Mrs Rafarty (vol. VI of the Longford Edition) pp 88–9.   **52** *Ennui* contains the barely-occluded violent past in the attempted kidnapping and the rebels meeting in the cave, but this is turned more into an adventure story than an encounter with a sublime revenant (pp 340–9). *The Absentee* contains an even more proximate past – the after-effects of the Act of Union (pp 82–3), and the hint of even nearer unrest in Count O'Halloran's spy mission (pp 218–19; 223).

Yet more work remains to be done. Should the category of the Irish sublime do no more than enable us to descry that more than one sublime might be operative in a text, we might thereby be able to weigh the versions and their concomitant political attitudes with greater exactitude. Recognizing that these texts represent Ireland as both legible and illegible, as ordered and chaotic, we can perhaps appreciate better the extent to which we need to remain agile if we are to chart our way through this vexed land with grace and integrity.

Notes on contributors

FRANCESCA BENATTI is a post-doctoral researcher currently working for the Thomas Moore Hypermedia Archive at the Moore Institute, National University of Ireland, Galway. Her research interests include nineteenth-century Irish popular periodicals and their role in Irish cultural nationalism.

MAURA CRONIN is a lecturer in the department of History, Mary Immaculate College, University of Limerick. She is the author of several articles on nine-teenth-century Irish social history and of *Country, class or craft: the politicisation of the skilled artisan in nineteenth century Cork* (1994).

FINTAN CULLEN is professor of art history at the University of Nottingham. His most recent book was *The Irish face: redefining the Irish portrait* (National Portrait Gallery, London, 2004).

LAURA DABUNDO is professor of English and founding director of the Kennesaw State University Press in Kennesaw, Georgia. She is the editor of *The encyclopedia of Romanticism* (1992), and *Jane Austen, Mary Shelley and their sisters* (2000), and has contributed to a variety of publications on Wordsworth, Austen, Edgeworth, and Owenson.

SUSAN EGENOLF is an assistant professor in the department of English at Texas A & M University. She is the author of several essays that explore the writings of Anglo-Irish and Irish women writers. She is currently completing a book entitled *The art of political fiction in Hamilton, Edgeworth and Owenson* (forth-coming).

IRENE FURLONG is a former post-doctoral research fellow in the department of History, NUI Maynooth. Her main research interests lie in the history of Irish tourism, and she is currently writing a book on Irish tourism and the State in the period 1880–1980. Other areas of interest include Irish social, economic and cultural history in the nineteenth and twentieth centuries, and the attitudes of Irish literary figures towards Ireland.

ANDREW J. GARAVEL SJ is an assistant professor in the department of English, Santa Clara University, California. Another essay on Somerville and Ross is forthcoming in a volume titled *Ireland's great hunger: representation and preservation.*

GLENN HOOPER is an honorary research fellow in the department of English, University of Aberdeen. He is co-editor of *Irish and postcolonial writing: history, theory, practice* (2002), editor of *Landscape and empire, 1770–2000* (2005), and author of *Travel writing and Ireland, 1760–1860: culture, history, politics* (2005).

SIOBHÁN JONES is an instructor in the department of History at the University of San Diego. She was an IRCHSS Government of Ireland Scholar, 2002–5, and completed her PhD on 'Southern Irish Unionism, press and politics, 1860–1960' at University College Cork. She is currently an editor with Cambridge Social Scientific Abstracts, and has contributed articles based on the southern unionist media to *Saothar - Journal of the Irish Labour History Society*, and to 'Made in Limerick', published by Limerick Civic Trust.

WILLIAM H. MULLIGAN, JR. is professor of history at Murray State University in Murray, Kentucky, USA. His current research involves Irish copper mining in the nineteenth century and migration from Irish copper mining areas to the Michigan Copper Country. His most recent edited publications are *The shoemakers of Lynn, Massachusetts, 1850–1880: family during the transition from hand to machine labor* (2006), and *Badger boy in blue: the Civil War letters of Chauncey H. Cooke* (2007).

JAMES H. MURPHY is professor of English and Director of Irish Studies at DePaul University Chicago. He writes on the politics, literature and culture of nineteenth-century Ireland. His recent books include, *Abject loyalty: nationalism and monarchy in Ireland during the reign of Queen Victoria* (1991), and *Ireland: a social, cultural and literary history, 1791–1891* (2003). He is a former president of the Society for the Study of Nineteenth-Century Ireland and has edited or co-edited three volumes of the proceedings of its conferences.

ÚNA NÍ BHROIMÉIL is a lecturer in the department of History, Mary Immaculate College, University of Limerick. She is the author of *Building Irish identity in America, 1870–1915: the Gaelic Revival* (2003) and her publications include works on the Irish American press and the gender construction of female teachers in late nineteenth- and early twentieth-century Ireland.

MÁIRÍN NÍ CHEALLAIGH recently completed her PhD in the school of Archaeology in University College Dublin, where she held both an IRCHSS Postgraduate Research Scholarship and a Humanities Institute of Ireland Postgraduate Research Scholarship. She is the author of a number of papers on the history of Irish archaeology and on nineteenth-century perceptions of Irish monuments, and is currently working in the archaeological private sector. In September 2007 she will take up an IRCHSS Postdoctoral Research Fellowship in the Department of Modern History, Trinity College Dublin.

MARY S. PIERSE teaches courses on nineteenth-century literature and literature of empire at UCC. Editor of *George Moore: artistic visions and literary worlds*

(2006), her current research concerns early literary impressionism in George Moore's writings. Other publications include articles on Moore's art, landscapes, and European connections, and on the poetry of Cathal Ó Searcaigh and Dennis O'Driscoll.

OONAGH WALSH is a senior lecturer in the department of History, University of Aberdeen. She is editor of *Ireland abroad: politics and professions in the nineteenth century* (2003), and author of *Ireland's independence: 1880–1923* (2000), and *Anglican women in Dublin: philanthropy, politics and education in the early twentieth century* (2005).

TONI WEIN is associate professor of Romanticism at California State University, Fresno. Her publications include works on the Gothic and the role played by Ireland in Gothic novels, on eco-critical pedagogy, and on women writers. She is currently at work on a book about theatrical representations of Jews in late-eighteenth century England.

Index